BRITANNIA RULES

C. Northcote Parkinson

BRITANNIA RULES

THE CLASSIC AGE OF NAVAL HISTORY 1793–1815

BOOK CLUB ASSOCIATES
LONDON

This edition published 1977 by
Book Club Associates
by arrangement with Weidenfeld and Nicolson

Copyright © 1977 by C. Northcote Parkinson

Printed in Great Britain by
Cox & Wyman Ltd
London, Fakenham and Reading

Contents

Illustrations

ILLUSTRATIONS

British towing the Danish fleet into harbour (*Nelson–McCarthy Collection
    RN Museum, Portsmouth*)
Lord Cochrane (*Radio Times Hulton Picture Library*)
Sir Nesbit Willoughby (*Radio Times Hulton Picture Library*)
Battle of Grand Port (*National Maritime Museum*)
Sir Philip Broke (*National Maritime Museum*)
Napoleon on board *Bellerophon* (*Mansell Collection*)

For Jonathan

PART I

THE WARS OF THE FRENCH REVOLUTION

1793-1801

ONE

Government and Admiralty

At daybreak on 19 June 1793, the lookout on board the frigate *Nymphe* (of 36 guns) reported a strange sail, which turned out to be the French national frigate *La Cleapatra* (of 40 guns). When the two ships came within hail Captain Edward Pellew ordered his men to the shrouds and called out 'Long Live King George the Third!' for whom the crew gave three cheers. Captain Mullon, his opponent, manned ship with the same formality, shouting 'Vive la Nation!' at which his men cheered three times in their turn. On hailing, Pellew had taken off his hat to the French captain. His replacing it was the signal to open fire, so beginning an action between two ships of roughly equal strength. Half an hour later the *Cleopatre* after losing her wheel and mizzen mast, collided with her antagonist, bows-on to the British broadside. Swarming on board the French frigate, boarders found that few of her men were still on deck. Mullon, mortally wounded, was trying to eat what he took to be his signal code but was actually his commission, and three of his lieutenants with sixty other men had been killed or wounded. The flag of the *Cleopatre* was hauled down and the second officer surrendered his sword to Mr Amherst Morris. On 21 June the *Nymphe* brought her prize into Portsmouth amidst the cheers of every other ship in harbour. When the news reached London, George III himself announced it from his box at the Opera. On 29 June Captain Pellew received the honour of knighthood at St James's Palace. He was the hero of the hour and could have which ship he liked. British monarchy had triumphed over French democracy and Britannia was still, after all, to rule the waves.

The significance of this almost ritual encounter has to be seen in its political context. The last war, that of American Independence (1775–

3

83), had ended in British defeat but the French, by taking the side of the rebels against George III, had undermined the moral strength (and financial solvency) of their own monarchy. By 1789 their government was bankrupt and the revolution began, offering a dangerous example to other peoples ruled by monarchies. War inevitably followed and the revolutionary armies of France fought successfully against the troops which were sent to restore order. French armies in which the aristocrats had been guillotined or otherwise removed, led by captains who had suddenly become generals, by colonels who had recently been subalterns, by former corporals who had just been commissioned, had defeated regular forces commanded by senior officers of long experience. Against discipline and training the French had successfully deployed sheer numbers and ideological enthusiasm. They had finally declared war against Britain on 1 February 1793, and all Europe waited to see the result. Would the forces of democracy prove as effective at sea as they had proved on land? Could naval battles be won by promoted boatswains and by the masters of merchantmen? Would their revolutionary fervour prove sufficient? And would it undermine the morale of their opponents? Would the slogans of liberty, equality and fraternity find a ready response on board the British men-of-war, causing mutiny, desertion and treachery? Were that to happen, the ascendancy of France would be established and with it the principle of republican rule.

The action between the *Nymphe* and *Cleopatre* did not mark the beginning of the war at sea. That had begun, in a sense, when the *Childers* sloop had been fired on by the batteries at Brest (3 January 1793). It had continued with the skirmish between the *Iris* (of 32 guns) and the French privateer *Citoyenne Française* (13 May) and the action, as indecisive, between the British *Venus* (of 32 guns) and the French frigate *Semillante* (40). Then there followed the capture of the sloop *Hyaena* (24) by a French squadron headed by the *Concorde* (44). Not one of these incidents proved anything conclusive. It was Pellew who was able to report the result of a decisive action between two equally matched ships. The report led to two important conclusions. It was clear, in the first place, that British seamen were so far unaffected by the French revolutionary example. They evidently regarded the war as another phase in the long drawn-out conflict between Britain and France; a war which offered them the chance of revenge for their past defeat. It was clear, in the second place, that discipline in the French Navy had more or less collapsed. If the *Cleopatre* were typical – and she was said

4

to be above average – the proclamation afloat of liberty, equality and fraternity must lead to complete disaster. Ordered by Mullon to board the *Nymphe*, the Frenchmen had not even tried to defend their own ship. The action lasted only fifty minutes, ending because the French had refused to fight. Theirs had been, finally, a miserable performance.

Reflecting on the result of this action, senior British officers would have remembered that the French successes of the last war had been tactical and technical. There had been the Academie de Marine, a French staff college, since 1752. Tactical theory had been first formulated by the jesuit Père Hoste but was greatly advanced by Sebastien-Francois Bigot, Vicomte de Morogues, first director of the Academie, whose *Tactique Navale* was published in 1763. The French Navy's great period was during the reign of Louis XV, the age of Choiseul, but the work continued under the leadership of Sartine during the next reign. Useful work was done by the Map and Chart Office and by the School of Ship-Construction. There was a new emphasis on hygiene and a Royal Marine Corps was formed by the Duc de Praslin in 1769. French naval officers of distinction included Comte D'Estaing, Comte D'Orvilliers, the Chevalier de Fleurieu, Comte de Guichen, the Bailli de Suffren and Comte de Grasse. These and other leaders could count on a body of other officers drawn from the Breton or Provencal nobility. Although always rather weak in discipline, the French Navy had a great tradition of its own, intellectual, scientific and systematic. The effect of the revolution was to sweep away all that was strongest, except in naval architecture, and place all future reliance on the patriotism to be found on the lower deck. It would take years to repair the damage and there would, in the meanwhile, be an obvious weakness in direction and leadership. The result of the action between *Nymphe* and *Cleopatre* was to pinpoint that weakness. That the French Navy had but a shadow of its former efficiency had still to be proved in battle but the early encounters, of which this was one of the first, gave the British a growing sense of confidence. If the French were no better than they seemed to be, the war at sea was as good as won.

The ministers of George III who had to study the balance of sea power were headed by William Pitt, a bachelor aged 34, who had been in office since 1784. His chief adviser was Henry Dundas (Secretary for War). William Grenville (Foreign Secretary), Lord Chatham (First Lord of the Admiralty), and the Duke of Richmond (Master-General of the Ordnance) were among the other ministers directly concerned with the war. Pitt had done great work in restoring British finances and prosperity after the loss of the American colonies. He had no comparable gift as a war leader and it may be doubted whether Dundas was very much better. Neither man was particularly popular and one anonymous critic expressed in these words what may have been a widely accepted opinion:

A POLITICAL CREED

I believe in Billy Pit, Chancellor of the Exechequer, Maker of Lords and Commons and of all court intrigues visible and invisible, and in one Secretary, Henry Dundas, the only beloved of Billy Pit, beloved before all women, man of men, Head of Heads and Minister of Ministers, beloved and hated, being of One Opinion with the Patron by whom all Ministers are made. Who for us men and for our taxation came down from Scotland and talked of his integrity; was appointed East India Director and went into Scotland and was burnt in effigy and the third day came back again according to the Newspapers and ascended into office and sitteth at the right hand of Billy Pit and shall come again to judge both the loyal and the disloyal whose folly shall have no end: And I believe in one George the 3rd, the lord and giver of all places who, together with Billy Pit are both worshipped and glorified, who spake by Proclamation. 'And I look not for the reduction of taxes till the resurrection of the dead and I hope for better government in the world to come. Amen.'

Cabinet decisions, whether wise or not, were conveyed to the Royal Navy by the First Lord who presided over the Lords Commissioners of the Admiralty. We know from the Minutes that the Board was busy putting ships into commission from December, 1792. Seven more ships of the line were so listed on 11 January 1793 with some forty-two frigates and sloops placed on higher establishment. Similar orders went out on the 22nd, 25th, 28th and 29th. Then came the following entries:

Wednesday 30 Jan^y
Res'd that a Memorial be laid before his Majesty, proposing an augmentation of Lieutenants, Schoolmasters and Pursers in the Fleet. . . .
The Navy Board are to cause the *Queen Charlotte* at Ports^m and the *Royal Sovereign* at Plym^th to be put into condition for Service at Sea and to report when they will be ready to receive men. . . .
Thursday, 31st Jan^y
. . . the *Captain* and *Fortitude* to be fitted out at Plym for Channel Service, manned with 600 men each, victualled to three months of all species of Provisions, except Beer, of which they are to have as much as they can conveniently stow and to be supplied with wine or spirits in lieu of the remainder.

6

Raisonable and *Agamemnon* at Chatham to be fitted out at that Port for Channel Service, manned with 500 men each, victualled for three months . . . etc.

Res'd that the following officers be ap'd to the ships against their names expressed: VIZ.

Rt. Hon. Captn Jas. Lord Cranstown	*Raisonable*
Captn Horatio Nelson	*Agamemnon*

Come now to the Admiralty Board Minutes for the day on which war was actually declared. It would seem that the Earl of Chatham came late, as from the Cabinet, Lord Arden taking the chair until he arrived:

Friday 1st Feb.ʸ 1793
Present:

Lord Arden	Earl of Chatham
Lord Hood	Honble. Mr Townshend
Captn Gardner	Mr Smyth
Mr Pybus	

A Letter was read from Mr Thos Parker, informing the Lords that a new Mechanical Power has been discovered which is thought applicable to the making of Cordage and Iron Work for the public service with much greater despatch than at present and a considerable saving of personal labour: Res'd that the said letter be sent to the Navy Board . . .

Other routine business followed, including a favourable report on Captain Pakenham's invention for steering a ship after the tiller in the gunroom has been shot away. All this took place, no doubt, before Lord Chatham arrived. With his arrival the Board dealt with a more important matter, the decision about which had already been taken:

In pursuance of the King's Pleasure, Res'd that the Right Honble Richard Earl Howe be appointed Admiral and Commander in Chief of His Maj'ty Fleet employed and to be employed in the Channel Soundings, or where ever else His Maj'ty Service shall require; and that he be empowered to wear the Union Flag at the Main topmast head on board any ship of the said Fleet where his Lordship may happen at any time to be.

There being no probability of a sufficient number of Volunteers offering in due time for manning the Ships fitting for Service at Sea, notwithstanding the Bounties which have been offered; Res'd that application be made to his Majesty for an Order in Council empowering this Board to issue Profs Warrants as usual . . .

7

These references may suffice to indicate the extent and the limits of their Lordships' authority. They could commission ships. They could appoint Captain Horatio Nelson to the *Agamemnon*. They could issue orders on a great variety of ship movements. But major decisions were made in Cabinet and the choice of a Commander-in-Chief on the Channel Station was (in this instance) made, almost certainly, by the King himself. Richard, Earl Howe, was an Admiral of the White Squadron, aged 67, and vastly senior to the other officer whose name had been put forward, Vice Admiral Lord Hood, aged 69, the First Sea Lord himself. There can be no question about Howe's ability but his position had always been unassailable for another reason. His mother was an illegitimate daughter of King George I, making him a cousin, in effect, of George III; he and his brother, the General, being always treated as such. Disappointed over the Channel Fleet, Lord Hood managed to secure his own appointment as Commander-in-Chief in the Mediterranean.

Until his departure on active service Samuel, Viscount Hood was the effective chief at the Admiralty. The custom was to appoint a politician as First Lord – in this instance Lord Chatham, Pitt's elder brother. The senior naval member of the Board represented the Admiralty in the House of Lords and did most of the actual work but was always assisted by a junior naval member who had to represent the Admiralty in the House of Commons, being often Member of Parliament for a dockyard constituency. There might be, as at this time, two other politicians, one in either House, and there were finally the 'signing members' Mr Smith and Mr Pybus, who signed documents when other and busier people were not available. The key man in the organization was the Secretary to the Board, Sir Philip Stephens, aided by the Assistant Secretary, Mr John Ibbetson; also assisted by the Chief Clerk, the Senior Clerks (who had 'Esq.' after their names), the Junior Clerks (No 'Esq.'), the Extra Clerks, the Supernumeraries, the Private Secretary to the First Lord and the Keeper of Records and Papers. The civilian staff was quite small and numbered only 88 in 1830, as compared with 800 in 1924 and about 8,000 in 1964. An anomaly, not the only one, was the position of the Treasurer of the Admiralty, no other than the Rt Hon Henry Dundas who drew emoluments (£4,000 p.a.) but performed no duty of any kind, save by deputy. More or less subordinate to the Board of Admiralty and each with an authority of its own were the Navy Board, the Victualling Office, the Ordnance Office, the Pay Office, the Sick and Hurt

Office, the Receiver's Office, the Marine Office, the Transport Board, the Board of Longitude and the Royal Naval Academy at Portsmouth. The Admiralty Building was, and physically still is, in Whitehall, the other offices being distributed between Somerset House, Tower Hill and Broad Street. Of these subordinate offices the most important was the Navy Board, of which Captain Charles Middleton had been Comptroller from 1778 to 1790, assisted by his surveyors, who were the leading naval architects, and by the Clerk of the Acts (whose office was first held by Samuel Pepys). The Navy Board had charge of the ships as opposed to the officers and men, but worked mainly through the Commissioners at the several dockyards. Portsmouth Dockyard had been founded for war against France, Plymouth for war against Spain and Chatham for war against Holland. Of less importance were the dockyards at Deptford, Woolwich and Sheerness. In Parliament the Navy had been voted about £4,000,000 for 1793, covering the cost of maintaining 45,000 seamen and marines. The naval shore establishments included Haslar Hospital at Portsmouth, completed in 1762 and providing accommodation for 2,000 sick and wounded. Communication, between the Admiralty and the naval bases were slow until 1796, the year in which the semaphore type of telegraph was set up to Portsmouth and to Chatham, the system being later extended to Plymouth and Falmouth. There were overseas dockyards at Gibraltar, at Halifax (Nova Scotia), at English Harbour, Antigua and at Port Royal, Jamaica. There were bases in India at Bombay, Madras and Calcutta. There was a smaller establishment at Kinsale in Ireland. What Britain lacked, however, since the previous war, was a naval base in the Mediterranean; notably Port Mahon in Minorca, lost to the Navy in 1782.

At the beginning of the war there were 26 sail of the line in commission, 32 frigates and 34 sloops; making, with other vessels, 135 units in all. Laid up in ordinary, maintained but neither rigged nor manned, were another 169 vessels including 87 of the line and 29 frigates. To commission all of these in less than a year was impossible because the seamen to be recruited were, many of them, in the East or West Indies. So ships were brought into service as they were completed, and as they could be manned. No major battle was likely until 1794, the enemy's difficulties being much the same as ours. There were theoretically over 300 men-of-war available, with others under construction. All were in very good order, copper-bottomed and ready for service and Middleton had accumulated naval stores to the value of £2,000,000 by 1790. He had discovered that the proper number at the Navy Board's meetings was five: 'More members are unnecessary and indeed inconvenient, because, having little to do, they naturally fall into familiar conversation and interrupt those who are employed in business.' He met this problem by using the other members as assistants; one, for example, to deal with accounts and returns and another responsible for army-victualling ships. He was no longer in office when war began but he left behind him the material upon which future sea-power could be based.

The previous war had involved defeat and disaster, being saved from ignominy by two successes at the eleventh hour; the relief of Gibraltar and the Battle of the Saints. A factor in the latter achievement was the introduction of the carronade, a new type of short-range 'smasher' cannon manufactured by the Carron Company in Scotland. Used originally in merchantmen, the carronade was adopted by the Royal Navy in 1779 more by way of addition than substitution. Carronades, being at first experimental, were not included in the ships' nominal number of cannon, with the result that a 1st-Rate ship of 100 guns actually mounted 110, a 3rd-Rate of 74 guns actually mounted 82, a Fifth-Rate frigate of 36 guns mounted 44 and an 18-gun sloop mounted 26. The contemporary usage remains among naval historians but we must remember that the number which follows a ship's name, while significant, is also to some extent fictitious. Thus while the *Minotaur* (74), built in 1793, mounted 74 guns, eighteen of them were 32-pdr carronades, the *Impetueux* (74) mounted 78 guns with her carronades included. Among the frigates, Pellew's ship *Nymphe* (36) mounted 38 guns in fact, a dozen of them being 24-pdr carronades, and the guns mounted by the *Amphion* (32) numbered 38 in all. Throughout this period the French ships, inherited from the old regime, were bigger, on average, and better designed than the British, and were established for a larger crew, but they mostly fired a lighter broadside. It may be added that the British conquest of Bengal had given Britain the world's best supply of saltpetre, the principal ingredient of gunpowder. There are reasons for believing that the propellant used in British cannon gave a higher muzzle velocity and with it a more or less permanent advantage. A parallel invention was that of the gun-lock, which did something to increase the rate of fire. The carronade was adopted by the French Navy but more slowly and with more reluctance; nor did the short-range weapon suit the French tradition in naval warfare.

Perhaps more important than the carronade was the British success in conquering scurvy, the traditional disease of which thousands of seamen used to die. Scurvy, as we now realize, was due to a lack of Vitamin C and arose, in fact, from a shortage of fresh provisions. It affected crews on a long voyage or those who spent long spells at sea and its nature and cure had been a matter for usually futile discussion over the last century and more. The turning point had been reached when Admiral Rodney assumed command of the American and West Indies Station in 1780, bringing Gilbert Blane with him as his personal physician, appointed soon afterwards as Physician to the Fleet. Finding that the fleet had a mortality rate of one in seven, he gave orders for the issue of lemon juice. A big effort was made in 1781 with the result that in the flagship only one man died in four months. Soon after war began again in 1793 Dr Blane, now Sir Gilbert, became a Commissioner for Sick and Hurt. In 1795 he persuaded the Board of Admiralty to sanction a regular issue of lemon juice to mix with the rum ration. By that date the problem had been solved, but for which many operations would have been impossible, especially those involving close and continuous blockade. In the tropics the grim alternative had been to remain at sea and lose men from scurvy or enter port and lose men from malaria. The cause of malaria was not to be discovered for another century but the control of scurvy had removed the age-old dilemma; malaria could be checked by putting to sea.

The British had made important progress in a number of directions, as for example in navigation, but to their progress in signalling we must give particular attention. For a very long period, from 1692 to 1783, British tactical theory was dominated by *The Permanent Fighting Instructions*, based on experience gained at the Battles of Barfleur (1692) and Malaga (1704). Only very rigid manoeuvres were possible and these were announced by a very limited number of signals. Some additional instructions were added by Vernon and Anson but the real breakthrough was made by Richard, Earl Howe, who issued his new signal book in 1776. This applied only to his own fleet on the American Station but the same numerary system, allowing ships actually to 'converse', was accepted by Admiral Rodney and was used by him at the Battle of the Saints. It proved a great success but was revised and improved by Admiral Kempenfelt whose system was based on nine flags. Howe, who was First Lord of the Admiralty from 1783 to 1788, secured the adoption of the new signal code by the Navy as a whole. With its issue in 1790 the *Fighting Instructions* were cancelled and a new era began. Instead of following a printed book of rules, captains were in future to obey the signals made from the flagship. And admirals, on their side, were able to explain themselves in some detail and in varying tones of encouragement or reproof. The change made is best shown by example. The *Fighting Instructions* read:

To draw into a line of battle one ship ahead of another, and keep two cables' length asunder. . . .
. . . When the signal shall be made . . . by hoisting an Union flag at the mizzen-peak and firing a gun.

From 1790, by contrast, the system was based on nine flags, each representing a numeral, together with certain other flags with a separate meaning (e.g. Negative). The numbers, used in groups, referred to entries in the signal book, a record of signals made would thus read:

General No.1 An enemy in sight
Frigates No.9 Leave off chase
General No.78 Tack in succession

The last signal would be formed by flag 7 (yellow diagonal cross on blue) and flag 8 (yellow and blue, divided vertically). By this system of signalling, tactics became infinitely more flexible.

So the British fleet of 1793 was generally well prepared for war, partly as the result of recent discovery and invention. There was, however, a change in professional attitude which is more difficult to explain or even date. One must realize, first of all, that eighteenth-century warfare on land had become highly formalized – one might even say, civilized. Armies were small and professional, being commanded by noblemen who fought in a gentlemanly way. They might salute each other before they opened fire. Having won the battle, they were more keen on collecting trophies than on pursuing the beaten foe. When a fortress was besieged, the fall of one bastion was enough to make the defending general capitulate with full military honours; he was not expected to sacrifice his life in a final scene of carnage. It was assumed that every war would end in a reasonable peace treaty, not in a massacre of the defeated side. When the siege of Gibraltar was in progress the Duc de Crillon, commanding the allied armies, was joined by the Comte d'Artois (the French King's brother) who brought with him some letters addressed to persons serving in Gibraltar. They were sent into the fortress under a flag of truce, the Duc de Crillon assuring General Eliott:

... of the highest esteem I have conceived for your Excellency, of the sincerest desire I feel of deserving yours, and of the pleasure to which I look forward of becoming your friend, after I shall have learned to render myself worthy of the honour, by facing you as an enemy ...

Permit me, Sir, to offer a few trifles for your table, of which I am sure you must stand in need ... I shall add a few game for the Gentlemen of your household, and some ice, which I presume will not be disagreeable in the excessive heat of this climate at this season of the year ...

When peace was made the Duc de Crillon came to visit Gibraltar, where he was cheered by the garrison and where the British officers were introduced to him.

Something of the same ceremony prevailed at sea. When France entered the War of American Independence, Admiral Sir George Rodney was actually living in Paris and it was a loan from a French nobleman which enabled him to return to England. After his victory at the Battle of the Saints he was urged by his second-in-command, Sir Samuel Hood, to pursue the enemy and complete their destruction. But Rodney had taken five sail including the French flagship. 'Come, we have done very handsomely,' he replied, and historians have suggested since that he was an elderly man and desperately tired. All this may be true, but it is still a very eighteenth-century reply. It was enough to defeat the enemy, there was no need to plan his destruction. Rodney and De Grasse were now friends and might expect to meet again – perhaps back in Paris? – and they were both gentlemen. Peace would follow, as it soon did, and there had been bloodshed enough. This was a civilized attitude towards war but it was not to survive for long. In this respect, Hood represented the future and Rodney the past. After the revolution the French officers need no longer be treated as gentlemen: they were mostly nothing of the sort. But something of the old attitude remained. Edward Pellew (see page 3) doffed his hat to one opponent and afterwards became close friends with another. And what of Richard, Earl Howe? Was he closer, in this matter, to Hood or to Rodney? Only time would show. But there was a change in atmosphere, foreshadowed perhaps during the American War and manifest in the days of Robespierre. Nelson's object, when he reached flag rank, was not merely to gain victory. His aim was to destroy the enemy.

TWO

The Opening Moves

First British move in the war was the appointment of Richard, Earl Howe, to the Channel Fleet which comprised, initially, between twenty and twenty-five sail of the line. Disappointed of this command, Lord Hood now made himself Commander-in-Chief in the Mediterranean with a fleet of similar size but better quality. While still the senior naval member on the Board, Hood, with Chatham's concurrence, was able to secure priority for his own fleet. As Codrington wrote:

The greater part of the men that entered for the '*Queen Charlotte*' at the Tower were taken by Lord Hood for the ships he was to command in the Mediterranean, which occasioned great delay in preparing the grand fleet for Channel service. The 64's and inferior ships were allotted to Lord Howe and the superior ones to Lord Hood . . .[1]

On his side Howe secured a strong staff with Sir Roger Curtis as Captain of the Fleet, Captain Christian as Flag Captain, Captain Barlow as captain of his repeating frigate the *Pegasus*, that fine seaman James Bowen as Master of the Fleet and Lieutenant Edward Codrington as his signal lieutenant. He was not ready for sea until July. Meanwhile, Rear-Admiral Alan Gardner, with 10 or 12 ships, had been appointed to command in the West Indies. There were no ships available at this time for the East Indies but there were supposed to be about 25 ships in reserve.

Apart from the ships, the Royal Navy had at its disposal a great deal of talent. Its senior officers had all gained experience in the previous war, and some were already distinguished. Rodney was dead and Howe was the only full admiral of the White Squadron but Sir Peter

Parker, aged 72, and Sir Edward Hughes, aged 73, were still alive and the Vice-Admirals included Thomas Graves, Sir Alexander Hood and Lord Hood himself, William Hotham, Sir Charles Middleton, Sir John Jervis and Adam Duncan. The Rear-Admirals included Sir Hyde Parker and the Hon. William Cornwallis. Post captains of note included the Hon. G. Keith Elphinstone, James Gambier, Peter Rainier, Charles Pole, Horatio Nelson, Cuthbert Collingwood, John Duckworth, Sir Richard Bickerton, Sir J. B. Warren, James Saumarez, Edward Pellew and Richard Keats. These officers varied in age from 50 to 34, Nelson, at 35, being among the youngest of them and owing his seniority to his having achieved post rank (through influence) at the age of 21. Their proper French opponents, on the active list in 1787, should have included D'Estaing de Guicher, Le Comte de Treville, De Grasse Tilly, La Motte-Picquet, de Vaudreuil, Bougainville, de Rioux, Des Touches, De la Clue, De la Perouse, Comte de Flotte, Chevalier de Borda, de Bouncial, de Kersaint and La Bourdonnaye. We hear of none of these after 1792 and while Morand de Galles, who had served under Suffren, lasted a little longer, we hear nothing of him after 1793. The effect of the Revolution was thus to give the British a decided advantage in experienced officers. More officers of ability would no doubt emerge, but would they appear in time?

The French position at sea would have been more secure if the deposition and execution of their King had been agreed by a majority of the population. In point of fact the revolution was bitterly opposed in several of the provinces, including some adjacent to the major sea-ports. Had the British devoted all their efforts to restoring the French monarchy, something might well have been achieved. But while George III might deplore all French ideas of equality, the British generally regarded the war as one more in the series between Britain and France; a series in which they had lost the last round. What help they offered the French royalists was very incidental to a war in which France was the enemy. But the activity of French monarchists was an important factor in the situation, especially in the area around Toulon. Sailing for the Mediterranean with 21 sail of the line, Lord Hood arrived off Toulon in August, 1793, to find there a French fleet of comparable size paralysed by political disagreement. The fleet was commanded by the Comte de Trogoff, a firm royalist, who was opposed by Rear-Admiral St. Julien, a sound republican. Provence generally was royalist but was threatened by a republican army under General Carteau. To add further confusion, Hood was presently joined by 17 Spanish ships under Don Juan de Langara and various other detachments (both ships and troops) from Naples and Sardinia. The result of a complex negotiation left Lord Hood in possession of Toulon, by invitation of the inhabitants, but the place could not be held for long against the republican armies. The evacuation was agreed, following a council of war, and orders were given for the destruction of the arsenal and the French fleet. In the confusion these orders were only partly obeyed. Of the ships of the line 9 were destroyed, and 4 brought away, leaving no less than 18 in French possession. A further result of the affair was that the French Navy lost still more of its more aristocratic officers, who were regarded, not unreasonably, as politically unreliable. While this Toulon episode was somewhat inglorious, it had all the effect of a major naval victory, leaving the Mediterranean open to British sea power. Having no base there, Lord Hood attacked and eventually secured the island of Corsica, once more assisted by a local rebellion. It was lost again, however, in 1796, leaving the British yet again without a Mediterranean base.

The Channel Fleet had merely skirmished with the Brest Fleet in 1793. It put to sea again on 2 May 1794, Lord Howe being ordered to escort the outward-bound convoys clear of the Channel and then seek to intercept a French convoy expected from the United States. Off Ushant with 26 sail of the line, Lord Howe failed to intercept the French fleet of 25 ships under Villaret-Joyeuse, which put to sea and successfully covered the expected convoy. In doing this, however, Villaret-Joyeuse could not avoid an eventual meeting with Lord Howe in battle. The main fleets were in contact on 28 May and there followed the action which came to be known as the Battle of the First of June. The two fleets were very evenly matched and the resulting victory for Britain showed, convincingly and on a large scale, that democratic principles would provide no recipe for success in a naval battle. Villaret-Joyeuse could claim afterwards that he had successfully protected the French convoy, a fact which saved him from the guillotine. Tactically, the battle showed Howe as heir to Rodney. In the first phase, on 29 May, his aim was to divide the enemy's fleet from to leeward, cutting off his last five ships. In the event the French lost two ships, taken, and three others badly damaged. They lost, at the same time, the weather gage (i.e. their windward position) and all further chance of avoiding battle. On 1 June, Howe's orders were to divide the enemy at all points, attacking from to windward, and then engage from to leeward. In point of fact, 7 ships broke through the French line and 6 prizes were taken, one other ship being sunk. The action ended, the French fleet escaped into Brest without immediate pursuit and without being effectively challenged by a fresh squadron just arrived under Rear-Admiral Montague.

Lord Howe's fleet fought in almost classical formation, forming three squadrons, each of two divisions. The Van Squadron was led by Admiral Thomas Graves, with Rear-Admiral Pasley commanding the first division. The Central Squadron was led by Howe as Commander-in-Chief, with Rear-Admiral A. Gardner commanding the second division. The Rear Squadron was commanded by Admiral Sir Alexander Hood but without a flag officer to lead the second division. Like Rodney, Howe was satisfied with his victory and did little to complete it. On the French side the battle was remarkable for two things. First, the National Convention had decreed that the captain and officers of any ship which hauled down her colours to the enemy, however numerous, 'unless the French ship should be so shattered as to be in danger of sinking' should be liable to the death penalty. Second, Villaret-Joyeuse was accompanied to sea by a politician, Jean-Bon Saint-André, the equivalent of a Russian Commissar in more recent terminology; a sort of joint commander and official observer. To understand the force of this decree, backed by this sort of inspection, we have to realize that wooden ships were hardly ever sunk in battle. They were sometimes burnt but the damage they sustained by gunfire was nearly all above the waterline. Shots between wind and water could usually be plugged and leaking could usually be countered by manning the pumps. The result was that it was thought perfectly honourable and correct to surrender, as on land, after further resistance had become pointless. The result of the French decree was the extraordinary duel between the *Brunswick* and the *Vengeur*. After four hours of battle at minimal range, the *Vengeur* surrendered but sank soon afterwards with most of her surviving crew. According to the French legend she sank, still fighting, with all hands. In fact, her captain, among many others, surrendered and became a prisoner of war. What is significant is that the captain dared not strike his colours any sooner. Other ships which had struck their colours re-hoisted them later, their captains influenced no doubt by fear of the consequences if their ship should be taken. The French were trying, in effect, to introduce a new kind of war to the death. They failed in this but they did alter the nature of war and the later actions were fought far more for mutual destruction. We have no record of Lord Howe saying, like Rodney, 'Come, we have done very handsomely', and we know, in fact, that he was almost too exhausted to stand. But he was evidently quite satisfied with his success and George III, no less satisfied, wrote of Howe that 'The 1st June must be reckoned as a proud day for him as it will carry down his name to the latest posterity.' His name is indeed remembered but we must admit that he represented an earlier age. By later standards he might be said to have failed sufficiently to exploit his success.

At the end of 1794 Pitt's ministry was joined by some of the Portland Whigs with a consequent reshuffle in which Lord Chatham was replaced as First Lord by Lord Spencer. At about the same time Lord Howe went ashore, remaining in nominal command but entrusting the Channel Fleet to his deputy, Admiral Sir Alexander Hood, Lord Bridport. On 12 October Lord Hood, his elder brother, quitted the Mediterranean Fleet, leaving Vice-Admiral Hotham in command, and returned to England, no doubt with Admiralty permission, for reasons of health. There had been from the beginning a jealousy between the Channel and the Mediterranean Fleets, made worse by a close association between Chatham and Hood. With Chatham's replacement the priority of the Mediterranean was lost. Hood was told that only five ships were available to reinforce his fleet. He remonstrated with the Board in outspoken terms, being (as one admirer put it) 'a stranger to any feeling of nervous diffidence'. His last letter on this subject, written from on board the *Victory* at Spithead, was so improper that the Board replied with an order to him to strike his flag and come ashore. As Earl Spencer told the King:

. . . the discipline and subordination so necessary to be maintained between the Board of Admiralty and the officers entrusted by that Board with the conduct of your Majesty's naval forces would be entirely at an end, if public and official representations of this kind were allowed to pass unnoticed.

On his side, Hood revealed that Lord Spencer's indifference and inattention extended to 'all who have any connection with me'. He never went to sea again and ended as Governor of Greenwich Hospital. 'Oh, miserable Board of Admiralty', wrote Captain Horatio Nelson, 'They have forced the first officer in the Service away from his command . . . Upward of 70, he possesses the mind of 40.' The removal of Howe and

Hood would have been more fortunate if they had been succeeded by abler men in the prime of life. Howe's successor, Lord Bridport (Lord Hood's younger brother) was aged 68 and even Hotham was 59. The results were unfortunate for Bridport fought an action with Villaret-Joyeuse on 22 June 1795, took three prizes and then called off the chase while still in a position to gain a real victory. In the Mediterranean, meanwhile, Hotham had an encounter with the French Rear-Admiral Martin off Genoa on 11 to 14 March 1795. The result was the capture of the *Ça Ira* (80) and *Censeur* (74) largely through the efforts of Nelson in the *Agamemnon* (64). Then Hotham broke off the action and refused Nelson's plea to renew it, adding the significant words 'We must be contented. We have done very well.' Luckier than most admirals, Hotham encountered the French fleet again in July, but once more threw away his opportunity, to Nelson's fury. Towards the end of 1795 Hotham was relieved of his command leaving Sir Hyde Parker as his successor on 1 November who was shortly afterwards succeeded by Sir John Jervis. By then, however, the damage had been done. All Europe could admittedly see that the British fleet was unaffected by revolutionary doctrines and that the French fleet was not as good as it had been under Louis xv. As against that, the French had not been decisively defeated at sea. Their Mediterranean fleet was still in being, their Brest fleet was still active and their war against British commerce was not unsuccessful. On land, moreover, the French success was complete and led to the treaties of 1795. Under these the Netherlands, now a French satellite, agreed to provide 12 sail of the line for service against Britain in the North Sea and agreed at the same time to admit a French garrison into Flushing. Spain made peace with the French and later (July 1796) turned that peace into an alliance, adding her fleet to that of France and declaring war on Britain in October. Prussia made peace with loss of some territory, Britain being left with no allies other than Portugal, Piedmont and Naples, the last two countries increasingly threatened by France. With the Dutch fleet to reckon with, the British had to form a third fleet in European waters, one which was placed under the command of Admiral Duncan. But this made it all the more difficult to reinforce the Mediterranean Fleet, which was barely equal to the French and was now faced by the Spanish as well. Corsica had become untenable and its evacuation was carried out under fire and not without loss.

On 4 August, just before the Spanish declaration of war, Admiral

Don Juan de Langara sailed from Cadiz with 19 sail of the line and 10 smaller vessels. He almost immediately encountered Rear Admiral Mann, whose 7 sail of the line were supposed to join Sir John Jervis's flag. Mann found refuge under the guns of Gibraltar but was so unnerved by the situation that he sailed for England; the result, it was said, of brooding on imaginary ills and difficulties. Calling at Carthagena, where he was joined by 7 more ships, the Spanish admiral eventually came into Toulon with 26 sail to add to the 12 he found there. With 38 sail of the line, Langara could thus bring overwhelming force to bear against Jervis, whose fleet (after Mann's withdrawal) numbered no more than 15. With the troops on board who had embarked at Bastia, Sir John sailed for Gibraltar, arriving there on 11 December 1796, but going on to Lisbon which was now his only base. There was no longer a British fleet in the Mediterranean. About this situation there had been a great deal of argument, more especially between Dundas and Spencer. As soon as the abandonment of the Mediterranean was discussed, Dundas wrote to Spencer in protest:

... Whatever calamities this country in the course of war has sustained in the persons of its allies, its own glory has at least remained untarnished, and the sentiment is universally acknowledged and publicly boasted of by us that our naval superiority stands unrivalled. Did we mean to boast only that we were superior to France? Surely not. We meant to say what every man feels, that a union of the naval power of France and Spain would be brought to confusion by our naval exertions, and we begin the war by running out of the Mediterranean and allowing immense fleets of theirs to parade and ride triumphant in these seas. It is impossible to figure a more humiliating circumstance. It amounts to a distinct confession that whenever France and Spain are at war (which will always be the case when one is) we must abandon all connection with the Mediterranean and in truth with the whole South of Europe.[2]

Spencer replied at length, his letter including the following comparison of strength on either side:

We have now belonging to the Channel Fleet ready, or nearly ready, twenty-four sail of the line and two more which may be ready by the end of December – say in all thirty-six. We have in the Mediterranean twenty-one. The total therefore of the line in Europe, exclusive of the North Sea, is fifty-seven. Take from that number thirty-five for the Mediterranean and you leave twenty-two sail of the line for the defence of this country ...
[When the French have twenty-five ships of the line in their Atlantic port and the Spanish another twelve between Cadiz and Ferrol.][3]

Spencer's answer was to leave Jervis with about 21 ships based on Lisbon. This was an almost purely defensive deployment but what else could he do? The fact was that a fleet in the Mediterranean could not be maintained. With no base nearer than Lisbon – Gibraltar offered no more than an anchorage – a fleet in the Mediterranean would use up its strength in protecting its supply lines. Corsica had been useful in itself, and doubly useful in denying its timber supply to the French, but it was too remote and was impossible to defend without decisive naval superiority in the Mediterranean. There was no alternative, but the British withdrawal gave great encouragement to the Corsican General Bonaparte. 'The expulsion of the English has a great effect upon the success of our military operations in Italy,' he wrote. 'It has the greatest moral influence on the minds of the Italians. It assures our communications and will make Naples tremble.'

The withdrawal from the Mediterranean had all the impact on Britain of a major defeat. So far as southern Europe was concerned, it represented British prestige at its lowest. It was at the same time that effective preparations began for victory. Our difficulty is in seeing that the preparations were more important than the current setback. Books on naval history must tend to concentrate on battles, ignoring other aspects and events. Readers are given a diagram and told a story of tactical brilliance. They are spared an account of the process by which the fleet was fitted, recruited, provisioned, disciplined, inspected, encouraged and inspired. It is a fact, nevertheless, that the Commander-in-Chief's orders and example on the day of battle may matter less than the work he has done over the previous months or years. In the present instance, Sir John Jervis's arrival in the Mediterranean as Commander-in-Chief was a turning point in the war. He found a fleet in complete disorder, the result of indiscipline under Hood and Hotham. On this subject a quotation from J. S. Tucker's biography of Jervis (later to become Earl of St Vincent) would seem relevant:

The writer of these pages has been often told, by an eye-witness to the fact, that, before the smoke of the salute to the Commander-in-Chief's flag was blown off, the signal to unmoor flew. Whether on that incident memory were or were not accurate, it is not too much to assert, that at this period and in this fleet commenced, and chiefly to the command of this Admiral was due, the creation of that naval system which, when carried out, he perfected the discipline, the health and the activity – in a word, the unrivalled efficiency of the British Navy.[4]

We are told that Jervis restored discipline but how did he set about it? Admiral Sir William James gives us a clue:

Within a few hours of his arrival officers and men knew that the easy-going days were over . . .

He found everything in the fleet far below his standard; there was a serious lack of stores, discipline was lax, insufficient attention was being paid to health, and after a few days at sea he knew that his captains had a lot to learn . . .

He constantly inspected his ships and his captains soon knew that he would accept no excuse for untidiness or dirt on the mess deck. One of his many orders for improving the health of the fleet directed that the bedding of the ships' companies was to be shaken and aired every week, a custom that has endured ever since.

By never relaxing for a moment or permitting any of his officers to relax he succeeded in keeping his men in good health. . . .

Nor would he allow the slightest relaxation in the strict discipline he had soon enforced in all his ships. He expected the officers to set the example. 'The Admiral having observed a flippancy in the behaviour of officers when coming upon the *Victory*'s quarter-deck, and sometimes in receiving orders from a superior officer, and that they do not pull off their hats, and some not even touch them; it is his positive direction, that any officer who shall in future so far forget this essential duty of respect and subordination, be admonished publicly. . . .'

Officer or man who committed a disciplinary offence received short shrift and the lazy and incompetent went in fear of coming under his eagle eye . . .[5]

Sir John's system of discipline began with the officers and with their public behaviour. Having secured their mutual respect he went on to demand obedience to orders:

He was fretful if he saw anything done in a careless or slovenly manner, whether at his table, or on exercise; and if he could not reclaim a young man in these particulars, he gave him up. He could not endure to hear of the word "trouble"; 'there ought,' he said, 'to be no such word in the naval dictionary.' Where any one said they could not do a thing they were desired to do, he used to tell them to 'rub out "can't" and put in "try"'. He would forgive an officer for losing or springing a topmast in carrying sail; but he never overlooked splitting a topsail in handing or reefing it, because he said such accidents were the effect either of ignorance or carelessness . . .

There was a remarkable trait in the character of Lord St Vincent, which tended greatly to extend the energies of naval officers under his command. Whenever he saw any one zealous, but diffident, he always gave him encouragement; but if arrogance and self-sufficiency appeared, he rebuked and repressed it with an irresistible moral power.

Lord St Vincent never liked to hear of an officer getting married in war time. He would say, when any one asked permission to go home to England for a short period, 'Sir, you want to go on shore and get married, and then you won't be worth your salt.'[6]

Having dealt with the officers as individuals he went on to discipline the ships. He would have no ship out of station and soon had occasion to issue the following order:

The Commander-in-Chief observes with concern, that the ships of the squadron do not preserve the prescribed distances from each other in the order of sailing, with the precision necessary for making a sudden impression upon the enemy, or to avoid accidents by falling on board each other, which will happen continually if they do not keep their station correctly. He thinks many ships are too sparing with their mainsails when to leeward or astern . . .[7]

There were two secrets of maintaining formation. The first lay in the knowledge that the Admiral was always watching and never, apparently, slept. The second lay in the fact that each captain, under the Admiral's eye, would always be on deck when the signal was made to tack or wear at night. But Jervis was not merely a fanatic about sail-drill. He was just as emphatic about gunnery and the need for constant practice. While a terror in the enforcement of discipline, however, he knew how to relax on occasion:

There was one point in Lord St Vincent's character which peculiarly fitted him for Commander-in-Chief on our most important stations: he had no disposition to hoard up his money, but always entertained his own officers, as well as foreign visitors, with the greatest liberality. This may appear to be a matter of trivial importance: but, when duly considered, it ranks high as a public virtue. It promotes harmony, and makes people well acquainted with each other . . .[8]

With Jervis, discipline came first but economy came second. He did his utmost to supply his fleet with all necessary stores, defying the Navy Board, if need be, and resorting to local purchase. But, having done his utmost in that direction, he would not tolerate any waste in any form. Captains were to practise 'the utmost frugality'. Spars or cordage might be condemned as unfit for their original purpose but that did not mean that they could not be used in some other way.

Officers were encouraged to improvise and any instances of waste would bring on them a stinging reprimand. Jervis wanted to know the exact stores available on board every ship down to and including the last pound of nails and the last ball of twine. Nor did his inquiries stop there for he established the practice of attaching store-ships to the fleet, considering that the stores would be safer afloat as well as more immediately available. He specialized in a procedure for refitting at sea. When a ship was crippled or in need of a repair which would ordinarily have meant sending her into port, he would, by signal, order all the carpenters' crews from the other ships to go aboard the ship in question and make a concerted effort to complete all necessary repairs and even finish the work with a coat of paint; all this without a pause in the fleet's movement at the time. His interest extended to the dockyards ashore and to establishments which were none of his business; places well known for every evil varying from pilfering to industrial dispute. This sort of curiosity would eventually do him no good but the situation in 1796 was such as to justify his interference. It came to be realized that he was doing his utmost to ensure that his fleet would be properly supplied.

The Admiral's sense of economy extended to the sick and the wounded. There could be nothing more wasteful than having men on the sick list.

The health of the crews was preserved by attention to their food and by great care that they were not overworked. They were kept at three watches; one watch being sufficient on common occasions, and two watches on any emergency; while the third was always left in repose, to mend their clothes, or amuse themselves as they liked.[9]

Jervis did much to ensure that each ship had a proper sick-bay, well-equipped and regularly inspected. But he relied still more on having a hospital ship with the fleet:

. . . This was usually a 44, upon two decks; the only use that vile class of ships could ever be applied to, and for which they were admirably adapted. This hospital ship always kept her station on the weather-beam of the admiral, supplied with every comfort, and even luxury, for the use of the sick, who quickly recovered, under the skilful care and kind treatment of the medical man in charge of them. Thus the ships had no serious cases on board, all of that description being immediately transferred, in cots, to the hospital, and returned to their proper ships when cured.[10]

So it became apparent that the tough disciplinarian had a kinder side. Was it merely in order to have his men back on duty again? That was one motive undoubtedly but it transpired that good care was also taken of the men invalided out of the service and sent back to England. There were moments, rare and fleeting as they might be, when Jervis appeared almost human.

The secrets of leadership are perpetually lost in times of peace and as regularly rediscovered in time of war. One secret is to ensure that the leader, who cannot be everywhere, will be talked about when he is not actually there. He has to be a colourful figure, one about whom stories are told. Jervis knew all about this simple technique and the stories told about him were legion and some of them quite possibly true. One significant story concerns a petty officer, Roger Odell, who inadvertently went swimming with all his money (£70 in notes) in a pocket. They were reduced to pulp and he was reduced to tears. Jervis witnessed the man's grief and presently called all hands aft and told Odell to step forward. He accused him publicly of being seen in tears. What defence had he to offer? Odell could only plead that he had, through his own fault, lost the savings of a great many years. Jervis replied that this was no excuse for tears. He added that Odell was one of the best men in the ship and concluded 'To show, therefore, that your Commander-in-Chief will never pass over merit, wheresoever he may find it – there is your money, sir,' (giving him £70), 'but no more tears, mind, no more tears, sir.'[11] So the old tyrant had really a heart of gold! Or had he? The real object of this exercise was obviously to build up the legend of an Admiral whose gruff manners concealed the kindest feelings for his men. Here, after all, was an anecdote that would be repeated for ever. The sum lost had been substantial and the loss had been made good with all possible publicity. The kind deed was done with a very deliberate purpose, the preliminary harshness calculated to emphasise the later generosity which was itself accompanied by the final rebuke. There were other stories about Jervis, some for the officers and some for the men, and they were mostly planned to give the same impression. These are tricks known to every leader and Jervis was evidently a master at playing to the gallery on occasion. We can note the process by which his legend was created and we can be sure that each step was planned, improved and coldly deliberate.

The Mediterranean Fleet gradually acquired the sort of reputation with which a more recent leader endowed the Eighth Army. But we do wrong if we concentrate too exclusively on the stately line of battle. The sight of the Fleet under sail in precise formation must admittedly have been breath-taking, the more so in that it included at one time no fewer than 7 three-decked ships. But Jervis also had under his command some 24 frigates, 15 sloops, 5 storeships, a hospital ship, a fireship, a prison ship, 4 cutters and an armed transport; well over 70 vessels in all. Nor should we forget that fleet actions were the exception and that other fighting was almost continual. During the twelve months or so which followed Jervis's hoisting his flag in the Mediterranean, the *Southampton* (32) took the French corvette *Utile* (24) and the *Terpsichore* (32) captured the Spanish frigate *Mahonesa* (34) off Malaga – the first Spanish ship to be taken after Spain entered the war. Then the *Terpsichore* took the French frigate *Vestale* (36) off Cadiz – a prize which was afterwards retaken. Finally, Commodore Horatio Nelson in the *Minerve* frigate (38) took the Spanish frigate *Sabina* (40) while the *Blanche* (32) took the *Ceres* – both prizes being retaken. Actions such as these helped to build up the fleet's morale and lessen the confidence of the enemy. But these actions led to two other general conclusions. First of all, Nelson was plainly the genius of the fleet. This had been perfectly obvious even before Jervis arrived and the Admiral had since decided to make full use of his talents. Nelson was a senior captain and soon to receive his flag, being promoted Commodore meanwhile. His only rival was Richard Bowen of the *Terpsichore*, whose distinguished career was to end when he was killed in action at Teneriffe in 1797. The other general conclusion must be that the British ships in the Mediterranean were clearly outnumbered. The *Minerve* could force the *Sabina* to haul down her colours but the sequel was one in which the *Sabina* was re-captured and the *Minerve* was lucky to escape. There were enemy ships everywhere and Jervis had in effect to fight a rearguard action as he withdrew from the Mediterranean. The different encounters were creditable in themselves but they could not turn a retreat into a victory.

Hope for the future lay in two factors which only a few people could properly assess at the time. There was, to begin with, the process by which Sir John Jervis trained the Mediterranean Fleet; a process regarded with horror by officers who were based on Portsmouth. Admiral Sir William James writes of Jervis:

... those thirteen months during which he welded a fleet, lacking in discipline and good seamanship, into a splendid fighting machine, and by continual endeavour succeeded in providing his ships' companies with food in circumstances that would have daunted most men, were perhaps the greatest period in his life.[12]

Of Jervis at this time Sir Gilbert Elliot wrote: 'The Admiral is as firm as a rock.' As for Nelson, he wrote to his wife on 17 October 1796:

We are all preparing to leave the Mediterranean, a measure which I cannot approve. They at home do not know what this Fleet is capable of performing: anything and everything. Much as I shall rejoice to see England, I lament our present orders in sackcloth and ashes, so dishonourable to the dignity of England, whose Fleets are equal to meet the World in arms; and of all the Fleets I ever saw, I never beheld one in point of officers and men equal to Sir John Jervis's, who is a Commander-in-Chief able to lead them to glory.[13]

What Jervis was doing and had done was not of course generally known. Still less, however, did anyone appreciate the other factors, which were at this time no more than the glimmering of an idea. In a letter to his wife dated 1 April 1795, Nelson made this comment on Hotham's indecisive action: 'Now, had we taken ten Sail, and had allowed the eleventh to escape, when it had been possible to have got at her, I could never have called it well done.'[14] Nelson's aim, one new to the naval history of his generation, something he had copied, in effect, from Bonaparte, was revolutionary, dramatic and simple. His aim was to destroy the enemy.

THREE

Britain at Bay

Holding the initiative in 1793–95 the British offensive action had been directed mainly against the West Indies, where Sir John Jervis and Lieutenant-General Sir Charles Grey conquered Martinique, St Lucia and Guadeloupe; Jervis being afterwards sent to the Mediterranean. An attempt against Haiti failed, Guadeloupe was reconquered by a French expedition and the losses from yellow fever were appalling. Some half-hearted efforts were made to help the French royalists in Brittany, more especially in 1795, but it proved impracticable to co-ordinate the operation of the rebels with those of their British friends. Farther afield an effort was made to provide a squadron for the defence of India and when the Dutch entered the war a British expedition had little difficulty in capturing from them their colony at the Cape. Some of these colonial conquests were valuable but little had been achieved against France itself. The French Navy had suffered some losses, particularly at Toulon, but it was still very much in existence. In desultory fighting it had become apparent that the French ships were seldom a match for their British opponents. Such opportunities as there were would seem to have been rejected, however, and then, with the Dutch and Spanish as our enemies, the balance of strength was in favour of France. The position would have been still more dangerous if the Dutch fleet had been more heavily gunned. The Dutch harbours and coastal waters were so shallow that their ships were limited in draught and therefore in tonnage. The fleet which was detached to operate against them comprised, therefore, the ships which were thought sufficient; the older and weaker ships, some converted East Indiaman and other vessels regarded as more or less obsolete.

Britain's allies on the continent having made peace with France, there was nothing to prevent the French planning a major attack on Britain. Nor was there much doubt as to where the attack should fall. Britain's weak point was then, as it has always been and as it still remains, Ireland. Here was a province ripe for rebellion, its catholic inhabitants as bitter against protestant England as were the Breton catholics against atheist France. It is a separate island, moreover, and its English reinforcements, like its French invaders, would have to come by sea. No better target could be found. Given French naval superiority in the western approaches its conquest would have been relatively easy. No such naval ascendancy had been established but now that the Spanish fleet could be added to the French, victory at sea did not seem remote. In the meanwhile it was decided to secure a bridge-head in Ireland. This decision, like that made by other invaders before and since, was a mistake. Without a naval victory the plan was not feasible, and, given a naval victory, it was not even necessary. As against that, a blow against Ireland would cause alarm and despondency, drawing into Ireland the British forces which might otherwise have been used in an attack upon France. The French royalists, whose armies had numbered up to 100,000, had been finally crushed by General Hoche, whose army was still in Brittany or thereabouts and who had readily available the muskets and bayonets, shoes and greatcoats, saddles and sabres with which the 'Chouans' had been supplied from Britain. With these an Irish army could be equipped and might, with French help, keep the British occupied for years. With all his experience of arguing with a catholic peasantry, Hoche was the ideal leader for such an expedition. It remained to make a plan by which his army might be safely transported to Ireland.

The difficulty in this sort of scheme is the timing. The factors in the situation include the invading force, the exiles, the potential rebels, the available tonnage, the tide and the moon and, finally, the weather. Planning is somewhat easier if the rebels are regarded as merely ancillary; the position as in 1588 or in 1944. Where, however, the rebels are to provide the bulk of the army, the invaders being merely ancillary, the timing becomes crucial, and the difficulties multiply. The exiles will be optimistic and must be regarded as liars. Contact with the rebel leaders may be intermittent and slow. The leaders' control over the partisan forces may be doubtful and there may be disagreement and jealousy between the leaders themselves. Yet, somehow, the rising and the landing must be made to coincide. If the partisans act too soon they will be defeated before help can arrive. If they act too late the landing may be opposed in force. After the initial success it will be essential to capture a deepwater seaport with facilities for landing artillery. As from that point all will depend upon the speed of the build-up, which must depend in turn upon the distance between the points of embarkation and landing; which could not, in this instance, be much under four hundred miles. With the British fleet undefeated, the French planners had to decide on a winter campaign, using long, dark nights to cover the operation and hoping that the enemy fleet would remain in port. They were given encouragement by the Irishman, Wolfe Tone, who reached France in February 1796, and told the Directory about the United Irishmen and other such improbable organizations. He assured his hosts that he could find 15,000 troops in Ireland, with 16,000 militia (3000 cavalry included) all ready to co-operate. He convinced them that the Irish seamen in the British fleet were on the point of mutiny. The French, oddly enough, believed him. They based their expedition on Brest, and chose Bantry Bay as their point of disembarkation with Cork as the seaport they were to occupy. They allocated 20,000 men to the enterprise with Hoche in command and Wolfe Tone (now Brigadier-General) as his political adviser. They collected 30,000 arms with other equipment for their expected recruits in Ireland. Villaret was to have commanded at sea but he was replaced, at Hoche's request, by the more submissive Morard de Galles. By 5 December 1796, the fleet was ready to sail. It sailed in fact on the night of the 16th, comprising seventeen sail of the line, thirteen frigates, eight corvettes and seven transports; 15,000 troops were embarked. Hoche and Morard de Galles were together in one of the frigates. The original plan had involved the Spanish fleet as well but this failed to appear and the French sailed without them. Even so, the fleet was stronger than the British squadron which might, in theory, have opposed it.

At this momentous time the Channel Fleet was still commanded by Richard, Earl Howe, who was ashore and often, in fact, at Bath. That he retained the nominal command was a reflection, perhaps, of doubts expressed about his deputy, Lord Bridport. The distrust he inspired in some people went back to the court-martial on Admiral Keppel in 1779, an affair which split the Navy at the time and was not yet forgotten.

. . . it appeared from the evidence given by the Master of the *Robuste*, on Admiral Keppel's trial, that Captain Hood [Lord Bridport] had taken out such leaves of the log-book as could alone tend to throw a proper light on the evidence which he had given to criminate the Admiral, and that he had caused *other leaves* to be substituted in their room. This was a transaction of so unprecedented a nature, as not only laid Captain Hood open to the censure of the Court, but cast such a *dark shade* upon his naval character, as neither time, nor a series of praise-worthy actions, can ever remove from the minds of the Officers of the fleet.[1]

This affair was more vividly remembered by his political opponents, Sir John Jervis being one of them, he having been conspicuous in this court-martial on the other side. Bridport is otherwise described as 'rather penurious and very rich' and 'supposed to be cautious'. Caution was certainly his characteristic when he had a skirmish with the French fleet in June 1795, and exercised what the historian, William James, calls 'unaccountable forbearance'. Whatever doubts may be felt about Bridport's character, his position was a difficult one as representative afloat of a Commander-in-Chief who lived ashore. It was made worse by the recent construction of the semaphore telegraph between London and Portsmouth, a device which tended to keep the Channel Fleet at Spithead and so within easy reach. The French threat was actually met, after a fashion, by forming an inshore squadron of frigates off Brest; a covering squadron of ships of the line off Ushant under Colpoys; a squadron in the Channel and to the westward under Sir Roger Curtis and the main fleet with Bridport at Spithead. It was not a fortunate arrangement but it was deliberate. Kempenfelt had fairly expressed Lord Howe's opinion when he wrote about the possibility of the French putting to sea in winter: 'Let us act wiser, and keep ours in port; leave them to the mercy of long nights and hard gales. . . . A large fleet never tacks or wears when it blows hard in a dark night without risking damage.' As Collingwood said, rocks and tides 'have more of danger in them than a battle once a week'.

First move in the invasion of Ireland took place on 11 December when Richery's squadron from the Isle d'Aix joined Morard de Galles at Brest. This move was reported by Sir Edward Pellew, commanding the inshore squadron. Then Morard de Galles sailed after dark, changing his mind at the last moment. His intention had been to leave by the Passage du Raz but he decided against it, making his signal with guns and rockets. Pellew, with the *Indefatigable*, had come close into the harbour mouth and now fired off his own rockets and guns, making the signal meaningless. In the confusion the *Seduisant* (74) was wrecked, adding her signals of distress to the confusion. The other ships duly put to sea but in different directions, some by the Passage du Raz, and never managed to concentrate. Bouvet brought most of the ships into Bantry Bay on 17–18 December but among the ships missing was the *Fraternité* with Morard de Galles, Hoche and Bruix. Then the wind increased to a gale and many of the ships' anchors dragged. They accordingly cut their cables and put to sea. The fleet was badly dispersed and new arrivals in Bantry Bay, finding no other ships there, returned to Brest. No forces were landed in Ireland and only a few of the French stragglers were lost. Most other ships reached base but the failure was complete on either side. For Britain the only crumb of comfort lay in the destruction of the *Les Droits de l'Homme* (80). This large ship of the line was intercepted on her way home by Pellew with two frigates, the *Indefatigable* and *Amazon*. A night action followed in such rough weather that the French ship dared not use her lower-deck guns. She had more than 700 soldiers on board but was apparently short of ammunition for her guns. There was a running battle which ended in the *Droits de l'Homme* being wrecked on the French coast with the *Amazon* for company. The *Indefatigable* was brought off by superb seamanship and Pellew's reputation stood higher than ever. The same cannot be said of Bridport or Colpoys.

Colpoys' error was in being absent from his rendezvous when Pellew sent news to him of the French being at sea. The official explanation was to the effect that he had been blown off his station by an easterly gale. He was certainly some forty miles west of Ushant, but why? The log of his flagship records only fresh breezes on the 15th and 16th. And if Colpoys could not remain at his rendezvous, how is it that Pellew could remain at his? With a force roughly equal to that of the French, Colpoys had done little or nothing to bring on a general engagement. He was not a coward in the ordinary sense of the word but his aim was merely to avoid defeat. As he put it in a letter to Pellew, he considered that a drawn battle would be fatal to England at that period of the war. As for Bridport, the call to action found him at his home ashore, at Cricket Lodge, near Chard in Somerset, and it took him two days to reach Portsmouth. He hoisted his flag in the *Royal George* on 19 December, three days after the French had put to sea.

On the 25th the signal was made to weigh, but the departure of Lord Bridport from Spithead was attended with even less happy results than that of Morard de Galles from Brest. The *Sans Pareil* and *Prince* collided and both ships anchored; the *Atlas* got aground; and the *Formidable* collided with the *Ville de Paris* and had to anchor too. With only eight sail of the line in company, the Admiral anchored at St Helens at half-past four. For the next two days it blew so hard from the east that the ships at Spithead were unable to join those at St Helens. On the 29th the weather moderated and the Admiral was joined by six more sail of the line, but now the north-westerly gales which were driving Colpoys up Channel held Bridport at St Helens. Only at 4 a.m. on January 3rd was the signal made to unmoor, and at day-break the squadron, comprising fourteen of the line and seven frigates, got under way with a fresh breeze from the east. Bouvet, Grouchy, Tone and the staff, with the first division of French line of battle ships, had got back safely to Camaret two days before.[2]

The delay over the Channel Fleet's sailing, and the bad seamanship displayed by some of its ships, were not alone responsible for Bridport's reaching Bantry Bay on 8 January. He had not steered directly for the Irish coast but had headed at first for the vicinity of Brest. But for this divergence he might have been off Bantry Bay on the 6th, just in time to intercept the last of the French ships. As things were he was back at Spithead on 4 February without having achieved anything. Nor had he learnt anything from experience for his slack methods were pursued as long as he commanded the Channel Fleet. His low reputation was shared by his flag officers, Colpoys and Sir Roger Curtis. Had Bridport been reasonably successful, Lord Howe might have sooner hauled down his flag and allowed Bridport to inherit the nominal, as well as the real, command. But Howe (aged 70) had some cause to think himself indispensable and was reluctant to make way for Bridport (aged 69). The only men to emerge from this campaign with an enhanced reputation were Vice-Admiral Kingsmill and Captain Sir Edward Pellew. Kingsmill was the flag-officer at Cork, whose ships did what little damage was done. Pellew, whose capture of the *Cleopatre* had more or less begun the war at sea, was a dashing frigate captain and the established hero of Cornwall and Devonshire. All had to admit that his destruction of *Les Droits de l'Homme* had been an epic story. A frigate was ordinarily thought so inferior to a ship of the line that it played no part in a battle and was not normally fired upon if present. But here was Pellew's frigate attacking an 80-gun ship and finally driving her to destruction on her own coast. However dull Bridport's record might be, there were younger men whose names were already becoming a legend and whose deeds are not forgotten even now.

We have touched upon the misfortunes of the French in their failure against Ireland but their worst setback occurred before they had even sailed. The French plan had originally depended upon the Spanish fleet coming to join them. 'Those damned Spaniards!' Tone exclaimed, 'Why are they not at this moment in Brest waters?' Given a junction of the two fleets, he said, it would be possible to 'cripple the naval power of England for ever'. This was an interesting possibility but the Spanish looked at the problem from a different angle. To send their main fleet northward would have left their coasts and their trade at the mercy of Sir John Jervis. The Spanish fleet joined the French at Toulon and sailed thence in company with Rear-Admiral Villeneuve on 10 December. Villeneuve was under orders to sail for Brest, late as he would be for the invasion of Ireland, but Admiral Langara went no farther than Carthagena. He was there superseded by Admiral Juan de Cordova who again had no orders to go beyond Cadiz. Owing to a gale, Villeneuve passed the Straits of Gibraltar without interception, reaching Brest alone with his own ships. The Spanish who had been last seen off Ireland in 1588, were not eager to revisit that country. Nor can we blame them. They had manned their ships with the greatest difficulty. Their officers were mostly without any operational experience. Their ships were magnificent but their seamanship was poor. Nor were they moved by any of the democratic zeal which was supposed to animate the French. It was a French war into which they had been dragged and from which they stood to gain nothing. Under French pressure, Admiral Cordova may have been theoretically on his way to Bantry Bay but he had evidently no intention of arriving in time. His immediate concern, when he sailed, was with a small convoy laden with mercury and bound from Malaga to Cadiz.

The Spanish came nearest to success on the night when Commodore Nelson, in the frigate *Minerve*, sailed through their fleet on his way from Elba to the fleet rendezvous. With better luck or vigilance they might have captured Nelson at the outset. From Nelson and from other sources Sir John Jervis, off Cape St Vincent with his fleet, knew of the Spanish approach. Cordova's fleet was blown far into the Atlantic, however, and finally headed for Cadiz on an easterly course. It was first sighted by a Portuguese frigate, commanded by an officer with the untypically Portuguese name of Campbell. On 14 January 1797, the two fleets were in sight of each other but a foggy morning made for poor visibility. Cordova had learnt from an American ship that Sir John

Jervis had with him nine sail of the line. This was perfectly true on the 4th but Sir John had since been reinforced by Rear-Admiral Sir William Parker with five more sail of the line. He had, in fact, fifteen in all, two of 100 guns (*Victory* and *Britannia*), three of 98, one of 90, eight of 74 and one of 64 guns; together with four frigates, two sloops and a cutter. With twenty-seven sail of the line, Cordova's fleet included the *Santissima Trinidad* (130 guns), six 112-gun ships, two of 80 and eighteen of 74 guns; together with twelve frigates and one corvette. With allowances made for the Spanish three-deckers, Jervis had little more than half the strength of his opponent. He had, nevertheless, decided to fight, saying that 'a victory is very essential to England at this moment'. A lesser man, a Hotham or a Bridport, would have said, and very rightly, that 'a defeat would be fatal for England at this moment'. But Sir John had brought his fleet up to a standard of training which gave his men confidence. Against odds which would have fully justified him in refusing battle he decided to risk a general engagement.

In the actual event, the odds were not as adverse as they might have been. Cordova had left three ships at Algeciras and detached five more to escort his convoy. Only seventeen of his ships were in action and these in such disorder that they tended to mask each other's fire. There was a big gap between Cordova's main fleet and his convoy and Jervis steered for this wide opening. Hoping to rejoin his lee division, Cordova altered course so as to pass astern of the British line. Observing this, Jervis signalled his fleet to tack in succession. The manoeuvre was promptly carried out but Cordova's leading ships were still in a position to join up with his group to leeward. Commodore Nelson in the *Captain* (74), third from the rear, saw what was happening, wore ship, quitted his place in the line and with the *Excellent*, threw himself athwart the *Santissima Trinidad* and her two supporting three-deckers. This brought the Spanish move to a halt and started a confused fight in which four Spanish ships were taken: the *San Nicolas* (80) by the *Captain*, the *San Josef* (112) by the *Captain*, the *Salvador del Mundo* (112) by the *Orion* and the *San Ysidro* (74) by the *Excellent* (74). The Spanish flagship *Santissima Trinidad* (130 or 136) also surrendered at one time but the Spanish eventually managed to bring her away, covered by fresh ships belonging to their lee division. In order to secure his prizes and rescue the damaged *Captain* Sir John Jervis rallied his ships, formed line and shaped his course for Lagos. The Spanish fleet pulled itself together went into Cadiz and was soon blockaded there. The *Santissima*

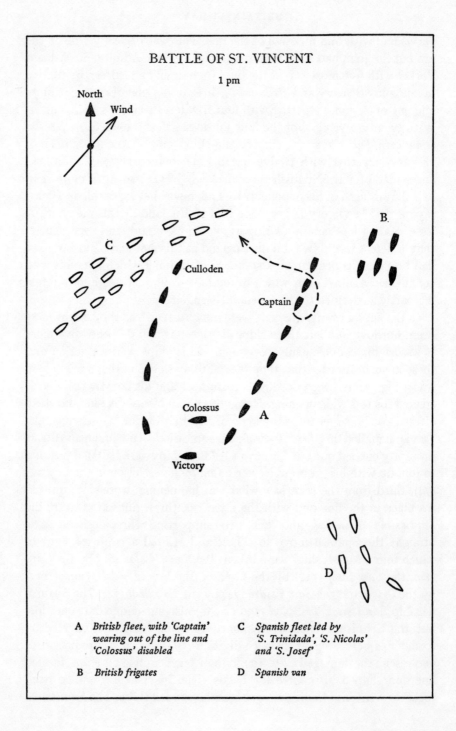

BATTLE OF ST. VINCENT

1 pm

North

Wind

C

Culloden

Captain

B

Colossus

A

Victory

D

A *British fleet, with 'Captain'*
   wearing out of the line and
   'Colossus' disabled

B *British frigates*

C *Spanish fleet led by*
   'S. Trinidada', 'S. Nicolas'
   and 'S. Josef'

D *Spanish van*

Trinidad was dismasted and three frigates were sent after her, located her but failed to make an attack. The curious sequel was that the *Terpsichore* frigate, commanded by Captain Bowen, subsequently engaged the *Santissima Trinidad* and only broke off the action when other Spanish ships appeared, allowing the Spanish flagship to escape into Algeciras. A more vigorous pursuit in strength would, no doubt, have made her a prize.

The Battle of St Vincent is remembered as the occasion that made Horatio Nelson a hero. This is not entirely true because he was a hero – for the Mediterranean Fleet – before the battle took place. He had been famous since the action between the *Agamemnon* and *Ca Ira* in 1795 and had been acknowledged as 'one of the first characters in the Service' before that. His hardest fight had probably been that between the *Minerve* and the Spanish *Santa Sabina*, in which the latter frigate, commanded by Don Jacobo Stuart, a great-grandson of James II, lost 164 killed and wounded out of a crew of 286. But Nelson gained national acclaim when he personally boarded the *San Nicolas* and then went on from her to board and capture the *San Josef*. Hearing of three desperate doings Nelson's wife begged him not to board again, adding 'Leave it for captains'. What she did not realize was that this task was usually left to lieutenants. A captain was not supposed to quit the ship for which he was responsible and a Commodore was supposed to be too senior for merely personal heroics. The only rival to Nelson in the Mediterranean Fleet, Richard Bowen, would have drawn level with him again had he managed to capture the *Santissima Trinidad* – the biggest ship in the world taken by a 32-gun frigate. As for Nelson's initiative in quitting position in the line, it certainly showed his presence of mind but was not quite as important as it has been made to seem. The effect was to acquire for Nelson some of the laurels which properly belonged to Jervis. As Captain Brenton says: 'From this day the old fashion of counting the ships of an enemy's fleet, and calculating the disparity of force was entirely laid aside, and a new era may be said to have commenced in the art of war at sea.'[3] If the rule was now to attack the enemy at sight and count the guns afterwards, the innovation was due to Sir John Jervis.

Put in arithmetical terms, the Battle of St Vincent was one in which fifteen British sail of the line attacked twenty-seven Spanish ships, several of them individually superior, captured four of them and inflicted heavy casualties among the rest. It could not be said that the

Spanish fleet was destroyed or even seriously weakened. The effect of the battle was rather to transform morale on either side. The Spaniards had been at least toying with the idea of sending their fleet to Brest so as to assist in the invasion of Ireland. How seriously was this plan considered? We hardly know. All that is certain is that we hear no more of this idea after 14 January 1797. In the immediate future the Spanish fleet was unfit for battle at all. The shock to Spanish pride is fairly shown by the official treatment of their senior officers: Admiral Cordova was deprived of his command and declared incapable of serving again in any rank. His second-in-command and four captains were dismissed and several other captains were reprimanded. In effect, the whole fleet was thought to have disgraced itself. On the British side the result of the battle was to raise morale in proportion. Nelson had written beforehand (p. 27) 'They at home do not know what this fleet is capable of performing; anything and everything'. This fact had now been proved and seamen of the Mediterranean Fleet were ready to fight the world. On a higher level the formula for victory had been discovered – Jervis to direct and Nelson to lead. It was seemingly only a question of time before Jervis would re-enter the Mediterranean. In the meanwhile there was a great sense of relief in Britain, where the news saved the government. This found expression in the honours immediately announced. Jervis was to have had a peerage in any case as Baron Jervis of Meaford but he now became, in addition, Earl St Vincent. Vice-Admirals Thompson and Parker became baronets and Waldegrave (a man St Vincent detested) obtained an Irish peerage. Calder, who carried home St Vincent's despatches, was knighted, and the childless Nelson, who might have had a baronetcy, became a Knight of the Bath. After the Battle of the First of June Howe had caused tremendous ill-feeling by his despatches in which some captains were mentioned and others ignored. St Vincent, at Calder's suggestion, avoided this mistake by the simple device of mentioning nobody. The ill-feeling he created was thus at least evenly spread.

The Battle of St Vincent is not remembered for tactical innovation. The Spanish fleet was in such disorder that it never achieved a proper formation. We should remember, in this connection, that the Spaniards had recently been on the same side as the British. Their ships were perfectly well known, having been moored almost alongside the British at Toulon. They had been in close touch, as allies, on a later occasion when their seamanship proved quite unequal to forming line and keeping station. That they should have been huddled in two groups was not surprising and it required no tactical genius to sail into the gap and attack the windward division before those to leeward could play any part in the action. Nelson's initiative in quitting the line created a sort of precedent for breaking formation and even for disobeying a signal. As against that, the Spanish example proved once more the value of the line ahead for the Spanish ships not only masked each other's fire but would seem, on occasion, to have fired into each other by mistake. It cannot be said that Jervis followed up his victory in a very ruthless fashion. It must be remembered, however, that he was still out-numbered at the end of the battle and that many of the Spanish ships had played no part in it. Of the British ships several, moreover, had all but exhausted their ammunition. They were fortunate in meeting opponents whose gunnery was so feeble. The art in which the Spanish excelled, however, was shipbuilding. Their captured ships were much admired at the time and the *San Josef* was later at sea under the British flag. The *San Nicolas* (built 1769) and *San Ysidro* (built 1768) were both commissioned but were too old perhaps to have much future. As for the famous *Santissima Trinidad*, which escaped on this occasion, the British had no dock in Portsmouth in which she could have been repaired.

In the aftermath of the battle, Earl St Vincent took his fleet back to Lisbon where his Portuguese allies were more obviously loyal than they had been in the past. St Vincent was not enthusiastic about Lisbon, assuring Lord Spencer that the government there:

... exhibits the most melancholy picture I ever read or heard of ... the com-mander-in-chief an imbecile ... the minister of education a bigot ... an empty treasury ... crimes go unpunished; honours and rewards bestowed profusely without distinction; the court filled with monks and friars; and the capital become so offensive, by the dereliction of the police, that it cannot be long without pestilence.[4]

Partly to avoid a longer stay at Lisbon, St Vincent put to sea on 31 March and began a blockade of Cadiz. The place was bombarded on two occasions but the Spanish fleet, being warped out of range, suffered no further damage except to its morale. There followed an expedition to Teneriffe with the object of capturing the Manilla galleon. Nelson, now Rear-Admiral in the ordinary course of promotion, was given a squadron of three ships of the line and three frigates, one of them the *Terpsichore*. An attempt was made to capture the town of Santa Cruz but the attack was repelled with heavy casualties. Nelson, leading in person once more, was badly wounded, losing his arm, and Bowen was killed outright. This was a sad postscript to the Battle of St Vincent. It is also to be remembered that Earl St Vincent was still excluded from the Mediterranean, where French squadrons roamed at will and where one of them captured the Ionian Islands. To re-establish Britain in the Mediterranean the first need was for a base. While none existed, British influence in southern Europe was practically non-existent. As against this, the Mediterranean fleet was decidedly formidable. It compared favourably in this respect with the Channel Fleet which had achieved little success since 1794. Richard, Earl Howe, was still popular with the seamen but he had gone ashore, leaving the command to the elderly and ineffective Bridport. The French had staged their attack on Ireland, admittedly achieving nothing but showing their flag at sea for weeks without being challenged. Bridport had made no serious effort to intercept them and such credit as resulted went to a couple of frigate captains. In the Channel, in contrast with the Mediterranean, the morale of the fleet was very low indeed, especially in the ships of the line. Here was the background for mutiny.

As another factor in the situation we have to notice the way in which government treated the army. The scales of army pay had been fixed under the Commonwealth on a basis which implied that each man would buy his own food, his own pipeclay (to whiten his cross belts) and his own boot blacking. The private soldier was thus paid 8d per day, of which sum he received very little in cash. Inflation had made this pay scale insufficient and there was a mutiny of the Oxfordshire Militia, suppressed with vigour, as a sequel to which three of the ringleaders were tried by court martial and shot. In 1795 Pitt's government raised the army's rate of pay but did so in an indirect manner. A regular pay increase would have required an Act of Parliament but Pitt avoided this, announcing a temporary increase under Royal Warrant with a consolidation of various allowances and an addition proportionate to the high price of bread. This in fact gave the soldiers 1s per day, most of it going as hitherto on food. For purposes of comparison we should note that ordinary merchant-seamen might expect to be paid 30s per month in addition to their food, while a skilled workman might receive 3s 9d per day. In general, the seamen's pay compared favourably with the pay of many people on shore but the man-of-war's crew were paid less than the seamen in a merchant ship. As men were pressed into the navy, moreover, the owners of merchantmen had to pay higher wages to such men as were left. What may seem odd, in retrospect, is that Pitt, recognizing the insufficiency of army pay, did nothing for the navy. The answer would seem to be that internal sedition and tumult was not improbable and that the government, lacking any regular police force, were relying on the army to maintain law and order. For this purpose there was a vast programme of barrack construction, begun in 1792 and entrusted to Colonel Oliver Delancey, who was made Barrackmaster-General. He had spent over nine millions of public money by 1804 but without keeping accurate accounts. He was then retired on a pension of £6 per day while retaining the Colonelcy of the 17th Light Dragoons until he died in 1822. Whatever the speculation, however, which may be attributed to him and to others, the barracks were somehow provided and their siting was related not to a possible invasion but to equally possible industrial unrest. The object was to separate the troops from the civilian population, a result never achieved while the soldiers were billeted in the towns and villages. But this use of soldiers as police would not have been practicable if the troops themselves were in a state of mutiny. From 1795 the army was controlled, for administrative purposes, by the Duke of York, as great a disciplinarian as was Collingwood in the navy. He was to do his utmost for the soldiers' welfare. Nor should we forget that the army was better represented in both Houses of Parliament. So it was easy to overlook the inadequacies of naval pay. After all, the seamen were not there. They spent most of their time at sea. They were normally neither vocal nor literate. Give them more money, it may have been felt, and they will only get drunk on it.

So the army had its rise of pay in 1795 and the navy did not. It would have been as well, therefore, if the army's pay increase had been kept from public knowledge; which, in effect, it was. But news of the pay rise was bound to reach the navy and this for the very good reason that many soldiers were serving on board ship. Two line regiments were thus well represented at the Battle of the First of June. Nothing in the world could prevent the soldiers talking to the seamen about their rise in pay. Nor could anything prevent the seamen reflecting that their recent record in war had been more distinguished than that of the army. They gained the impression in 1795–96 that their wants had been forgotten, that their case had gone by default. Nor can it be denied that they were right. They were very ill-used indeed.

FOUR

Mutiny

When discussing the Naval Mutinies of 1797, modern authors are apt to emphasize the darker side of naval history; dwelling on the press-gang, the salt beef, the weevil-infested bread, the harsh discipline, the starving and flogging, and the hardships generally of life in the navy. Hardships there certainly were, some of them common to the merchant service and others common to life in the army, or common, indeed, to any other life ashore. It is true, moreover, that only a minority of the men could be described as volunteers. But how else are the armed forces to be recruited in time of war? Conscription in the twentieth century is the updated press-gang, lacking the picturesque details but lacking also the sporting chance of escape. Our only progress has been in bureaucratic efficiency. For all practical purposes the press-gang is still in use and unlikely to be abolished. But all our discussions are apt to be pointless because the Mutinies of 1797 were not the result of harshness or cruelty. They were almost entirely concerned with pay. The pay scales had been fixed in the reign of Charles II and had never been revised in the light of inflation. Prices were rising during the last years of the eighteenth century and the seamen and their wives were not being paid enough to live on. The grievance was a very real one and the seamen of the Channel Fleet, in port for months at a time, had leisure to consider it. They had also among them a proportion of landsmen who could read the newspapers and who knew how wages had risen ashore. They had every reason to be profoundly dissatisfied.

The first petitions about pay were sent to the Admiralty, and were ignored, during the winter of 1796–7. Other petitions (unsigned) went to Lord Howe in February 1797, and were then sent on to the Admiralty.

Some perfunctory inquiry was made by Lord Hugh Seymour but no action followed and no reply could be sent. On 15 April when Lord Bridport, Commander-in-Chief at last after Lord Howe's resignation, made the signal to weigh anchor, the crew of the *Royal George* ran up the shrouds and gave three cheers. All the other ships of the Channel Fleet cheered in reply and all ships remained at Spithead. On the following day, the 16th, two delegates from each ship attended a meeting on board the *Queen Charlotte* at which two further petitions were drawn up and signed, one to Parliament and the other to the Admiralty. The demands had now been raised. In addition to higher pay, the seamen now wanted increased and improved food, vegetables (not flour) to be served while in port, better treatment of the sick and an entitlement to shore leave after absence at sea. Responding rather well, Lord Spencer came down to Portsmouth on the 18th, with Lord Arden, Rear-Admiral Young and Mr Marsden, and agreed to most of these demands. The delegates repeated the demands which had been ignored and added others, including the demand for the King's pardon for all who had taken part in the mutiny. Worried by these new grievances, which might prove endless, their Lordships sent three flag-officers to reason with the delegates on board the *Queen Charlotte*. This turned out to be a false step, for Vice-Admiral Sir Alan Gardner fairly lost his temper with the men. 'You're a damned mutinous blackguard set that deserves hanging!' he roared. Grabbing one man by the collar, he went on to bawl 'I'll hang you, and I'll hang every fifth man in the fleet.' A meeting which had been planned as a measure of conciliation was thus brought to an untimely end in a far from friendly atmosphere.

Following this unfortunate encounter it became clear that the seamen would never return to their duty until they had the King's pardon for all their acts of mutiny. Lord Spencer hastened back to London with the object of obtaining it. After a Cabinet meeting, Pitt and other ministers went to Windsor where the King agreed to sign the document and issue it as a proclamation. This was a step forward but the increases of pay needed authorization by Act of Parliament which would take time. When copies of the royal proclamation arrived in Portsmouth the crews of some ships were satisfied and Lord Bridport sailed with these ships to St Helens, leaving at Spithead the four ships still in a state of mutiny, one of them being the *London*, flagship of Sir John Colpoys. As negotiations dragged on the men became suspicious and hostile. In order to prevent the entry of visiting delegates from St Helens, Colpoys sent all hands below and had the gunports closed. The men tried to storm the hatchways and the officers, with Colpoys' permission, fired at them. The fire was returned and Colpoys ordered the marines to fire a volley. The order was not obeyed and an ugly scene followed when the men threatened to hang the first lieutenant by whose pistol one of the seamen had been mortally wounded. Colpoys pleaded an Admiralty order (one which had been generally ignored) in which officers were urged to suppress the mutiny by 'the most vigorous means' and 'to bring the ringleaders to punishment'. News of this quickly circulated and the situation grew worse, most officers being put ashore and Colpoys himself being held prisoner. When reports reached the Admiralty Lord Arden told Pitt 'Total destruction is near us!' and was dissuaded, with difficulty, from resigning. What might the French attempt, with the Channel Fleet paralyzed? Another awful possibility existed, that the mutinous seamen would take the fleet to France. The government turned in despair to Richard, Earl Howe or 'Black Dick' as the sailors called him, a man the mutineers would be inclined to trust.

The eleventh hour appeal to Lord Howe was an admission, in itself, of the bad appointments which had led to the mutiny. It was a sad fact that Bridport and Colpoys had failed to intercept the French fleet in 1796. In the mutiny Bridport failed again. A first-rate Commander-in-Chief would have sensed the mutiny coming. When it did (and if it did) it would have been his cue to storm the Admiralty on the seamen's behalf and then make a passionate appeal to the fleet on behalf of the King. He did nothing effective and had to be superseded, when the crisis came, by the old hero he had replaced. Bridport did not finally retire until the end of 1799, on which occasion Sir Edward Pellew wrote:

You will have heard that we are to have a new Commander-in-Chief, heaven be praised. The old one is scarcely worth drowning, a more contemptible or more miserable animal does not exist. I believe there never was a Man so universally despised by the whole Service. A mixture of Ignorance, avarice and spleen.

As for Colpoys, he was commemorated in a ballad:

> The murdering Colpoys, Vice-Admiral of the blue,
> Gave order to fire on the 'London' ship's crew;
> While the enemy of Britain was ploughing the sea,
> He, like a base coward, let them get away
> When the French and their transports sailed for Bantry Bay.

He was to hold no sea-going appointment after the mutiny but was consoled with a knighthood of the Bath in 1798 and the Command-in-Chief at Plymouth in 1803. After a stint at the Admiralty he ended up as Governor of Greenwich Hospital.

With the twittering Bridport pushed aside, Howe went on board each flagship in turn, bringing with him a copy of the Act of Parliament in which the seamen's main demands were met. Howe brought to his difficult task a tremendous asset, that of limitless patience. Collecting the delegates together, he talked with them for hours. Their demands included the removal of about a hundred officers. Colpoys' name heading the list. As a face-saving gesture, many of the more senior officers had resigned or asked for a transfer and Howe was thus able to reduce some-what the list of those actually dismissed. The Spithead mutiny came to an end and Howe visited each ship in turn amid scenes of general rejoic-ing and enthusiasm. Bridport finally sailed on 17 May, undermanned and under-officered, but at last finally at sea. Unfortunately, the mutiny, begun at Spithead, could not end there. It was bound to spread to Plymouth and Torbay, which it did, and it was bound to reach the foreign stations, the West and East Indies. It was bound, above all, to reach London River and the adjacent ports, Chatham, Sheerness, Yarmouth and the Nore. The mutiny at Spithead lasted from 15 April to 17 May 1797. The mutiny at the Nore began on 12 May and ended on 12 June. Britain was almost defenceless for about two months, being in greater danger than at any other period of the war.

As compared with the mutiny at Spithead, the mutiny at the Nore was more sinister. It was, to begin with, a strike in sympathy with the original mutiny, beginning without a stated object. All the more reasonable demands of the seamen had been met, in fact, before the Nore mutiny began, and were known to have been met soon afterwards. In the second place, it began not in a fleet but among the odd ships that happened to be in the Thames Estuary at the time. In the third place it began after the great danger was all but over, so that the Admiralty, with a fleet at sea, was no longer so willing to bargain with mutineers. As against that, a mutinous fleet in the Thames Estuary was in a posi-tion to blockade the Port of London; the mere threat of which lost the mutineers all popular support. Last of all, the Nore affair had a more political atmosphere. Why? Because the ships on this station were more likely to receive the riff-raff from London. The bounty and quota systems of enlistment had supplied the navy with some men not usually to be found on the lower deck.

Of these, several were discovered afterwards to have been disqualified attorneys, and cashiered excisemen, clerks dismissed from employment, and other individuals in similar cases. It was also suggested that, besides these, many persons had entered on board the ships, as common seamen, completely qualified to breed disturbances, by acting in that station, and selected, for that very purpose, by the enemies of the government.

Certain it is, that the plan of operation, concerted among the disaffected, evinced great judgement and sagacity. They were conducted with spirit and ability, and plainly shewed, that the authors were persons of no contemptible capacities . . .[1]

What evidence exists for this deep-laid plot is not, perhaps, sufficient, but the seamen at the Nore clearly had among them some sea-lawyers of better than average education, whose views were more or less republican. When assured that the grievances expressed at Spithead had all been met by King and Parliament, the Nore mutineers added some demands of their own. They demanded shore leave, punctual pay, pardon of former deserters who had re-enlisted and more equal distribution of prize money. The Admiralty, through Vice-Admiral Charles Buckner (flag officer at the Nore) rejected all these demands. Members of the Board came down to Sheerness but refused to meet the delegates. The mutiny soon spread to the North Sea Fleet, based on Yarmouth, and Admiral Duncan, blockading the Texel, was left with only two loyal ships, the *Venerable* (74) and *Adamant* (50). By making signals to more distant (and imaginary) ships, the form of blockade was maintained. There was deadlock, meanwhile, at Chatham and Sheerness, and the Admiralty ordered coercive measures, depriving the ships of provisions and water and refusing to receive the sick into hospital. On shore there was a concentration of troops and artillery under General Sir Charles Grey and steps were taken for the defence of Tilbury and Gravesend. Buoys were removed from the channels in the estuary, to prevent other ships joining those involved in the mutiny. The mutineers retaliated by blockading the river, at news of which 3 per cent Government Stock fell to $47\frac{1}{2}$ per cent, at that time the lowest quotation on record. This time, however, the Admiralty stood firm and public opinion was against the mutineers. The ships gradually returned to their duties, most of the men being pardoned but the ringleaders arrested and brought to court martial. In the end some 412 men were tried and 59 condemned to death, of which number 29 were executed, 9 were flogged and 29 were imprisoned, the remainder being acquitted or pardoned.

As from the time of the mutiny the petty officers and able seamen obtained an additional 5s 6d a month, bringing an able seaman's pay up to 1s a day.

Ordinary seamen received an additional 4s 6d per month and landsmen an additional 3s 6d. All were now to receive their full weight of provisions without deduction for leakage or waste. Full wages were to be paid to the wounded and marines were no longer to lose their shore allowances when embarked. There were considerable improvements in the seamen's conditions of service and there was, eventually, a changed and fairer allocation of prize money. Conditions of service were improved at the same time in the army. By the proclamation of 25 May 1797, the private soldier was promised 1s daily, a net increase of 2d a day. From this 1s a day a sum not exceeding 4s a week was to be applied to his messing, a sum not exceeding 1s 6d was to be applied for necessaries and the remainder, 1s 6d per week, less certain deductions, would be paid to the private soldier, thus:

	Infantry	Dragoons
	7s 0d a week	8s 9d a week
Stoppages	5s 6d a week	7s 1½d a week
Remains	1s 6d a week	1s 7½d a week

Drummers received 1s 1¾d per day; Corporals, 1s 2¼d; Sergeants 1s 6¾d. Since the soldier and sailor were both to receive 1s per day, they might appear to be on the same footing. In fact, the seamen were better off, their food being provided for them in addition to their pay.

When considering this time of crisis, we should remember that the mutiny, serious as it was, did not extend to the whole navy. The call to mutiny met relatively little response in the Mediterranean, where the morale was high after recent victory and where Earl St Vincent ruled with a rod of iron. Nor was there any comparable trouble on board the frigates and sloops. Men serving in frigates were less interested in pay and more interested in prize money. Their chief ambition was to move to a more profitable station but they had no reason to quarrel with their officers about that. Men serving in sloops, which were used mainly for commerce protection, spent little time in port and being at sea kept them out of mischief. The objection, in the long run, to Howe's policy of keeping the fleet in port was that men so kept in ships at anchor would desert or mutiny. If at sea and in the presence of the enemy the men felt that they were fighting a war. At anchor and actually in sight of their home country, the men had more leisure than was good for them. As compared with a merchantman every warship was wildly over-manned for every purpose except that of firing its guns. There was a daily routine and regular drill but the men were relatively idle. They could talk sedition or politics or think wistfully about the pleasures of going ashore. For discontented muttering the best remedy was to put to sea. For actual mutiny, the best remedy was a fleet action; a victory in which everyone could claim a share of heroism. As for the complaints made, the one nobody could ever remedy was the grievance about the denial of shore leave. For men allowed ashore would simply disappear. There were particular ships under exceptional captains in which one watch would stand surety for another, but shore leave, for the great majority, was to remain an idle dream; nor is it easy to see how it could have been otherwise.

In theory the period from 15 April to 12 June 1797, should have given the French a tremendous opportunity. That they made no use of it is proof, first of all, that it took them by surprise. It was not something they had planned and instigated. Their blow against Ireland had been attempted but had failed. Now was the time to try again, as Wolfe Tone advised Lazare Hoche. When news came that pay concessions had been made and various officers put ashore, Tone argued that Pitt's government must be on the point of collapse, which at one time it was. Hoche proposed a new invasion attempt and was told at the Ministry of Marine that it would take two months to organize. 'That means six', groaned Wolfe Tone on 5 June and added that anything done must be done at once. Hoche agreed with him but discovered that the Directory, having no fleet immediately available, had a new plan which depended upon using the Dutch fleet under Admiral de Winter to transport a partly French army under Hoche's command. After negotiation, it was finally agreed that a Dutch army of 15,000 men should be commanded by General Daendels, with Tone to serve as Adjutant-General. Troops were actually embarked at one time but other preparations were slow and Duncan's fleet off the Texel was still on station. Early in August Wolfe Tone was losing hope:

There seems to be a fate in this business. Five weeks, I believe six weeks, the English fleet was paralysed by the mutinies at Portsmouth, Plymouth and the Nore. The sea was open, and nothing to prevent both the Dutch and French fleets to put to sea. Well, nothing was ready. That precious opportunity which we can never expect to return was lost; and now that at last we are ready here, the wind is against us, the mutiny is quelled and we are sure to be attacked by a superior force.[2]

This summary was correct and he might have added that summer would be over before anything could be done. Hoche was optimistic, however, proposing that while the Dutch struck their blow his own army should concentrate at Brest for a new attempt on Ireland. Tone's proposal was that the Dutch fleet, without troops embarked, should give battle to the British North Sea Fleet. With Duncan defeated, troops would embark for an attack on Edinburgh, would march from there to Glasgow and use that as a base for invading Northern Ireland. This was a hare-brained idea but no scheme, however sensible, had now much prospect of success because the Dutch army had already been kept waiting for too long and was dwindling through desertion and disease. The invasion plan was no longer possible but the first part of Tone's plan appealed, nevertheless, to the Dutch politicians. Why should not Admiral de Winter repeat the successes of Tromp and De Ruyter? Then the French could launch their planned invasion of Ireland. At this point General Hoche died of consumption, leaving General Bonaparte as France's only military genius. Bonaparte showed no immediate desire to invade Ireland (he had already had another idea, about Egypt) but the Dutch politicians were still dreaming of naval victory. Considered as a prelude to invading Britain such an achievement was now pointless, but the dream remained. The naval committee of the Batavian republic was also convinced that the British ships might be lured into destruction on the Dutch coast. It did not occur to them that Duncan, after blockading the Texel throughout the summer, knew the shoals at least as well as they did. Ordering Admiral de Winter to sail, the committee members urged him 'to draw the enemy as near the harbours of the republic as will be possible in conformity with the rules of prudence and strategy'. What rules, one wonders? Not for the last time in history, the members of a committee had not the least idea what they were talking about.

The Dutch fleet which finally put to sea on 8 October 1797, comprised four 74-gun ships, each of them a flagship, seven ships of 68 or 64 guns, five ships of 56–44 guns, four frigates and six corvettes. By the accepted ideas of the day, the 56–44 gun ships were obsolete and not fit to appear in battle. The 64-gun ships were semi-obsolete, only one of this class appearing in the British fleet at the Battle of St Vincent. As against that, the Dutch knew that Duncan's fleet comprised many ships that were equally obsolete and that all or most of his seamen had been involved in the mutiny. John William de Winter, the Dutch admiral, had entered the Dutch navy in 1762 and rose to the rank of lieutenant. Having republican views, he joined the French army and returned to Holland with it, as a general, in 1795. He was now an admiral, having never even commanded a ship. Few of his officers can have had any experience in war. Given the vaguest of orders, the Dutch Admiral took his fleet to sea and cruised rather aimlessly southward. He was unopposed in the first instance because Duncan, after eighteen weeks at sea, had returned to Yarmouth roads for repairs and supplies. To watch the Texel he had left Captain Henry Trollope in the *Russel* (74) with the *Adamant* (50), two frigates and a sloop. Shadowing the Dutch fleet, Trollope sent the *Speculator* lugger to inform Duncan that Admiral de Winter was at sea. He received this signal on the morning of the 9th and sailed that afternoon, making contact with Trollope on the 11th and finding the Dutch fleet heading northwards in order of battle. Fearing that the Dutch would enter port, Duncan attacked at once, bringing on what was to prove the most hard-fought action of the war, taking its name from the Dutch village of Camperdown, opposite which the action took place.

Adam Duncan, a tall man aged 66, had been a follower of Keppel and spent a lifetime in worthy but undistinguished service. He owed his position to the fact that he had married the niece of Henry Dundas. He was a great admirer of Lord St Vincent but the admiration was not returned. St Vincent was strongly prejudiced against all Scotsmen. 'You will never find an officer, native of that country, figure in supreme command,' he once told Evan Nepean, Secretary of the Admiralty, 'They are only fit for drudgery.' The man he had chiefly in mind was Middleton, the ex-Comptroller, 'that Scotch packhorse', but his prejudice would be later confirmed by Cochrane. Duncan had been given more than his share of drudgery but his moment had now come. He was well supported by Vice-Admiral Richard Onslow and by Captain Henry Trollope. Without attempting to form line, Duncan hurled his fleet at the enemy. Of his sixteen sail of the line he himself led a group of seven against the leading Dutch ships and Onslow led nine against their rear,

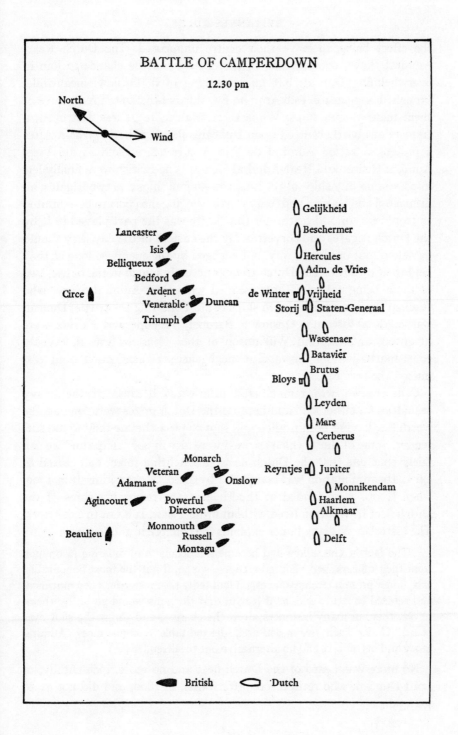

BATTLE OF CAMPERDOWN

12.30 pm

the effect being to leave their centre unopposed. The Dutch Rear-Admiral Bloys, commanding in the centre, had the chance to join in overwhelming Duncan but made nothing of it. Onslow, meanwhile, brought his squadron to bear upon five ships of the Dutch rear, three of them mere 50-gun ships. While these were more or less destroyed, a tremendous battle centred upon Duncan's flagship the *Venerable*. After a prolonged action Admiral de Winter surrendered and so did Vice-Admiral Reuter and Rear-Admiral Meures. The British were finally left in possession of 7 ships of the line, two 50-gun ships and two frigates, all dismasted and leaking and 'only worth bringing into port to be exhibited as trophies'. An odd feature of this battle was the part played in it by the Dutch frigates and corvettes. By the custom of the day they should have kept out of harm's way, not engaged by the enemy so long as they held their own fire. The Dutch frigates actually joined in the battle, two of them being taken. Others escaped with Rear-Admiral Story, who reached the Texel with eleven ships in all. Following the battle, Duncan was made a Viscount, Onslow a Baronet, Trollope and Fairfax were knighted, and Captain Williamson of the *Agincourt* was deservedly court-martialled for 'cowardice, negligence or disaffection' and dismissed the service.

Camperdown was remembered afterwards because of the heavy casualties on either side and because the Dutch prizes were found to be worthless, having been riddled and shot to pieces before they would surrender. Some of those which escaped were also in poor shape and we can fairly conclude that the Dutch fleet, as a fighting force, had ceased to exist. Its annihilation was completed by Lord Duncan himself in 1799, when troops were landed at the Helder. The remaining ships of the Dutch fleet then surrendered without firing a shot. It is fair to ask 'why?' The historian William James explains the collapse in these words:

... The fact is, the sailors had become politicians; and differing in opinion from their officers, had adopted a course which, if not the most honourable, was, under present circumstances, undoubtedly the most safe. They mutinied, and refused to fight; and, as if fearful that the guns would go off by themselves, they, in many instances, drew the charges, and threw the shot over board. Under such, we must add, discreditable circumstances, Admiral Story and his officers had no alternative but to surrender . . .[3]

No more was heard of the Dutch fleet and no more, incidentally, of Lord Duncan, who retired soon afterwards, in 1800, and did not go to sea again.

The Battle of St Vincent ended any likelihood of the Spanish co-operating with the French in an invasion of Ireland. The Battle of Camperdown ended any likelihood of the Dutch playing a similar role. The French were still convinced, however, that Ireland offered them their great opportunity. A rebellion started there with French encouragement might distract the British for years. Where else could as small an investment pay as large a dividend? And the Bantry Bay campaign was, in a sense, a source of satisfaction. Little had been achieved but the fact remained that the French ships had reached Ireland and that most of them had returned safely to France. With the same supine Commander-in-Chief at Portsmouth, the same thing could be done again but with improved direction and better results. Thinking on these lines led to three more expeditions. The first, under Commodore Savary, sailed from Rochefort on 6 August 1798, carrying troops under General Humbert. The troops were duly landed at Killala Bay but, numbering less than a thousand, were forced to surrender to Lieutenant-General Lake. At about the same time General Rey and Napper Tandy made a brief appearance off Donegal but did not land. The second expedition, under Commodore Bompart, sailed from Brest on 16 September 1798, carrying 3,000 troops under Generals Hardy and Ménage. Located at the outset by Captain Keats, Bompart was never able to shake off the frigates which shadowed him. He reached Lough Swilly but with Sir John Borlase Warren from Plymouth in close pursuit. Of the French squadron comprising one ship of the line and eight frigates, seven were taken and only two escaped. The third expedition, under Commodore Savary, was meant to be a repetition of the first and was launched on the assumption that Humbert's force was still in the field. Savary, sailing on 12 October, could achieve nothing but brought his four frigates safely back to Rochefort.

It cannot be said that these results were encouraging in themselves. There had been no great Irish rebellion, least of all after Humbert had surrendered. As against that, the threat to Ireland had attracted there a considerable British army, one which would remain there as long as the threat was a reality. Forces for the defence of England were correspondingly weakened and French planners began to evolve a new strategy. They had come to realize that a full-scale invasion of Ireland was impossible without a previous naval victory. To land a few thousand men on the Irish coast was practicable enough but they could be neither maintained nor reinforced. This had been proved by experience.

The question now asked was whether England could be invaded by the shortest route? Discounting the likelihood of a naval victory, could the Channel be crossed at its narrowest point? Could boats row across during a dead calm sea while the British men-of-war were unable to intervene? Could the invasion take place on a dark night? So possible did this seem that General Bonaparte was appointed Commander-in-Chief of the Army of England. More than that, the Directory, firmly in power from September 1797, ordered the construction of landing craft and gunboats. Base line for the invasion was from Cherbourg to Antwerp. Rear-Admiral La Crosse had four Commodores to assist him (Ganteaume, Decrès, Casabianca and Dumanoir-le-Pelley). Landing craft were designed by the celebrated Swedish architect, Chapman, and built under the immediate supervision of Merskein of Antwerp. Eight million francs were allocated to boat construction and the work was continued during the winter of 1797–8. By 21 March the following return could be made:

Frigates and Corvettes	18	
Gunboats	276	
Landing craft, cavalry	319	
Landing craft, infantry	718	
Troops available	70,034	
Horses	5,394	

Bonaparte was himself active, visiting Dunkirk and sending Kleber and Desaix to visit Havre and Brest. He sent engineers to examine Boulogne, Etaples, Ambleteuse and Calais, and others to Holland. By February he was expressing doubts, writing on 23 February 'There are fitting out at Brest but ten ships of the line, which have no crews, and are still far from being in condition to keep the sea.' He doubted whether the invasion could take place in 1798.

Make what effort we will, we shall not, for many years, acquire the control of the seas. To make a descent upon England, without being master of the sea, is the boldest and most difficult operation ever attempted.

Difficult as the operation was likely to prove, it was not entirely abandoned until the proposed technique had been tested. There followed, therefore, a raid on the two islands of St Marcouf on the coast of Normandy; islands which lie to the east of the Cherbourg Peninsula and some four miles off the land. They each measured at the time about 200 yards long and 120 yards wide. Conquered by Sir Sidney Smith in 1795, they had been garrisoned since, armed with some cannon, and were said

54

to threaten communication between Cherbourg and Havre. It may be
doubted whether their capture represented a strategic masterstroke
but the French thought their occupation mildly irritating. Now was
the moment, however, for these islands to claim their moment in history.
The French decided to recapture them, not to gain glory for France
but to try out their landing craft. The isles were to be the scene, in fact,
of a rehearsal; an exercise in combined operations. For this purpose they
were ideally suited, being close at hand and provided with a real enemy
firing live ammunition. No training exercise could have been more
realistic. For Phase I thirty landing craft were loaded with troops and
escorted by a few gun-brigs. Sailing from Havre on 7 April, this flotilla,
commanded by Captain Muskein, encountered two British frigates and
withdrew under fire to the small port of Sallenelle. Reinforced by more
troops in another forty landing craft, Muskein decided to try again but
waited for the moment when a neap tide would accompany a dead calm.
These conditions prevailing on 6 May, the attack was repeated, being
opposed this time by the garrison alone. The landing craft withdrew
after six or seven had been sunk. We may fairly conclude that two
valuable lessons had been learnt. First, a dead calm in the Channel
is unlikely to last for long. Second, an opposed landing will probably
incur heavy casualties. Bonaparte had realized all this before Muskein
proved it. His conclusion was that the invasion of England must
wait until 1799. On 3 May he left Paris but went in the opposite direction, heading not for Dunkirk or Brest but for Toulon. We hardly
know to this day whether the invasion of England in 1798 was ever
seriously intended.

Considering the possibility of invasion at this and a later period of the
war, we must realize that what the French wanted was the steamboat
and especially the steam-tug. It would not have solved every problem
but it would have facilitated the Channel crossing on a windless day.
Journalists of the period talked happily of the fantastic schemes which
were theoretically possible, some of them involving the use of balloons.
We recall, however, that these great inventions came too late and that
balloons played no part in warfare until 1870. However, the steam
vessel did actually exist during the French wars. More than that, Wolfe
Tone, had he reached Glasgow from Edinburgh (see page 49) would
have been only a few years too early to see the *Charlotte Dundas* steaming on the Forth and Clyde Canal. But the earliest steamboats were
long before his time. One was invented by Denis Papin in about 1707.

Then came Jonathan Hulls, who designed but did not build a stern-wheel towboat.

> Jonathan Hulls
> With his patent skulls
> Invented a machine
> To go against wind and stream:
> But he, being an ass,
> Couldn't bring it to pass
> And so was ashamed to be seen.

There were many experiments between 1750 and 1783, one being the paddle-wheel steamboat built for the Marquis de Jouffroy at Lyons in 1783. James Rumsey built another in 1784 and showed it to George Washington. The propeller was invented by Joseph Bramah, engine-builder of Piccadilly, in 1785. In the same year John Fitch produced a steamboat, formed a company, and had his craft steaming on the Delaware. His fifth boat, launched in 1790, reached 8 m.p.h. and was in passenger service for four months. There were almost simultaneous experiments in Scotland, leading to final success in 1802. In other words there was nothing to prevent the French using some fraction of the available funds to finance the development of a steamboat suitable for combined operations. Why was nothing done? As always in time of war, the crucial factor was time. Granted that steamboats might have been built, would they have been ready by the summer of 1798? The answer may well be 'no', and who could guess in 1798 that they would be still more desperately needed in 1804?

Bonaparte believed that the threat to England and Ireland would keep the British out of the Mediterranean; the area in which he now meant to make his major effort. Nor was he mistaken. To the Channel and North Sea Fleets could now be added the army in Ireland. To these defensive measures could also be added the efforts made against the invasion flotillas themselves. As in World War II, the enemy landing craft attracted considerable hostility. When it became known that enemy landing craft were collected at Flushing and were expected to reach Dunkirk and Ostend by the Bruges Canal, a squadron embarked troops and sailed for Ostend. A landing took place (on 14th–15th May) and engineers blew up the locks and sluice-gates of the canal, also destroying all the gun-boats they found. This operation, which involved heavy losses, was in fact a failure and others, no doubt, had as little result. The point to notice, however, is that efforts were made and that British forces were absorbed in watching the invasion coast. Bonaparte had changed his mind by the middle of February, at latest, and had decided against the invasion of Britain. What he wanted now was to ensure that British forces were off-balance. So they would prove to be but there would be three consoling thoughts for Britain and they need to be kept in mind. First and foremost, the Portuguese alliance had not yielded to pressure. But for that, the British position would have been a great deal worse. Second, the Kingdom of the Two Sicilies was still independent and might be won over as an ally. Third, the Emperor of Austria was probably about to renew the war against France and bring pressure on Naples to do the same, provided that a British fleet would re-enter the Mediterranean. But how could it operate there without a base?

FIVE

Battle for the Mediterranean

Bonaparte's plan for an invasion of Egypt was more original than we can easily understand, in modern times. There had been European wars fought in Italy, Germany or the Netherlands. There had been colonial wars, fought on a much smaller scale in America, the West Indies and India. But the idea of leading a European army into Asia had not been considered (except by the Russians) since the time of the crusades. Bonaparte's interest in Egypt dated from 1796 when he found some books about that country in the Ambrosian library at Milan. He would seem to have discussed Egypt with Talleyrand, who reported to the Directory in July, 1797, supporting the idea of invading Egypt as a step towards conquering India. He also obtained the advice of Magallon, former French consul in Egypt. Active preparations began at Marseilles, Toulon, Genoa, Civita Vecchia and Corsica. Admiral Brueys was ordered to leave for Toulon on 12 February 1798. The sailing of ships from Toulon to Brest was countermanded on the 13th. On 5 March Bonaparte was appointed to command the expedition, he providing the Directory on that day with detailed plans for the conquest of Malta and Egypt. On 2 April Admiral Brueys assumed command of the thirteen sail of the line at Toulon. Bonaparte arrived there himself on 8 May and the expedition sailed on the 19th. Its destination was completely unknown, even to the senior naval officers. That it should sail for Egypt would cross no ordinary person's mind. As for an overland attack on India, there had been no thought of that since the time of Alexander the Great. Nor would the possibility of this have seemed worthy of serious discussion.

The preparations at Toulon and elsewhere could not, of course, be concealed. When the first report reached London the Cabinet was already considering whether the fleet should re-enter the Mediterranean, using Neapolitan bases to give confidence to Austria. These discussions ended with the orders sent to Lord St Vincent on 29 April.

. . . The armament at Toulon, Genoa etc. is represented as being very extensive, and is very probably in the first instance intended for Naples. . . . This armament is in truth more likely to be destined either for Portugal or Ireland; for the former most probably, by landing somewhere in Spain; for the latter, by pushing through the Strait and escaping our vigilance, which, while you are occupied by the fleet at Cadiz, it is not impossible they may succeed in. Whatever may be its destination, its defeat would surely be a great object for this country . . .

It is proposed to be left to your lordship's determination whether this purpose should be obtained by a detachment from your fleet or by taking your whole force into the Mediterranean. At the same time I cannot help suggesting that it would be extremely desirable not to lose sight of the great advantage which has hitherto been obtained from the constant check which you have kept on the Spanish fleet at Cadiz. . . . If you determine to send a detachment into the Mediterranean, I think it almost unnecessary to suggest to you the propriety of putting it under the command of Sir H. Nelson. . . .[1]

On the assumption that St Vincent would send a detachment into the Mediterranean, Spencer proposed to reinforce him with eight ships from the Channel Fleet. Should he decide, however, to take his whole fleet eastwards, Spencer wanted to recall this reinforcement. Lifting the blockade on Cadiz would expose Ireland to the danger of the Spanish fleet coming north. Some rumours about the threat to Egypt reached Lord Grenville at the Foreign Office but were discredited. Dundas, however, saw the possible danger and sent warning to Lord Wellesley in India. Spencer sent a parallel warning in May to Rainier, the Commander-in-Chief on the East Indies Station. Left to make his own decision, St Vincent sent Nelson (on 2 May) to reconnoitre with three sail of the line. The reinforcement from the Channel Fleet, under Sir Roger Curtis, joined St Vincent off Cadiz on 24 May and changed places with the blockading squadron, the new ships being painted to imitate the old. The Spaniards thus deceived, St Vincent sent Troubridge with ten ships to join Lord Nelson, bringing his squadron up to the number of thirteen. Sir Edmund Berry states:

It was only characteristic of the general tenur of Lord St Vincent's command that every ship destined to compose the squadron of reinforcement was ready to put to sea from Cadiz Bay at a moment's notice; and it is a fact worthy of permanent record, as illustrative of the energy and activity of British seamen, that as soon as Sir Roger Curtis, with the squadron under his command, was visible from the masthead of the Admiral's ship, Captain Troubridge and his squadron put to sea and were actually out of sight, on their way to Gibraltar, before the former cast an anchor on the British station off Cadiz.[2]

The story is so well known that we are apt to take its sequence for granted. It was unavoidable, we feel, that St Vincent should detach a squadron and as logical that Nelson should be given the command. It was not, however, as inevitable as all that. St Vincent was unwell and was already talking of retirement. Apart from that, however, what decided him was the central fact that his reinforcements came from the Channel Fleet and were therefore, in St Vincent's opinion, completely useless. It was his immediate task to restore discipline in them and re-train such of their officers as he might not replace. Months would pass before he would consider these ships fit for active service: 'The Captains Aplin and Ellison are drivellers and there are others in this squadron totally unfit to command ships of war in these times.' As for sending Nelson into the Mediterranean, in doing so, he brushed aside the claims of Rear-Admirals Sir John Orde and Sir Roger Curtis, both senior to him. Orde was furious about it, protesting and grumbling so much that St Vincent sent him home. Nelson, meanwhile, had what amounted to an independent command and Curtis, if he objected, did well to keep his views to himself. The ships which had come from England were all more or less mutinous: The *Marlborough* (Captain Ellison), the *Lion*, the *Centaur* and the *Princess Royal* especially so. There followed a series of courts-martial, a number of executions and a spate of admonitions addressed to the captains and officers. Little by little, discipline was being restored. The more active task was entrusted, meanwhile, to ships which had been longer in the Mediterranean Fleet.

The French sailed from Toulon, as we have seen, on 19 May, immediately heading for Malta, the capture of which was to be its first task. The expedition comprised thirteen French sail of the line and 8 frigates, two Venetian 64's and 8 Venetian frigates, 8 corvettes and 400 sail of transports carrying 36,000 troops. The naval commander was Vice-Admiral Brueys whose flagship of 120 guns had been the *Sans Culotte* and now became *L'Orient*. He was assisted by Rear-Admirals Villeneuve, Blanquet-Duchayla and Decrès. Some rumours about the proposed invasion of Egypt had already reached London. In a letter of 9 June, Dundas had asked Spencer whether he had suggested to St Vincent that Egypt might be the destination of the French fleet. 'It may be whimsical, but I cannot help having a fancy of my own on that subject.' Information then reached the Foreign Office that General Bonaparte had taken with him a collection of books relating to Egypt, the Near East and India. Writing to Spencer again, Dundas began 'My dear Lord – India has occupied my thoughts all night . . .' Nelson was not looking so far afield but he knew of a possible threat to Egypt. Unluckily, the *Vanguard* lost her foremast in a gale and his two frigates had returned to Gibraltar, thinking that he would be forced to do the same. He was thus left without means of gaining intelligence at the very time when he heard about the French having sailed from Toulon. He was consoled, however, on 7 June by the appearance of Troubridge and the ten ships sent him by St Vincent. With a squadron of thirteen sail of the line, Nelson entered the Straits of Messina and presently learnt that the French had captured Malta and Gozo, meeting little or no resistance from the moribund Order of the Knights of St John, and had sailed again on 18 June, their destination unknown. Nelson guessed (correctly) that they were going to Alexandria, and followed them with all speed. His only scouting vessel was the *Mutine* (16) and he now sent her to Alexandria to see whether the French were there. On 28 June the *Mutine* ascertained that they were not. Nelson ranged the Mediterranean and came into Syracuse for water on 20 July, having twice missed the French fleet by a matter of hours. The French had sighted Alexandria the day after he had gone. In three weeks Bonaparte had landed, taken Alexandria, won the Battle of the Pyramids and entered Cairo. His conquest of Egypt was complete and he had seen nothing of the British fleet since he left Toulon. Bonaparte ordered Admiral Brueys to take up a defensive position at anchor and he did so in Aboukir Bay on 8 July. He should really have had his fleet in Alexandria harbour, where his ships would have been safe, but *L'Orient* was too big for the harbour and he could not leave her outside. Nor could he supply her for the voyage back to France. He had been at anchor three weeks when Nelson reappeared. Had Brueys managed to sail again unchallenged the career of Nelson might well have been at an end.

The defensive position taken up by Vice-Admiral Brueys was weaker than it appeared to be and weaker, no doubt, than he thought it was. Men-of-war during this period needed a depth of five fathoms in smooth water. Brueys had anchored his ships more or less parallel to the four fathom line but insufficiently close to it. His flanks were unprotected, his ships were about 160 yards apart, at single anchor without springs, and half his men had been sent ashore. No proper survey of the Egyptian coast had ever been made and Brueys may well have assumed that the British would make a cautious approach, sounding as they went and correcting such charts as they might possess. He supposed, perhaps, that he would have time to prepare for battle, embarking his men again, tightening his line, improving his position and mounting some guns ashore on either flank. It was late in the day when the British squadron's approach was signalled and Brueys felt confident that the inevitable battle would take place on the following day, giving him the whole night in which to improve his position. He could not suppose that the British would risk a night action in uncharted waters. They came on, nevertheless, and at 5.30 pm he signalled his ships to clear for action on the seaward side. Some of his men were still ashore and he tried to make up for this by borrowing seamen from his frigates. His thirteen sail of the line included, besides his flagship, three 80-gun ships, the *Franklin*, the *Guillaume Tell* and the *Tonnant*. He had also four frigates, two corvettes, three bomb vessels and some gunboats. He placed his flagship in the centre of his line, supported by the *Franklin* and *Tonnant*. Rather belatedly, he ordered his ships to lay out a second anchor and send a stream cable to the next ship astern, thus ensuring that their broadsides would continue to bear.

Nelson had, of course, seen his opportunity. The fleets were equally matched but a fleet at anchor was at a tactical disadvantage. The attacking fleet could concentrate on a part of the defending line. Quite apart from that, the fact that the French were first seen at single anchor showed that there was room between them and the shoal, room for them to swing. It was possible, therefore, to pass them on the landward side and double them, ensuring that some would have an opponent on either beam. He had so often discussed all possibilities with his captains that he wasted little time in explaining what he intended. They could see for themselves what had to be done. Ships took up formation as they approached the enemy and Nelson's signals were few; first, to prepare for battle; second, to be ready to anchor by the stern; third, to concentrate on the enemy's van and centre. He had previously ordered his ships to fly the white ensign (not the blue, which would have been correct) so as to recognize each other more easily in the dark. The early dangers were navigational and one ship, the *Culloden* (Captain Trou-bridge) struck a reef during the approach and was saved with difficulty, playing no part in the battle. So Nelson fought with only twelve ships, all of 74 guns, together with the obsolescent *Leander* (50), which went first to the *Culloden*'s rescue and so arrived rather late on the battlefield. At 6.28 pm, as it grew dark Nelson's leading ship, the *Goliath* led the way inside the French line, the *Zealous, Orion, Theseus* and *Audacious* following suit. The *Vanguard*, Nelson's flagship, now came up on the outside of the French line, presently supported by the *Minotaur* and *Defence*. This was the tactical situation which Nelson had wanted, with five French ships overwhelmed by eight British opponents. They were the oldest and weakest French ships. They had been ready to engage with one battery only, on the seaward side, and were caught with their guns not even run out. Several, finally, had opponents on either beam. It was now dark and the *Bellerophon*, coming up, passed the *Franklin* and did unequal battle with the three-decked *Orient*. The *Majestic* went on to engage *L'Heureux* and ended up exchanging broadsides with *Le Mercure*. The three rear French ships were left without opponents. At this time, with victory already certain, Nelson was wounded and was taken to the cockpit. He was on deck again later and retained command.

In the centre of the French line the *Peuple Souverain*, after being trapped between the *Orion* and *Defence* was driven, dismasted and silent, out of the battle line. The *Leander* (50) moved into the gap and took up a raking position, under way, across the bows of the *Franklin*. A French frigate, the *Serieux*, rashly opened fire on the *Orion* and was sunk outright when the fire was returned. The *Bellerophon*, dismasted and severely damaged by the French flagship, drifted out of the line but her place was taken by the *Swiftsure* and *Alexander*. At 9 pm, a fire was seen on board *L'Orient* and the guns of the *Swiftsure* concentrated on the spot. The action continued and so did the fire and at about 10 pm, the French flagship blew up with a tremendous explosion. The nearer ships were in danger from the falling wreckage and even the more distant ceased fire. Guns were silent for about ten minutes and then the action was resumed by the *Franklin*, which, however, struck her colours at midnight. The *Tonnant* was then the only French ship still firing and she was dismasted by 3 am. At 4 am, the action was renewed and the *Heureux* and *Mercure* were cannonaded into surrender. The *Timoleon* had run herself ashore but the *Généreux* and *Guillaume Tell*, with two frigates, were sufficiently undamaged to make their escape. The

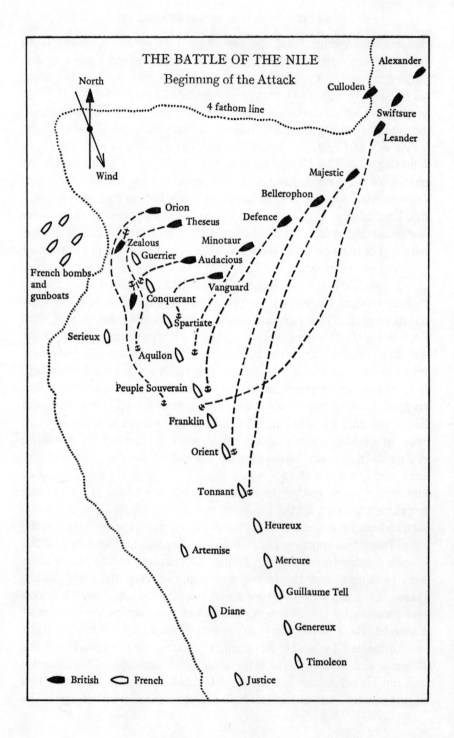

THE BATTLE OF THE NILE
Beginning of the Attack

North

Wind

4 fathom line

Alexander

Culloden

Swiftsure

Leander

Majestic

Bellerophon

Defence

Orion

Theseus

Minotaur

Zealous

Guerrier

Audacious

French bombs
and
gunboats

Conquerant

Vanguard

Spartiate

Serieux

Aquilon

Peuple Souverain

Franklin

Orient

Tonnant

Heureux

Artemise

Mercure

Guillaume Tell

Diane

Genereux

Timoleon

British   French

Justice

Tonnant then surrendered and the crew of the *Timoleon* set their ship on fire and escape ashore. The battle was over and of the French ships of the line one had blown up, nine had surrendered, one was wrecked, one was burnt and only two had escaped.

The Battle of the Nile is remarkable, first of all, as a battle of annihilation. Nelson's aim was to destroy the French fleet. He was not content with the sort of technical victory which had satisfied Rodney or Howe. He sought to do at sea what Bonaparte had done on land. He wanted to follow up success to its logical end, and it is typical of him that his obsession was now with the two French ships that escaped. He wanted them taken and he wanted to make the capture in person, as indeed he eventually did. The fact that the French chose to give battle while at anchor was an important factor in their destruction but the fact remained that it was a new kind of victory, not really typical of the century that was ending. Nelson had impressed on the battle a style of his own. Having said that, we should remember that Lord St Vincent, as Commander-in-Chief, must share the credit. It was he who had trained and disciplined the fleet, stamping out the last traces of mutiny. It was he who had done so much for the fleet's hygiene and diet that there was not a man sick when the day of battle came. Nor could Nelson have created the fleet he led. Superb as he was as leader and tactician, he had no comparable gifts as an administrator. His flagship at the Nile was far from being an example to the rest of the fleet. Where Nelson was incomparable was in careful planning for battle, in the leadership which made his fleet into a team and in the swift and often brilliant decisions he made when in the presence of the enemy. The Nile was a masterpiece in its way, much of its success due to Nelson's decision to attack at once but much due also to St Vincent's hard work over the previous years.

Behind the famous epic of the victory won lurks the ghost of the victory which Nelson failed to achieve. Central to the whole story is the fact that Nelson might have intercepted the French fleet and convoy on the way to Alexandria. Bonaparte might have been killed or captured before he could reach Egypt. His army could have been dispersed before it landed. We are all familiar with the contrast often drawn between Napoleon, supreme on land, and Nelson, supreme at sea. What we need to remember is that they once confronted each other and that Napoleon escaped destruction. Was it altogether a matter of luck? The element of chance was very much present but the story of the campaign also reveals Nelson's impatience and over-anxiety. A more solid chess-player might have achieved a better result on the Mediterranean chess-board. As for Bonaparte, he had done what he wanted to do. He had landed his army in Egypt very much as planned. It is true that his communications had been cut but this was a possibility he must have had in mind. Of the French land forces Nelson wrote 'I have little doubt but that the army will be destroyed by plague, pestilence and famine, and battle and murder, which that it may be soon, God grant.' That did not happen, at least not immediately, and Napoleon's Egyptian adventure was not finished. He was, in a sense, marooned, but India lay before him, no more nor less accessible than he had known it to be. In any future negotiation over a peace treaty his possession of Egypt would be a valuable asset; perhaps even a trump card. What Britain gained immediately, by contrast, was access to Naples, where British status had risen sharply with the news of victory. As Nelson was to remark 'The Kingdom of the Two Sicilies is mad with joy.' He went there, in fact, with some reluctance, but needed time ashore to recover from his head wound. From his station off Cadiz, Lord St Vincent wrote 'Tell Lady Hamilton I rely on her to administer to your health at Naples, where I have no doubt it will soon be re-established.' He need not have worried on that score. Lady Hamilton looked after Nelson very well indeed.

The victory gained and Nelson given his peerage, it remains to see what use was made of the situation created. With British influence restored in the Mediterranean, St Vincent was instructed to protect Naples and Sicily, co-operating (should war be renewed in Italy) with the Austrian and Neapolitan armies. He was instructed to cut off all communication between France and Egypt, befriending the Turks, now in alliance, and blockading Malta into surrender. All these duties he entrusted to Nelson, who was made responsible for the Mediterranean from Naples and Malta to Alexandria. Retaining direct responsibility for the western Mediterranean, St Vincent fixed his headquarters at Gibraltar and entrusted the blockade of Cadiz to his second-in-command, Lord Keith. His immediate concern was with a plan for the conquest of Minorca, the former British naval base taken by the Spanish in 1782. There were some troops available under Lieutenant-General the Hon. Charles Stuart and these were embarked in a squadron under the command of Commodore Duckworth. The landing took place on 7 November 1798, and the Spanish garrison presently surrendered without destroying the valuable naval stores at Port Mahon, which now became available again. At the other end of the Mediterranean, a squadron was left to blockade Alexandria, another to help the Maltese besiege the French garrison which held Valletta, and a strong detachment under Sir James Saumarez to escort the French prizes to Gibraltar, to Lisbon and so to England. Naples was the temporary base for Nelson's flagship and for some other ships, all damaged to some degree in the recent battle. By the end of 1798 the British Mediterranean Fleet was deployed over a wide area, its immediate opponents being scattered and weak. Valletta was bound to fall in the end and this would give the British the base they needed in the centre of the Mediterranean, adjacent to allies in Sicily.

How would the French react to this new situation with one of their armies marooned in Egypt and the British re-established in the Mediterranean? How would they respond to Bonaparte's appeals for help? Their obvious move was to send their Brest fleet southward and then join forces with the Spanish, presenting the British with a new challenge in an area where they had reason to feel secure. This was the plan on which they decided, placing the Brest fleet under the command of Admiral Bruix, who had been their Minister of Marine. Bruix was ordered to enter the Mediterranean, embark troops in Italy (3,000–4,000 in number), relieve Corfu, Malta and Alexandria and, finally, give battle to the British Fleet. The defect in this plan, which Bruix may well have drafted, was the confusion between two objects: that of relieving Alexandria and that of defeating the British fleet. Apart from that, the expedition was delayed by a shortage of naval stores and a still worse shortage of seamen. A deficiency of 5,000–6,000 men was made good by drafting dockyard workers and taking soldiers from the garrison of Brest. Meanwhile, there was an elaborate cover plan, made easier by a rebellion which had actually taken place in Ireland. Irish representatives were assured that help was on the way and troop movements gave the same impression, reinforced by press reports and instigated rumours. Dutch ships were prepared for sea and French troops sent to Holland. The stroke of genius was to allow the schooner *Rebecca* to fall into British hands with fake despatches aboard. Bruix finally sailed on the evening of 25 April with a formidable and well-manned fleet comprising twenty-five sail of the line (four three-decked ships and two of 80 guns, five frigates and two corvettes). Lord Bridport was actually off Brest on the morning of the 25th but obligingly moved his fleet

(16 sail of the line) to a position off Ushant leaving but a single frigate to watch the French fleet. When he realized that the enemy fleet had sailed he sent a warning to the Admiralty, to Keith and St Vincent and went with his fleet to protect Ireland. By the time Bridport realized his appalling error Bruix was far to the southward and approaching the Straits. There was a chance of his being joined by five Spanish ships from Ferral. Were he then able to release the seventeen Spanish ships at Cadiz, he would have forty-seven sail of the line; a fleet of almost incredible size. Lord Keith, warned of the French approach, was saved by a westerly gale which kept the Spaniards in port and blew fair for the Straits. Ignoring Keith's squadron, Bruix passed into the Mediterranean. On the evening of 5 May Lord St Vincent saw the French from Gibraltar, twenty-six sail being counted. 'The weather was so hazy, with heavy rain, their force could not be ascertained with precision.' For St Vincent this must have been among the worst moments of his life.

At this time of impending disaster Lord Keith was still off Cadiz with sixteen sail of the line, Duckworth had four off Minorca, Nelson had one at Palermo, Troubridge had four off Naples, Ball had three off Malta and Sir Sydney Smith had two at Acre. Racing eastwards with a far superior fleet, Bruix had the chance of a lifetime to destroy them in detail, and Nelson did not even know how the situation had changed. St Vincent had now to concentrate his fleet with utmost speed. First, he sent for Keith, who reached Gibraltar on 10 May. Second, he sent a warning to Nelson. Third, he sailed with his fleet for Minorca and added to it Duckworth's four ships. Fourth, having unavoidably released the Spanish fleet at Cadiz, he took up a position to prevent them joining the French at Toulon. Finally, fifth, he fell seriously ill and wrote his letter of resignation from Port Mahon, Minorca, on 16 June:

My Lord,

I am honoured with your lordship's letters of the 4th, 6th and 15th of May and feel very sensibly the credit you are pleased to give to my exertions, which, unhappily are sapped to the very foundation by such a rapid decline of health, as to bereave me of all power both of body and mind; and perceiving that a longer continuance in the command could be injurious to his Majesty's service, and unjust to Lord Keith, I determined to put him in immediate possession of it, in order to give full scope to his exertions, which I am sure will not disappoint his most sanguine friends. . . .

Lord Keith had inherited a difficult situation. The Cadiz fleet of seventeen sail (six of them three-deckers), released by his departure, put to sea on 17 May and reached Carthagena on the 20th. This passage was made in a gale during which two of their ships collided with each other and ten were more or less dismasted. While these indifferent seamen had been released from Cadiz, the Channel Fleet was now spared the trouble of blockading Brest. This enabled the Admiralty to send reinforcements to the Mediterranean, twelve sail of the line under Rear-Admiral Sir Charles Cotton. With this reinforcement, Lord Keith could finally muster about thirty sail of the line against a possible enemy concentration of about forty. But there was no actual encounter. Bruix, after entering the Mediterranean, went to Toulon, where he received orders to co-operate with the French armies in Italy. Subsequent orders told him to sail to Alexandria, embark Bonaparte's army and bring it back to Toulon. Knowing that the British fleet would now be superior in strength, he decided that he needed Spanish help and sailed accordingly to Carthagena. The Spanish would not sail for Alexandria but offered to sail with him to Brest via Cadiz. Pursued by Lord Keith, whose fleet had missed him in the Mediterranean, Bruix was back at Brest on 13 August. The combined fleet showed no further enterprise in 1799.

Bruix certainly missed a great opportunity but it would not be true to say that he had achieved nothing. He had released Bonaparte from his captivity in Egypt. On 25 August two frigates sailed from Alexandria: the *Muiron* flying the flag of Rear-Admiral Ganteaume, with Bonaparte and his staff, and the *Carrère*, commanded by Commodore Dumanoir-le-Pelley, with Lannes, Murat and Marmont among his passengers. With Lord Keith in vain pursuit of Bruix, with Lord Nelson trying to protect Sicily but having his ships taken from him by Keith, with the ships withdrawn that had been blockading Alexandria, the way was wide open for Bonaparte. The man to be feared was Commodore Sir Sidney Smith, whose ship, the *Tigre* (74) together with the *Theseus* (74) had played an important part in the defence of Acre, thwarting Bonaparte's attempted return overland through Syria. Smith, however, had gone to Cyprus and the French frigates reached Corsica without incident and went on from there to Frejus, where Bonaparte landed on 9 October. The general situation had made this voyage possible but there was also an element of luck. When General Kleber, left in Egypt with about 20,000 men, sent an important dispatch to France, the vessel which carried it was taken by a British sloop. This was at a rather later date, however, when the situation had become more normal. A result of this voyage was that Bonaparte came to a false assumption about the ease with which an unconquered sea can be traversed. Of naval warfare he was ignorant but of combined operations he now had some experience and it led him to conclusions which we now know to be wrong. From the date of Bonaparte's return began the rapid process by which Bonaparte made himself First Consul, virtual dictator, and finally Emperor, of France. Kleber's army in Egypt, lacking ammunition and pay, and faced by Turkish forces, seemed at this stage to have no future.

With the Mediterranean of less importance, following the French concentration at Brest, Lord Keith was able to devote his personal attention to the blockade of Valletta. He commanded a squadron there in February 1800, with Nelson as his second-in-command. The French made a last and desperate attempt to supply their garrison, entrusting the task to Rear-Admiral Perrée whose supply ships were escorted by his flagship, the *Généreux* with a frigate and two corvettes. At Valletta was the powerful French ship *Guillaume Tell*, the other survivor from the Battle of the Nile, which might sail (if unwatched) to help cover the entry of the supply ships. The relief attempt failed completely, the *Généreux* being taken by the *Foudroyant*, under Nelson's flag, together with the *Northumberland*. Perrée himself was killed and no supply ship reached Valletta. Satisfied that the victory of the Nile was now more complete, Lord Nelson pleaded illness, struck his flag at Leghorn and went home, with the Hamiltons, to England. Captain Manley Dixon remained off Malta and the *Guillaume Tell* made her expected attempt to escape on 30 March. She was promptly engaged by the frigate *Penelope* which so crippled the French ship that she was overtaken by the *Lion* (64) and, later, by the *Foudroyant*. After a tremendous fight, in which his crew sustained over 200 casualties, Rear-Admiral Decrès hauled down his colours. Valletta itself surrendered on 5 September and Captain Ball R.N. became the first British Governor. In Valletta the British now had an ideal naval base, impregnably fortified, with a deep-water harbour and all the shore facilities which the Knights of Malta had built up over the centuries. Some of the Knights had fled to Russia, where they elected the Tsar as Grand Master. Knowing of this, Bonaparte sought to make trouble by assuring the Tsar that Malta was his. 'Desiring to give a proof of personal consideration for the Emperor of Russia and to distinguish him from the other enemies of the republic, who fight from a vile love of gain, the First Consul wishes, if the garrison of Malta is constrained by famine to evacuate the place, to

restore it to the hands of the Tzar as Grand Master of the Order . . .'
We can all be generous in giving away what we do not possess. The
status of Malta was bound indeed to cause future difficulties but these
did not arise until peace was actually being made.

Once in supreme power, Bonaparte did not forget the army he had
left stranded in Egypt. Several vessels tried to get through with needed
supplies and a more serious attempt was made by a squadron under
Rear-Admiral Ganteaume in January 1801. Sailing from Brest with
seven ships of the line and two frigates, Ganteaume eluded pursuit,
passed Gibraltar on 9 February, and went on to Toulon. On receiving
reiterated orders to go to Alexandria, Ganteaume sailed again but
sighted a squadron commanded by Sir John Borlase Warren and put
back to Toulon. Ordered to try once more, he sailed for the third time on
27 April, found that Alexandria was blockaded and attempted to land
his troops at Benghazi. Before he could do so, against local opposition,
Lord Keith appeared and Ganteaume recognized that his efforts had
failed. He was, in any case, too late. The British had already landed in
Egypt, Lord Keith having arrived with an army of 16,000 men under
General Sir Ralph Abercromby. The campaign is of interest in being
the first during the war when a French army had been defeated by a
British army. From the naval angle it is chiefly interesting as a good
example of a combined operation. Credit for the direction went to
Keith's Captain of the Fleet, Philip Beaver, whose planning was
evidently meticulous, but he shared the credit with Captain Sir Sidney
Smith and Captain the Hon Alexander Cochrane. On 8 February 1801,
a boat flotilla of 320 craft landed the first division of troops, covering
fire being provided by gunboats, bomb-vessels and sloops. It was an
opposed landing under heavy fire but it succeeded and the boats returned for the second and third divisions, the whole army being ashore
by nightfall. The French fought a creditable campaign in Egypt but
finally capitulated, Alexandria being the last place to fall, on 2 September. Too late to be of great importance was the arrival of an expedition
coming up the Red Sea from India and under orders from Admiral
Rainier.

Before the French garrison in Egypt surrendered and while it was
still thought possible to save the situation, an agreement was reached
between France and Spain by which six Spanish sail of the line should
be transferred to the French navy. To complete the transaction, Rear-
Admiral Durand Linois was ordered to sail from Toulon with three ships

of the line, *Indomptable* (80), *Formidable* (80) and *Desaix* (74), and proceed to Cadiz, where Rear-Admiral Dumanoir-le-Pelley had already
taken over the Spanish ships. These nine were to join with six more
Spanish ships, embark troops in Italy and land them in Egypt, trapping
the British army between the opponents they were fighting and these
fresh forces newly landed behind them. The squadron duly sailed from
Toulon on 13 June and was seen from Gibraltar on 1 July. The only
British man-of-war at Gibraltar was a sloop, the *Calpé*, whose captain
watched the French ships drop anchor at Algeziras. Linois had been
warned, and might anyway have guessed, that there was a British
squadron blockading Cadiz. He went no farther than Algeziras, where
he had the protection of the Spanish shore batteries. The British squadron, commanded by Rear-Admiral Sir James Saumarez, comprised the
Caesar (80), six ships of 74 guns, a frigate and a sloop. A boat from
the *Calpé*, unnoticed by the French in the darkness, reached Saumarez in
the small hours of 5 July. At this time the *Superb* (74), commanded by
Captain Richard Keats, was detached to watch the entrance to the
Guadalquivir, eighteen miles farther north. Saumarez sent his frigate
to recall Keats, ordering him to follow the squadron to Algeziras. With
intermittent wind the squadron passed the Straits, the *Venerable*
leading, and sighted the French ships as they warped closer to the shore.
Making the signal for battle, Saumarez launched his squadron into
the attack, the more confident in that he had five ships to the enemy's
three.

The Bay of Algeziras is open, shallow and strewn with sunken rocks.
It was defended at this time by Fort Santa-Garcia, by a battery on the
Isla-Verda, by another called San-Iago and another named Almirante.
The Spanish had, in addition, fourteen gunboats, tactically placed in
groups round the bay. The French ships were moored close inshore,
forming a line with the frigate in still shallower water and close to the
Isla Verda. Leading the attack, the *Pompée* dropped anchor opposite the
Formidable and engaged her at short range. The *Audacious* anchored
opposite the *Indomptable* but at rather longer range, the *Venerable*
opposite the *Desaix* but still farther away. A fitful wind had prevented
their closing and the *Caesar*, coming up and engaging the *Desaix*, was as
handicapped as the *Hannibal* anchored near her. The *Spencer* came
under fire from the batteries but could not approach near enough for
her guns to have much effect. Seeing that the *Pompée* was hard pressed
and that the *Hannibal* was in a bad position, Saumarez ordered the

Hannibal to 'go and rake the French admiral' (i.e. the *Formidable*). Attempting to do this, the *Hannibal* ran hard aground opposite the Almirante Battery and could not be refloated. Linois now made the signal for his ships to cut their cables and run themselves ashore. The *Desaix* and *Indomptable* did so and Saumarez signalled his ships to cut their cables and renew the action but the breeze died away again and the attack never took place. The *Pompée* was towed out of action by the boat of the squadron, a planned landing on the Isla-Verda had to be cancelled and Saumarez hoisted the signal to break off the action. The other ships withdrew, not without difficulty, and the captain of the *Hannibal* had to haul down his colours. There had been much damage and heavy casualties and the British squadron had been defeated.

In studying the Battle of Algeziras we have to remember that there was a Spanish squadron in Cadiz and that Saumarez, in raising his blockade, had released it. His aim was to destroy Linois before the Spanish could follow him. With hindsight we might conclude that the Spanish were unlikely to act with undignified haste, but Saumarez dared not count on that. His recent experience, moreover, and the climax of his previous career, had been the Battle of the Nile; a classic example of an attack on a fleet at anchor. Nelson's method had been to avoid the slightest hesitation and go straight into action before the French could strengthen their position. It gave his men a moral advantage over their unenterprising opponents. His plans were already formed and explained (to meet this or any other situation) and required no elaboration at the last moment. This was the example which Saumarez tried to follow but the circumstances were not the same, nor is it likely that his captains had been properly briefed. Unless there were frantic need for haste his better plan would have been to drop anchor at Gibraltar, collect local pilots and ask their advice, study the battlefield, make a plan and wait for a steady wind. The planned capture of the Isla-Verda might well have been the opening move in a phased operation. A day's pause for reflection would also have given him another ship the *Superb*, commanded by an officer who was reputed to be the best seaman in the navy, better even than Sir Edward Pellew. As against that, Saumarez had the example of Nelson and the feeling that the Spanish might seize their opportunity. Who are we to say that his decision was wrong? It was certainly unfortunate. Where Saumarez showed his true quality was not at Algeziras but in his subsequent refusal to accept defeat. For him at least the battle was far from over.

Back at Gibraltar, Sir James's squadron was in a shattered condition, having suffered 375 casualties, with all the ships more or less damaged and one of them, the *Pompée*, a mere wreck. The French squadron had suffered at least as much and with heavier casualties. Linois therefore sent an urgent appeal to Cadiz, asking that a squadron should join him before the British could attack again. Agreeing to this, Admiral Massaredo ordered Vice-Admiral Moreno to go to Linois' help with six sail of the line and three frigates. He sailed from Cadiz on 9 July and dropped anchor at Algeziras, the detachment which had been watching Cadiz (The *Superb* (74), *Thames*, frigate; *Pasley*, sloop) reaching Gibraltar on the same day. Saumarez, with five ships of the line, was now opposed by nine ships gathered at Algeziras, six of them having played no part in the recent action. Linois had claimed a victory on 5 July but he and his allies showed no desire to follow it up. With the odds so much in their favour, they should have offered to give battle. In fact, their plan was merely to escort the three battered French ships into Cadiz; a reasonable idea in itself but unsuitable for the aftermath of what they claimed as a triumph. There was now a race to repair the ships that had been in battle. On the British side the *Pompée* was beyond immediate repair and her crew were distributed among the other ships. It was questionable whether the *Caesar* could be repaired in time, without which Saumarez would have to face the odds of four to nine. Nor were these the real odds because of the Spanish ships three were of three decks and of these two were among the biggest and most heavily armed ships in the world. The odds were unfavourable in any case but with the *Caesar* ruled out, they became impossible.

The *Caesar* had been the flagship in the action of 5 June and Brenton, the flag captain, was told by the Admiral that his ship would probably be still under repair when the enemy sailed, which would mean shifting his flag to the *Audacious*.

Captain Brenton, turning the hands up, informed the crew of the Admiral's intention, and called upon them to use every exertion to put their ship in a state to bear their Admiral's flag again into battle, should the enemy give them an opportunity. An universal cry was heard of all hands, 'All night and all day.' This however Captain Brenton would not permit; but he employed the whole ship's company, from four in the morning until eight in the evening; of the remaining eight hours, each watch was alternately allowed four of repose. He alone slept not, for his active mind, and disposition, were wound up to the highest pitch of excitement; and he has been heard himself to describe, the overwhelming sense of sleep and weariness, by which he was overcome when these exertions were happily terminated.[3]

At noon on Sunday 12 July, the enemy ships were seen to be leaving Algeziras and forming their line of battle off Cabrita Point.

. . . At one o'clock the enemy's squadron was nearly all underway; the Spanish ships *Real-Carlos* and *Hermenegildo*, of 112 guns each, off Cabrita point: the *Caesar* was warping out of the mole. The day was clear; the whole population of the rock came out to witness the scene; the line-wall, mole-head, and batteries were crowded from the dockyard to the ragged-staff; the *Caesar*'s band playing, 'Come cheer up my lads, 'tis to glory we steer;' the military band of the garrison answering with 'Britons strike home'. The effect of this scene is difficult to describe: Englishmen were proud of their country; and foreigners, who beheld the scene, wished to be Englishmen. So general was the enthusiasm among our gallant countrymen, that even the wounded men begged to be taken on board, to share in the honours of the approaching conflict.[4]

This is one of the most famous scenes in naval history. As the *Caesar* passed out of the harbour, the Rear-Admiral's flag was rehoisted and the signal made to prepare for battle. But the enemy was not in a similarly heroic mood. Vice-Admiral Moreno's squadron headed straight for the Atlantic. The allied formation, with its more powerful ships covering the retreat in line abreast, was originally planned so as to prevent the recapture of that status symbol, *Hannibal*. She made such slow progress, however, that she was sent back to Algeziras. The formation was unmodified even after it had become pointless and the retreat westwards continued as it had begun. One thing immediately obvious was that the British ships, jury-masted and somehow patched and mended, were never going to overtake their opponents, who gained distance and were soon out of sight in the gathering darkness. The *Superb* had not been in the recent battle, however, and Saumarez told Captain Keats to make sail ahead and attack the enemy's sternmost ships. Thus released, the *Superb* came up with the Spanish, still maintaining their formation in line abreast. Finding himself between the two great three-decked ships, Keats opened fire with both broadsides and then passed ahead of these huge antagonists. In the darkness and the smoke they continued the action, firing hopefully at where the *Superb* had been but actually hitting each other. Keats left them to it and closed with a smaller opponent, the *Sainte-Antoine* (74) which presently ceased fire and sur-rendered. She was then fired into, by mistake, by the *Caesar, Venerable, Spencer* and *Thames*. The *Real-Carlos* (112) meanwhile, was on fire and collided with the *San Hermenegildo* (112) setting that ship alight in her turn. At fifteen minutes after midnight the *Real-Carlos* blew up, the *San Hermenegildo* doing the same after another quarter of an hour, fewer than 300 men being saved out of 2,000. The pursuit continued during the night and the *Venerable* came up with the *Formidable*. An indecisive action followed, ending when the *Venerable* ran aground. By the time she had been rescued the battle was over and the last of the allied ships had reached Cadiz and safety. So ended the last of the French efforts to reinforce their army in Egypt. It had capitulated before any further attempt could be made.

The action of 12 July 1801, was an extraordinary affair from several points of view. It was made possible by tremendous efforts at Gibraltar, without which the squadron could not have sailed. In at least one ship the crew must have been totally exhausted before the enemy was even seen. Then the scene is presented of five ships pursuing nine. Of the ships pursued two, at least, were far more powerful than any of the pursuers. A night action followed during which all the damage was done by a single man-of-war, her consorts doing no more than fire into a single wretched ship which had already surrendered. Saumarez had earned his Knighthood of the Bath and the capture of the *Hannibal* had been sufficiently avenged. In purely naval terms this action emphasizes the differences between the professionals and the amateurs. Ships of the British Mediterranean Fleet had gained a complete ascendancy over their opponents. Trained and disciplined by St Vincent, inspired by Nelson, led by men like Saumarez or Keats, they were on top of the world. The French did surprisingly well but without the same level of competence. As for the Spanish, they seem to have had nothing but courage. To fight a night action in line abreast was lunacy. But how did the *Real-Carlos* come to burn? This was due, beyond question, to lack of training. Damage control was, after all, a matter of drill. Day after day, week after week, firemen had to muster and exercise, each man knowing exactly what he had to do and knowing that he would have to do it in any weather. A ship like the *Real-Carlos* had never been in action and had spent very little time at sea. There was no drill in Spanish ships which had become second nature, which men could perform when half-asleep (as the *Caesar*'s crew must have been). Even the drill would not always save a ship – it did not save the *Queen Charlotte* – but the Spanish managed to lose two three-deckers during the same night through sheer ignorance of what they were trying to do. It was, by contrast, a very professional squadron that Saumarez led into action and he was lucky to have, in Keats, a very exceptional seaman. He may be thought lucky and in a sense he was. His quality showed however, in the way he recovered after the first setback. Some men would have despaired when defeated by a smaller force and then confronted by a force which was so much greater. But despair did not enter into the true professional's vocabulary.

So Bonaparte's invasion of Egypt came to nothing. He reached that country with little difficulty and conquered it with less. But the implications of his plan brought the British navy into the Mediterranean. Whereas earlier operations had made Britain nervous about Ireland, tending to give British forces a merely defensive role, the Egyptian campaign changed the whole situation, taking the pressure off Britain, and leaving Bonaparte highly vulnerable. This was the cue for a British counter-offensive, reaching its climax in the Battle of the Nile. Exploiting this victory, the British captured Minorca, freed Malta and finally launched the expedition which, with Turkish help, drove the French out of Egypt. All the subsequent operations in the Mediterranean were the result of French efforts to reinforce or rescue their marooned army. These efforts failed and were bound to fail because their basic concept was wrong. To invade Egypt without establishing a naval ascendancy in the eastern Mediterranean was not really feasible. To secure Malta was a useful first step but the army which landed in Egypt, and which might very easily have been destroyed on the way there, could not be properly maintained. Without secure communications, without a flow of ammunition and other supplies, any further move eastwards, any actual threat to India, was out of the question. The situation thus created led to Bonaparte's first defeat. We need to remember, however, that it was for Britain a defensive victory. A French blow, wildly misdirected, had failed to hit a British opponent. No British effort, on the other hand, had as yet made any great impact on France. The British position in the Mediterranean, lost in 1796, was restored and somewhat improved in 1798–1801. Britain's success had brought her allies – Naples, Turkey and (for a time) Russia – but Bonaparte remained supreme in Europe.

While France was not very obviously weakened by the events of 1798-1801, the British had performed a feat of arms which they would have occasion to repeat with growing success. The expedition to Egypt already described comprised 22 ships of the line, 37 frigates and sloops and 80 transports carrying 18,000 soldiers embarked in Britain. With previous calls at Port Mahon, Valletta and Marmorice, this whole fleet reached Aboukir Bay in good order and performed a textbook version of an opposed landing. It was a long-distance operation with quite a large force and at any earlier period a high proportion of the men involved would have died on the way. By 1801 all the serious difficulties had been at least foreseen and an expedition of this sort, and at this range, had become technically possible without serious loss. In battles ashore the French techniques might still predominate but the British, in combined operations, had a technique of their own. It was taken very seriously, so much so that a *Report on Conjunct Expeditions* was written by John Bruce (Librarian of the India Office) in 1797, containing an account of all such operations going back to 1589. Printed by order of Dundas and circulated only among the members of the Cabinet, it emphasized a number of lessons concerning the chain of command, the provision of landing craft and gunboats, the importance of 'a large marine corps', the need for up-to-date intelligence and for a sound system of supply. This provided a basis for thought. By 1801, however, there were officers who had come to specialize in this work and we find that men seen on the beaches at Aboukir were to reappear on other beaches at a later date. Among British officers of either service there were some to whom all the problems had become familiar. No effective blow could be directed against France until all these problems had been studied and all or most of the difficulties had been overcome.

SIX

The Northern Alliance

Why Lord Bridport should have remained for so long as Commander-in-Chief of the Channel Fleet is a mystery still to be solved. He was admittedly well-connected, having married a niece of Viscount Cobham who was related to the Pitt and Lyttleton families. As against that, he had achieved little against the enemy and he presided over a fleet in which discipline had never been restored after the mutiny. By 1800 he was elderly, tired and sick. When all patience had been finally exhausted, the end came abruptly.

When he (Lord Spencer) returned from a Cabinet meeting with the news that Admiral Lord Bridport was to be ordered to haul down his flag, the naval members objected. Spencer told them plainly: 'If the necessary orders to Lord Bridport are not signed, the existance of the Board of Admiralty will be ended.'[1]

The orders were signed and Lord Bridport's flag was hauled down in April, 1800. King George III expressed his feelings between the lines of a letter to Spencer dated from Windsor on the 16th:

With infinite satisfaction I learn from Earl Spencer that Lord Bridport has resigned the Command of the Channel Fleet, and do not object to his being advanced to the rank of a Viscount.

I trust no time will be lost in appointing Lord St Vincent to succeed him with a civil letter from the Board to Sir Alan Gardner whose meritorious services certainly deserve every attention, though his inclination I am thoroughly convinced would not incline him to undertake the supreme command of the Channel Fleet.

George R.[2]

There were moments in his reign when George III would seem to have had more common sense than anyone else. In this instance his 'infinite satisfaction' and 'do not object' hint at a patience long since tried to breaking point. In this instance, however, he was wrong about Sir Alan Gardner, Bridport's second-in-command, who thought himself entitled to succeed as Commander-in-Chief. The trouble lay, to begin with, in the bad feeling which had existed, since the war began, between the Channel and the Mediterranean Fleets. This was symbolized by the fact that a captain at Bridport's table had proposed the toast 'May the discipline of the Mediterranean never be introduced into the Channel Fleet!' – and this without a rebuke from Bridport. When Sir Alan Gardner made his furious protest he based his case on the fact that he had served in the Channel Fleet for seven years and had therefore a right of inheritance, the ignoring of which would leave him disgraced and humbled in the eyes of the fleet. Remaining as second-in-command, Gardner behaved so badly that St Vincent concluded 'Either Sir Alan Gardner or I must retire.' That their differences lay deeper is suggested by St Vincent in writing:

I cannot account for his rudeness to me in any other way than his having been worked up by a party which considers my elevation as an obstacle to the further aggrandisement of them – I mean the Hoods, who have shown hostility to me ever since the court martial on Admiral Keppel . . .[3]

The problem was solved by sending Gardner to succeed Kingsmill on the Irish Station. But his sulks and tantrums were significant as illustrating the lack of discipline throughout the fleet. St Vincent realized that a big task lay ahead of him and that he was going to be extremely unpopular.

What the Channel Fleet lacked in discipline it made up for in numbers. With forty-eight French and Spanish ships of the line at Brest (see page 69) the Channel Fleet had to be almost as strong, numbering some forty sail all told, with six flag-officers in all. The business in hand was the blockade of Brest to which St Vincent began at once to apply a new kind of pressure. Bridport had tried, without complete success, to contain the enemy fleet. St Vincent's object was to strangle it. In France, as in Britain, nearly all heavy goods were carried by sea and river, only passengers going by road. With a close blockade, never relaxed for a day, the coastal traffic ceased, leaving Brest without its usual supplies. There would thus be such a shortage of naval stores and provisions that no fleet could be properly supplied. Apart from that, a fleet continually in port must deteriorate, partly by desertion and partly by sheer lack of practice. A sailing man-of-war needed about three months at sea before it had worked up to operational standards in sail-drill and gunnery. Under conditions of close blockade, exercised only in harbour, a crew could never gain precision, confidence and speed. Some might gain sea experience in privateers but this weakened the sense of discipline and still left each crew unexercised as a whole. So the blockade had to be maintained, for maximum effect, at two levels. Ships of the line were needed, to ensure that an enemy squadron leaving harbour would be immediately in action; and smaller vessels were needed to close with the enemy coast and interrupt all coastal traffic, forcing the enemy to supply his fleet (slowly and expensively) by road. Both operations required discipline. In the past it had been easy for captains to report damage to their rigging and ask permission to go into port, where they would stay for as long as they could find an excuse.

Under St Vincent nearly all repairs were to be done at sea with the aid of a storeship and any captain lingering in harbour was called upon to explain what had detained him. The keeping of ships at sea was made possible by improvements in diet and hygiene, supervised by Dr Baird. After one long period at sea, with 28,000 seamen and marines, the hospital cases numbered exactly sixteen. When the fleet had to shelter in Torbay the order was issued that no officer should sleep ashore or go more than three miles from the landing place. Rules such as these did not make St Vincent popular, but

. . . it must not be forgotten that there was another and more general side to his character, which made those who served under him submit cheerfully to much that they disliked at his hands. Knowing that the feeling in Lord Bridport's flagship, the *Royal George* was not in his favour – for ever since the days of Keppel and Palliser there had been considerable antagonism between the Channel and Mediterranean fleets – St Vincent shifted his flag into the *Royal George* and by his courtesy soon became very popular there . . .[4]

Discipline had to begin with the officers, and indeed with the flag-officers, but the Fleet had never wholly recovered from the mutiny. St Vincent's comments were caustic, his remedies drastic. 'The licentious-ness on board the *Pompée* and *Montague* is enough to ruin any fleet. I am most exceedingly anxious to get rid of them both.' The *Terrible* 'had two hundred Irish of the very worst description' and the *London* 'has a deal of mischief in her'. He suggested that the Post Office should open the letters to and from the lower deck. His final conclusion (10 June 1800) was as follows:

The execution of one man, who knowing of an intention to mutiny not revealing it, will have a million times stronger effect, than the like punishment inflicted on a score of actual mutineers.

It was this last discovery which later enabled the Duke of Wellington to suppress duelling in the army. The secrets of leadership and discipline have to be rediscovered, it seems, by each generation.

In point of fact, St Vincent had only a short period in which to restore discipline to the Channel Fleet. Hoisting his flag in April 1800, he went ashore again in February 1801. Pitt's government had fallen and Addington took office, appointing St Vincent as First Lord of the Admiralty. Accepting office, St Vincent set about disciplining the whole Navy by the same methods he had used in the Mediterranean and the Channel. He would appear in his Admiralty office at seven each morning and began, in the name of reform, to do with a hatchet what Nelson would have done (if at all) with a penknife.

While St Vincent and others had been restoring British sea power in the Mediterranean, a new threat had developed in the Baltic. It was not a sea in which Britain had normally any naval presence but it was an area in which British trade was important and upon which the navy relied for timber and naval stores. Swedes and Danes were apt to supply France with the same sort of goods under the neutral flag; goods which were often seized by the British as contraband. The resentment was there and Bonaparte used it to good effect, bringing the Tsar Paul over to his side and persuading the Baltic powers to revive the League of Armed Neutrality; an alliance of Russia, Sweden, Denmark and Prussia, plainly directed against Britain. Emphasizing the hostile purpose of the alliance, the Tsar detained all British merchantmen in Russian ports, relying on the fact that he and his allies had (at least in theory) about fifty ships of the line between them. Had Britain agreed to the terms offered, the neutrals could have supplied all the trade which Britain denied to France, bringing the blockade to nothing. Addington's government did not agree and St Vincent advised a 'great stroke at Copenhagen', not because the Danes were foremost in the alliance but because their capital was the nearest and most vulnerable. Ministers went further and

decided that a fleet should sail for the Baltic under the command of
Admiral Sir Hyde Parker, with Lord Nelson as second-in-command. It
was not a happy arrangement nor was Sir Hyde Parker a very fortunate
choice, but it was one for which St Vincent must be held responsible. In
explaining the appointment we have to realize, first of all, that the fleet
to be detached from the Channel Fleet and reinforced by ships com-
pleting repair or otherwise available, numbered eighteen sail of the line
and thirty-five smaller vessels; too large a fleet for a Rear-Admiral to
command. There were to be three flag-officers, in fact, the Commander-
in-Chief to be a full Admiral with considerable seniority over the other
two. Among the Admirals available (many senile and others already
employed) Sir Hyde was the one who was believed to have some knowledge of the Baltic. Nelson was thought too junior and unsuitable,
anyway, to command a fleet as opposed to a squadron. A Commander-
in-Chief had a vast administrative responsibility, with logistic problems
and diplomatic tasks. Hyde Parker had some reputation as an administrator and some experience of this work. He was not known as a
fighting admiral but neither was it certain that there was to be any
fighting. There was to be a demonstration of naval strength but preceded by a diplomatic mission. It seemed quite possible that the Danes
would see reason before actual hostilities began. In chief command
Nelson might be too bellicose. It was better, perhaps, to place over him
someone older and wiser.

It is just possible that St Vincent had another and less creditable
motive. He liked efficiency but he also enjoyed the process of spurring
people into unwonted activity. His appearance in the Admiralty at
seven in the morning was probably useless in itself but it was the sort of
scene St Vincent liked to stage. He was at last in a position to storm
through the dockyards, exposing the incompetence and dishonesty
which were ruining the service. The idea was excellent but there was a
touch of the malicious in what he actually said and did. To one who
liked to inspire activity Hyde Parker presented an ideal target. He had
been ashore for some time. He was prosperous, fat and comfortable. His
command at Jamaica had been uneventful from 1796 to 1800 and St
Vincent wrote of him:

I see by the papers Sir Hyde Parker is arrived and as he has had no work
whatever, or responsibility to affect his mind or body, during the whole of his
command, he is very well able to come out in the *Royal George* and give me a
spell, if he does not object to serve in the second post . . .

The moment had come, in fact, for Sir Hyde Parker to make himself useful. But Sir Hyde was not straining at the leash. Far from that, he chose this moment to marry.

> The 23rd inst. Admiral Sir Hyde Parker, to Miss Onslow, daughter of his brother Admiral. The difference of their ages is exactly forty-three years. Lady Parker has a settlement of £2000 *per annum*.[5]

St Vincent's particular abomination was an officer who married in time of war. He had himself married in 1785 in time of peace two years before he hoisted his flag, but he regarded a newly-married officer as all but lost to the service – as a man who would not put his duty first. Sir Hyde had not merely married but had made himself faintly ridiculous in marrying a girl of eighteen. St Vincent would have had a certain pleasure in routing Sir Hyde from his bridal bed and making him sail for the Baltic in March. It was time the old so-and-so did something to earn his pay. That the task might be beyond Sir Hyde was a fact which he could at the time have overlooked. After all, if there was to be a battle, there would be Nelson there to do the fighting. As this was the thought which would occur to other people, Sir Hyde's position was all the more difficult. If there was a setback he would be the man responsible. If there was a victory all the credit would be given to Nelson. It is no real advantage to have a known hero as one's second-in-command.

The expedition sailed from Yarmouth on 12 March, having embarked some troops under Colonel Stewart, the 49th Regiment, two companies of riflemen and a detachment of artillery. Besides Hyde Parker and Nelson there was a third flag officer, Rear-Admiral Graves. Ahead of the fleet, in a frigate, went the Hon Nicholas Vansittart, whose task was to persuade the Danes to adopt a friendlier policy towards Britain. The Skaw was sighted on the 18th and the fleet approached the Cattegat; presently dropping anchor, however, to see what diplomacy could achieve. It is possible that the Danes would have seen reason if the envoy had appeared with the fleet behind him. Instead, the fleet was out of sight, being eighteen miles from Cronenborg and Elsinore. Sir Hyde Parker hesitated, failing to realize that any further delay might add to the enemy strength, bringing their Russian and Swedish allies to join them. If Copenhagen were to be attacked the approach, it was realized, could be made in more than one way. A Council of War was held at which arguments were put forward in favour of one or another. Impatient with all this talk, Nelson ended by saying 'I don't care a damn which passage we go, so that we fight them.' He was chiefly anxious to end the affair before the Russians could arrive. At a further Council of War on the 31st he offered to annihilate the Danes with ten sail of the line. After some further hesitation while the channel was marked by new buoys, replacing those the Danes had removed, Sir Hyde accepted Nelson's offer but gave him two 50-gun ships as well together with some frigates and other vessels, including bomb ketches and fireships, numbering twenty-four vessels in all. Sir Hyde Parker retained eight ships as a reserve, including his two three-deckers, which were probably unsuitable for the task. He was to make some sort of a threat from the north but he evidently meant to keep his squadron intact. The object of forming this reserve was apparently to guard against the possible appearance of the Russians or Swedes. Considering the fleet as a whole, it is interesting to note that the ships were a scratch collection; about seven from the Channel Fleet, including the once notorious *London* (98), the rest drawn about equally from the North Sea and Mediterranean. They had no chance to exercise together as a fleet, nor had Nelson any previous acquaintance with many of his officers. They came together, as it were, on the eve of battle. Many of them were somewhat daunted by the navigational difficulties of the approach to Copenhagen; and the weeks lost by Sir Hyde's caution had obviously given the Danes ample time in which to strengthen their defences.

The harbour, arsenal and docks of Copenhagen lay in the city of Copenhagen itself, the entrance being guarded by the formidable Trekroner Battery. There were other batteries lining the shore to the southward and the Danish fleet was drawn up in shoal water covering the city front. It comprised a number of two-decked men-of-war interspersed with rafts and other improvised batteries. If all these were silenced it would be possible for the British bomb-vessels to take up a position from which they could destroy the arsenal and other shore installations. While they remained intact the bomb-vessels were effectively kept out of range. As at the Nile, Nelson was thus faced with an enemy fleet at anchor but with this difference, that he was outnumbered, the Danish ships and rafts totalling about twenty. One thing also apparent was that the Danes, fighting to defend their own capital and in view, some of them, of their own homes, would stand their ground. It was also obvious that they could be reinforced from the shore, more men rowing off to replace the casualties. A hard fight was inevitable. As at the Nile, however, the enemy fleet was at anchor, which made it possible for the attacking fleet to concentrate on a part of the enemy's line, leaving some of his ships without an opponent. Repeating the tactics used at the Nile would have meant passing inshore of the enemy line but this was impossible because of the shore batteries. Engaging the enemy ships from the seaward side would leave the shore batteries at least partly masked by their own vessels. As the strength of the Danish position centred upon the Trekroner Battery, Nelson decided to sail past Copenhagen by the Holland Deep and then attack from the south, engaging the weaker end of the Danish line. His squadron was in position by 1 April and the battle took place on the following day. By one of the ironies of history the Tsar Paul had been assassinated on 25 March. As his successor adopted a different foreign policy, the Northern Alliance had thus begun to disintegrate before the battle began. Unluckily for the Danes they knew nothing of this turn of events before 9 April.

On 2 April the British squadron moved into the attack. There was immediate disaster, the *Bellona* and *Russel* running aground and the *Agamemnon* failing to gain her proper position in the line. Lord Nelson took the remaining ships into battle and was soon hotly engaged with the Danish ships and floating batteries. After three hours of cannonade on either side the battle was still undecided. Seeing this and finding that ships he sent to reinforce Nelson, replacing the three lost at the outset, were making slow progress against the wind, Sir Hyde Parker made Signal Number 39, which meant DISCONTINUE THE ACTION. In his recent and definitive study of the battle, Mr Dudley Pope emphasizes that the signal was general, made not to Nelson but to the fleet as a whole. Each ship was thus obliged, in theory, to obey the signal without waiting for the signal to be repeated from Nelson's temporary flagship, the *Elephant*. That is the first fact to realize. The second fact is that for the ships of the line to have obeyed the signal would have been virtual suicide. Placed as they were opposite resolute opponents, they could not withdraw until the enemy's fire had been silenced. Withdrawal would have meant ceasing fire and sending the men to make sail. It would have meant presenting each ship's stern to the enemy's guns and to a raking fire which would have redoubled when the Danes saw the British retreat. It would have involved appalling casualties and damage and would have allowed the Danes to claim a victory. It would have destroyed British prestige in northern Europe. 'Leave off action!'

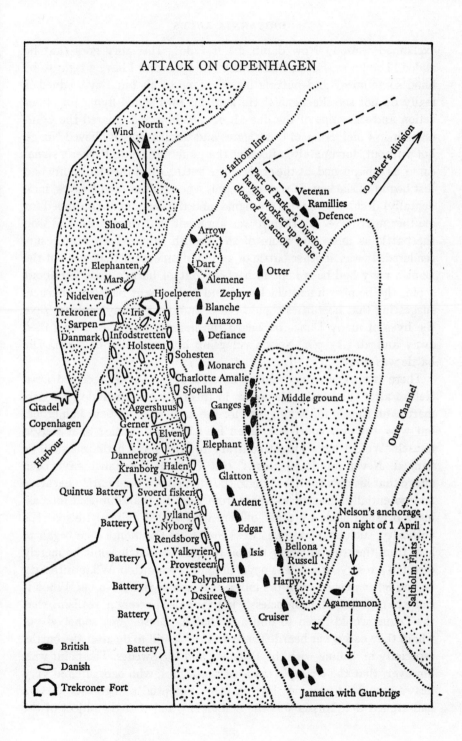

ATTACK ON COPENHAGEN

exclaimed Nelson, 'Now damn me if I do!' The story goes that he added 'You know, Foley, I have only one eye – and I have a right to be blind sometimes,' and putting his telescope to his blind eye, added 'I really do not see the signal!' He kept his own signal flying for closer action and the ships of the line all obeyed him and ignored the Commander-in-Chief. Some of the frigates and smaller vessels obeyed No. 39 but without, fortunately, affecting the issue. Sir Hyde Parker's signal came, as it happened, at the crisis of the battle, when the Danish fire had just begun to slacken. It was 12.30 pm, when Nelson (and Graves, incidentally) decided to ignore the signal, and the cannonade continued for another hour or so. By then it was apparent that the British had won the battle as more and more of the Danish ships ceased fire or surrendered. It was another battle of annihilation except that some of the Danish navy had been kept in harbour out of harm's way. By about 2 pm, the bombardment slackened and Nelson sent in a flag of truce, suggesting that hostilities should cease. In no other way could he save the lives of many Danes on board the floating batteries. Firing died away and at 3.15 pm, Nelson's flagship hoisted a flag of truce. The battle was over.

There is no known account of how Sir Hyde Parker received Lord Nelson after the battle. He could, in theory, have demanded a court-martial on Nelson for having, not for the first time, disobeyed an order; but who was ever court-martialled for winning a battle? Said Nelson himself 'Well, I have fought contrary to orders and perhaps I shall be hanged. Never mind; let them!' But Hyde Parker must have been aware that his own contribution to the victory had been purely negative and potentially disastrous. Apart from that, he found himself increasingly brushed aside by other officers who looked only to Nelson. His authority, such as it was, was weakened from the moment he began to lead from the rear, allowing Nelson to fight the battle while he merely directed a reserve which was never actually committed. What authority he had left vanished from the moment he made Signal No. 39. When it came to negotiation, he hopelessly left that also to Nelson, realizing that the Danes would listen to him and that he himself was somebody of whom they had never heard. There was much still to do after the battle, especially in dealing with the Russians and the Swedes. The point was, however, that the example made of the Danes, who had suffered very heavy casualties, was not lost on other potential antagonists. Nelson had argued that Russia was the real enemy and that the object of the exercise should be to destroy the Russian fleet, after which Denmark and Sweden would be the allies of Britain. He would have visited Copenhagen on the way back from Revel. In the event the plan worked as well in reverse, the Russians being strongly influenced by the example made of the Danes.

Negotiations proceeded at Copenhagen and the truce turned into an armistice. News of the Tsar's death was officially confirmed and it was rumoured that the new Tsar would be willing to release all British ships that had been detained. Meanwhile it was reported that the Swedish fleet was at sea. So it had been, but Sir Hyde Parker's fleet found it once more at anchor under the guns of Carlskrona. Soon afterwards orders arrived from the Board of Admiralty ordering Sir Hyde Parker to hand over his command to Lord Nelson and return to England. Nelson, now Commander-in-Chief in the Baltic, sailed for Revel, only to find that the Russian fleet had withdrawn to Cronstadt. Once contact had been made with Alexander, the new Tsar, Nelson was assured that the embargo on British merchantmen would be lifted and that friendly relations would be resumed between Russia and Britain. So ended the Baltic campaign and Nelson, handing over the command to Vice-Admiral Sir Charles Morice Pole, returned in the *Kite* brig to Yarmouth. He was made Viscount for his services at Copenhagen and Rear-Admiral Graves was made a Knight of the Bath. Back at Yarmouth at an earlier date, Sir Hyde Parker wrote an indignant letter to the Admiralty, asking what he had done wrong and why he should be recalled with such ignominy. The Board's reply, signed by St Vincent and Troubridge, was brief and to the point:

Whereas you have acquainted us . . . with your arrival in Yarmouth Roads in His Majesty's ship *Blanche*; and whereas we think fit that you shall strike your flag and come on shore; you are hereby required and directed to strike your flag and come on shore accordingly.

Once ashore, he was to stay there. Sir Hyde Parker was never employed again.

With the end of French efforts in Egypt and the end of French intrigues in the Baltic, the war had reached a sort of stalemate and negotiations began for a general peace treaty. Preliminary articles were signed on 1 October 1801, ratifications were exchanged on the 10th and King George III issued his proclamation on the 12th, ordering a cessation of conflict by sea and land. Further negotiations followed leading at last to the Definitive Treaty of Peace concluded at Amiens on 23 March 1802. By this treaty Britain restored all territories taken from France, Spain and Holland with the exception of Trinidad and Ceylon. Losing Minorca again, Britain was thus left once more without a base in the Mediterranean. Egypt was to be returned to the Sultan of Turkey but the boundaries of the French Republic were extended so as to include Belgium, the Rhineland, Savoy and Piedmont. The existence of the French satellites was acknowledged; the Helvetic, Cisalpine and Ligurian Republics. For all practical purposes France was left in control of Italy, with strong influence over Spain, Holland and Sweden. Put more briefly, France had and would retain, the predominant position in Europe. A curious feature of the Treaty was the agreement over Malta, Gozo and Comino. These islands had belonged to the monastic and military Order of the Knights of St John, a legacy from the Crusades. The celibate knights, who all had to be of noble birth, had been divided into linguistic groups – Castilian, French, English etc. – each '*Langue*' a subdivision of the Order, and each knight had drawn an income derived from property belonging to the Order in Spain, France or elsewhere. There were no Maltese Knights and the Maltese played no part in the government of the island. The knights had lost much of their original character and were easily expelled by Bonaparte. Then the French were driven out by the British with the help of the Maltese populace; the island had since been used as a British naval base. To settle the future of Malta was not easy but the problem was solved in these words:

The islands of Malta, Gozo and Comino shall be restored to the Order of St John of Jerusalem, to be held on the same conditions on which it possessed them before the war, and under the following stipulations

1. The Knights of the Order whose *Langues* shall continue to subsist, after the exchange of the ratification of the present treaty, are invited to return to Malta, as soon as the exchange shall have taken place. They shall there form a general chapter and shall proceed to the election of a grand master ... [any previous election to be invalid and there was to be no French or English *Langue*] ...

3. There shall be established a Maltese *Langue*. . . . Proofs of nobility shall not be necessary for the admission of knights of this *Langue* ... etc.

These antiquarian plans, perhaps admirable in themselves, were unrealistic. The order was disintegrating before it was destroyed. The knights depended for their incomes on properties elsewhere which had been mostly appropriated by national governments. The medieval concept of a monastic military order was not in line with current thought. It came too late or – in terms of the gothic revival – it came too early. Apart from that, moreover, the knights had been unpopular with the Maltese, who did not want to have them back and who felt by now that they had won their freedom. These provisions in the treaty were impossible to fulfil and this fact must have been known to many people at the time. Were they inserted by one protagonist (or by both) as an excuse for breaking the treaty at some future date? Whatever the purpose may have been that was certainly the effect. This does not mean that the peace was necessarily to be of only brief duration, but it does suggest that the resumption of hostilities was already foreseen by some or all of the signatories.

In many history books the Treaty of Amiens is described as the result of an indecisive war. We have often been told that the French had won the war on land, the British had won the war at sea. In a familiar British terminology there had been, we have been assured, a drawn match. But this view is entirely false. The war was not indecisive nor can it be described as a draw. It was a decisive war and the French had won. Britain itself, including Ireland, had been successfully defended and a number of French attacks had failed. Attempts to invade Ireland had come to nothing. An attempt to advance on India via Egypt had been defeated. The attempt to form the Northern Alliance against Britain had been foiled. But all these British victories had been purely defensive, no one of them posing any danger to France. Nor were these the issues which brought Britain into the conflict. The British object had been to prevent France from gaining a position of dominance in Europe and, above all, a position of dominance over the Rhine estuary. The British war aim had thus been to keep the French out of what we now call the Netherlands and Belgium. That was the aim and it had not been achieved. A secondary aim at this time had been to destroy the revolutionary movement in France by aiding the French royalists; and here again the failure had been complete. The only successful offensives had been in capturing distant islands and colonies, some in the Mediterranean, some in the West Indies, one at the Cape and some in the Indian Ocean. These were all the trophies to show for the efforts made, and they were practically all relinquished under the terms of the Peace of Amiens, Ceylon and Trinidad being the sole exceptions. Thousands of seamen and soldiers had given their lives to secure by warfare what would then be given away in negotiation. To all intents and purposes Britain had lost the war.

Had the Treaty of Amiens led to, say, twenty years of peace, it would have left Bonaparte permanently dominant in Europe; as supreme as Philip II had sought to be, more autocratic than Louis XIV had ever been, as oppressive as Adolf Hitler would ever be. The Treaty, as Bonaparte saw it, gave him a free hand on a continent in which Britain had no further interest or influence. It was at this moment that George III was induced to waive his title of King of France and delete the lilies from his coat of arms. He appears in the definitive treaty as no more than 'King of the United Kingdom of Great Britain and Ireland'. Addington and his colleagues saw this, no doubt, as a minor point and a concession to reality. It had, however, a symbolic significance. It underlined Britain's withdrawal from Europe. It negatives every tradition an Englishman would associate with the Battle of Agincourt. Nor did Bonaparte concede anything in return. He did not renounce his own plans to conquer an empire in Asia or America. Far from that, he had regained Louisiana from Spain and saw this as a base for expansion, not abandoning the idea until 1803. One of his first acts after peace was made was to send a fleet and army to suppress a revolt in Santo-Domingo (now Haiti) and re-establish French influence in the West Indies. In the other direction his agents were active in Tripoli, Egypt and Syria. He was busily creating a new fleet, saying that 'Peace is necessary to restore a navy – peace to fill our arsenals, empty of material, and peace because only then is the one drill-ground for fleets, the sea, open'. He was aiming, in fact, at world domination and there was nothing in the treaty which would be inconsistent with this aim. British diplomacy was admittedly feeble and Bonaparte made much of quitting Egypt, which had (unknown to the British negotiators) already fallen, but the treaty was mostly dictated by him as to a defeated enemy. While the British had held their own, France had become relatively stronger at the expense of the other countries in Europe.

Some ministers in England may have foreseen an early renewal of hostilities but one minister did not. This was Earl St Vincent, who launched at this time his plan for the reform of naval administration. He had introduced discipline and order into the Mediterranean Fleet, the Channel Fleet, and to some extent in the navy as a whole. With the aid of Sir Thomas Troubridge and Captain Markham, he now proposed to introduce the same order and discipline into the shore establishments.

The task was not going to be an easy one. The dockyard officials, clerks and craftsmen were not subject to the Articles of War. They formed a tight community bound by long-established custom and enjoying long-recognized perquisites. They were voters, many of them, in the dockyard constituencies. Nor were they directly responsible to the Board of Admiralty but to the Navy Board of which St Vincent was not even a member. The Third Surveyor, however, Mr Tucker, was a follower of his and he had long known of abuses which he was powerless to prevent. The one certainty about such a programme of reform was that it would take time. Given from five to ten years of peace the whole system could have been put right, at least for the time being. But the time available, as it turned out, was far too brief for so ambitious a task. It is also a question whether his quarterdeck manner created the right atmosphere.

As First Lord of the Admiralty, Lord St Vincent's piercing eye struck terror into those foul sinks of iniquity, the dockyards, which came the first under his notice. Then began the howlings, the yells, of the crew who for years had been 'battening' on the vitals of their country. When these people found that their menaces and abuses were unheeded, they had recourse to tears, to entreaties, to appeals in behalf of large and helpless families, and to former good character. All this Lord St Vincent was prepared for; and, like Ulysses, he stopped his ears and pursued his way.[6]

St Vincent's difficulties began before the war had even ended. Sending a fleet to the Baltic, additional to the fleets regularly stationed elsewhere, had strained all dockyard resources to the limit. The result was a strike in the dockyards, the men demanding higher wages. Their average earnings were £93 (as compared with a naval lieutenant's £105.16s.) and their demand was for double pay.

St Vincent found himself in a difficult position, for the Cabinet were pressing him for the ships, while the men necessary to fit out the ships were on strike. In this position he took forcible action by informing the delegates that the Board had decided to discharge them from the service, and that similar treatment would be meted out to any man in a dockyard who collected money in support of a combination to intimidate the authorities.

St Vincent suspected that the shipwright officers had actually encouraged this wage demand in April 1801. By September 1802, there was 'a combination entered into between the caulkers of Chatham and

Sheerness, and those in the merchant builders' yards in the Thames'. St Vincent had those in the naval yards discharged. He pursued the same policy when there was a combination (or trade union) among the victualling-office bakers, observing that 'frequent compromises with this description of people' had done 'infinite mischief'. This was an answer to some forms of industrial unrest but corruption in other forms did not yield to such drastic treatment.

... It was a common expression with the receiving clerks in the dockyards, to say that 'they had not been hampered', as a reason for refusing to receive inferior articles into store, when supplied by the contractors. The 'hampering' meant a bribe in the shape of a hamper of wine, or some other good thing, as the price of a certificate stating that the merchandize was fit for his Majesty's service, when it was known to be not so . . .[8]

The peculation, common and deplorable as it was, mattered less than the danger of accepting unsuitable or damaged materials. Perhaps the worst abuse of any concerned the use of copper bolts.

... Every ship was supposed to have a certain number of these bolts driven through her works, in order to secure the fabric well together. Some of these are two feet long; others, through the stem and breast-hooks or bows of the ship, and about the stern post and near the rudder, much longer: their diameter about one inch and three quarters. It is the most important part of the duty of the master builder and his confidential assistants to see that these bolts are driven effectually into their proper places; but in order to deceive or elude the vigilance of the inspectors, the wretches contrived what they called 'a Devil bolt.' These were neither more nor less than the heads and tails of bolts, about two inches long, cut off and placed where the builder supposed the entire bolt to have gone through, the intermediate part being filled up with a wooden plug or *trenail*, whilst the head on the outside and the tail forelocked within, gave the deceitful promise of security. Thus was the ship deprived of her most effectual fastening, and the diabolical act was only discovered when perhaps there was no remedy.

It is probable that the loss of the *York* of 64 guns, in the North Seas, and the *Blenheim*, 74, in the East Indies, was owing solely to this practice: and the *Albion* of 74 guns we know to have been very nearly the victim to this foul and hellish fraud. That ship had been sent out to India quite new. She was one of what we used to call 'the forty thieves' (that number of ships of the line having been built by contract in the merchants' yards, and found wanting in almost every good quality). After being on service about three years, this ship proved so loose and defective that she was ordered home, and had nearly foundered on her passage; and on being taken into dock it was discovered that her weakness was owing to the number of these 'devils' which had been put into her when building.[9]

The sale of copper bolts was only one fraud among a thousand and to prevent them all was beyond the wit of any one reformer. St Vincent came to recognize this and persuaded Parliament to pass the Act of December 1802 which appointed Commissioners 'for inquiry into irregularities, frauds and abuse in the navy departments and in the business of the prize agency'. The work of inquiry began thus on Whig insistence, was stopped later by the Tories but was resumed in 1806, the Commissioners reporting finally in 1809. It was the tenth report in this series which led to the impeachment of Henry Dundas, Lord Melville.

It cannot be supposed that there was any lack of opposition to St Vincent's reforms. His plan for doing all work in the naval dockyards, giving no further contracts to the private shipbuilding yards, created an outcry among the builders and the monopolistic suppliers of timber. Pitt and his friends in opposition took up the case against the government, suggesting that the navy was being dangerously weakened by St Vincent's policies. Pitt eventually moved for an inquiry into St Vincent's naval administration but there was a majority against him of 201 to 130. We can see, in retrospect, that there were valid arguments on either side. St Vincent was undoubtedly right in demanding reform and an end to long-established abuses. Had there been a prospect of peace over the next decade his case would have been unanswerable. When it came to be realized, however, that a renewed war was inevitable, it was fair to ask whether this was the time for reform, with all the dislocation and friction which was sure to result. Men-of-War built in the Thames were not as good as those built at Chatham – about this there could be little dispute – but any ship, in the last resort, was better than none. Long-established corruption was due in St Vincent's time, as it is due to-day, to the fact that Parliament takes little interest in the armed forces in time of peace and can find no time for inquiry in time of war. It was St Vincent's misfortune that he was not given time enough to do the work on which he had set his heart.

When Tierney replied to Pitt's demand for an inquiry into St Vincent's administration of the navy he told the House that men-of-war numbered 511 on 31 December 1803, with 373 lighters and other small craft for use in harbour, and 624 gun vessels for coastal defence. A more detailed return than was actually made on that occasion would have shown the following strength:

First Rate Ships	112–100	guns	6	
Second Rate Ships	98–90	guns	6	Ships of
Third Rate Ships	84–80	guns	7	the Line: 72
Third Rate Ships	74	guns	38	
Third Rate Ships	68–64	guns	15	
Fourth Rate Ships	54–50	guns	16	
Fifth Rate Ships	44	guns	13	
Fifth Rate Ships	40	guns	8	
Fifth Rate Ships	38	guns	15	Frigates etc.: 120
Fifth Rate Ships	36	guns	27	
Fifth Rate Ships	32	guns	18	
Sixth Rate Ships	30–20	guns	23	
Sloops	18–16	guns	58	

The Naval Chronicle (Vol. XI p. 477) adds the following information (for 1804):

The total number of his Majesty's Ships, and armed vessels of every description in commission on the 15th of March last, was 1,874; and the number of seamen mustered on the same day, was 84,431. The marines actually in pay on the 15th of March, 1804, were 15,663.

[*Note:* These totals of ships and other vessels are only approximate. They vary according to whether odd categories are included like hospital ships, prison ships, receiving ships and sheer hulks.]

The whole purpose of the Addington ministry was to make peace, which Pitt had refused to do. There are reasons to think that the peace they made was on disadvantageous terms. They partly made up for their diplomatic failures, however, by refusing to evacuate either Malta or the Cape. For this they had every excuse because Bonaparte had broken the treaty on his side, intervening in Switzerland (September 1802) and virtually annexing Piedmont, Liguria and Elba. He also failed to evacuate the Netherlands and persisted in plans for developing Antwerp as a naval base. It was clear by March 1803, that a renewal of war was certain and the issue of Malta had perhaps made it inevitable from the beginning. Bonaparte said on one occasion that he would sooner see the British on the heights of Montmartre than in possession of Malta. But Britain needed a base in the central Mediterranean and the nonsense in the peace treaty about re-forming the Order of St John of Jerusalem provided all the excuse that was needed for keeping the base already occupied. Bonaparte was encouraged in his warlike plans by the fact that the British had no allies. He would seem, nevertheless, to have wanted a longer period of peace. He even made some conciliatory gestures at the last moment. It is to the credit of Addington that he responded by declaring war on 16 May 1803. Not for the last time in their history the British mobilized their fleet and went to war against a European dictatorship. But the dictator's title was under discussion and the new war had not progressed very far before Bonaparte ceased to be First Consul and was crowned Emperor of France. As from 2 December 1804, he was the Emperor Napoleon and the war in which he was engaged had become Napoleonic.

PART II

THE WARS
OF THE
EMPEROR
NAPOLEON
1803-1816

SEVEN

Britain and the Third Coalition

The Emperor, as he was soon to become, began the war with an offensive plan already formed. Preparations for the invasion of Britain had been well advanced in 1801 and Napoleon had merely to order a renewal of activity based on existing plans. The invasion flotilla centred upon Boulogne but the landing craft, many of them built at inland ports like Paris and Strasbourg, were collected in all harbours from Boulogne to Flushing, with larger concentrations at Calais, Dunkirk and Ostend. There were 1,273 landing craft at Boulogne by the end of 1803 and they comprised vessels which fell into the following categories:

1 *Gun-vessels or Prames*, ship-rigged, mounting twelve 24-pounders, manned by 38 seamen and embarking 100 soldiers or more. Some vessels in this class had stalls for fifty horses.
2 *Gun-brigs*, mounting three 24-pounders and one 8-inch mortar.
3 *Schooners and Luggers*, mounting one 24-pounder.
4 *Peniches* or large flat-bottomed rowing boats, which looked (and were) very vulnerable indeed.

With unarmed transports included, there were supposed to be 2,293 craft in all.

As soon as invasion exercises began, certain awkward facts began to emerge. It became apparent, first of all, that these vessels were insufficiently seaworthy to be afloat between November and May. It then became clear that the actual embarkation of troops could not be accomplished in one tide. To embark 150,000 men, as planned, with 8,000 horses and 400 guns, would be no simple feat of organization. Napoleon began by stating that he needed command of the Channel for six hours, but he revised this estimate, extending it to twelve hours, to twenty-four hours, to several days and finally to as many weeks. One problem (not the only one) was that of accommodating the troops ashore. The actual invasion, depending on the weather, could not be on a date fixed in advance. Given this measure of uncertainty it was impossible to have troops waiting on the beach. They had to disperse, finding shelter in towns, villages and tented camps. This meant that hours would be spent in collecting them again. There would be traffic jams on converging roads, to avoid which there would have to be a detailed time-table. But there were limits again to the length of time which troops could spend in vessels at anchor, waiting for other units to embark. It was agreed in the end that this operation was impossible – as Decrès had been saying from the outset – without escort, and that an essential preliminary would be to establish a temporary naval superiority in the Channel; a task the more difficult in that France's traditional allies, the Spanish, were currently at peace. There were two other difficulties about this invasion project. First, there was no cover plan, nothing to distract attention from a known threat. Second, there was no possibility of surprise, all the invasion ports being under daily observation. Of all these obstacles Napoleon became aware, attributing some of them to his admirals' lack of enterprise. He persevered, however, in what he regarded as a feasible project and the only one which could lead to the defeat and destruction of his most persistent opponent.

On the British side Lord St Vincent, at the Admiralty, was entrusted with the country's naval defence. The Channel Fleet was under the command of Admiral the Hon William Cornwallis, who blockaded Brest and whose detached squadrons, commanded respectively by Collingwood and Pellew, were blockading Rochefort and Ferrol. The Mediterranean Fleet, blockading Toulon, was now placed under the command of Vice-Admiral Lord Nelson, with Rear-Admiral Sir Richard Bickerton as his second-in-command. The French fleets were all under close blockade as St Vincent understood the term and not in the way that Lord Bridport had thought sufficient. But who was to confront the threatened invasion itself? This central task was given to Admiral Lord Keith. Under his orders the North Sea Fleet was concentrated at the Nore but with three detached squadrons for particular tasks. One of these, under Rear-Admiral Montague, was based on the Downs and was responsible for watching the enemy coastline from Flushing to Calais. Another, under Rear-Admiral Thornborough, based upon Yarmouth, was responsible for trade and coast protection from Orford Ness to the Firth of Forth. A third, under Commodore Sir Sidney Smith, based upon Horsley Bay, was responsible for the defence of the Thames Estuary. By a clever deployment of quite inadequate forces, Keith was to harass the French, 'make such a show of defensive force as would keep the population on our coasts in good heart' and afford protection to the British coastal trade. One way and another, Lord Keith had quite enough to do.

Britain itself was in a ferment of warlike activity with 'fencibles' in every fishing village and volunteers drilling in every open space, but a meeting with the French on British soil was not really desirable. The better plan was to anticipate the French by launching a spoiling attack upon each of their invasion ports. This had been attempted by a flotilla under Lord Nelson's command in 1801. Boulogne had been the target and there were two attacks, one by bomb vessels in daylight on 4 August and the other by ships' boats at night on the 15th. Little was achieved in either operation and the damage done was fully balanced by the losses sustained. It was resolved, nevertheless, to try again in 1803. Each invasion port was, of course, strongly defended by shore batteries and gunboats, and these would have the advantage of position in any artillery duel. It was supposed, however, that something might be achieved by the use of shell as opposed to shot. Cannon of this period fired solid projectiles but bombs filled with explosive could be fired at long range from the howitzer or mortar, used commonly in siege warfare. These high-trajectory weapons were never used afloat, however, except in a specially-designed bomb vessel. To have attempted high-angle fire from an ordinary ship would have been appallingly dangerous for the bomb would most probably have hit the ship's own rigging and so dropped down again on the mortar crew. The bomb vessel, usually a ketch, had her mast stepped aft and space left forward, but guarding against the obvious danger had left her vulnerable to ordinary gunfire. The drill was, therefore, to engage the enemy first and then bring up the bomb-vessels behind a screen of ships already in action. This had been the technique used by Lord Nelson at Copenhagen and it might have proved effective against a well-defined and extensive target like the Danish arsenal. Used against landing craft, the bomb was wildly inaccurate, as was soon apparent. Dieppe was thus bombarded on 14 September 1803, and the port of Granville was attacked by a larger force, under Rear-Admiral Sir James Saumarez, on the 13th. There followed another attempt on Calais at the end of the month but again with very little result. The search began for some other weapon which would break the stalemate. Could something be done with fireships?

What both sides needed was the steam vessel and we note (see page 55–6) that steamboats were already to be seen on the Delaware and in Scotland. Consideration of this fact brings us to the career of Robert Fulton (1765–1815), the American artist who came to London in 1787 in order to study painting under Benjamin West. Falling under the influence of the Duke of Bridgewater, Earl Stanhope and James Watt, he turned instead to engineering and, moving to France, experimented with his 'torpedo' on the Seine in 1797. Napoleon was sufficiently impressed to give him a grant of Fr.10,000. With this encouragement he laid down his *Nautilus* submarine during the winter of 1800 and completed her by May, 1801. She was 21 ft 4 in. long, 7 ft in diameter, with a glass conning tower, a hand-driven propeller (for use under the surface), a mast and a sail. After some encouraging results he increased his crew from one to three and resumed his trials at Brest in June 1801. The *Nautilus*, it was found, could cover 500 yards, submerged, in seven minutes. Operationally, the idea was that the *Nautilus* should attach an explosive 'torpedo', with a delayed action fuse, to the bottom of an enemy ship. Using this method, Fulton blew up a schooner with 20lbs of gunpowder in August 1801. This experiment was watched by a commission appointed by Napoleon and the Minister of Marine, Admiral Pleville le Pelly, who finally rejected the invention (on the commission's advice) in February, 1804. In the meanwhile, in 1803, Fulton was propelling a boat by steam power on the Seine. Soon after the French rejection of his schemes he came to Britain in May 1804, and offered his inventions to the British government.

So far as Napoleon was concerned, the crisis of his invasion project came in July–August 1804. In our own time we date the German failure from the date on which the Luftwaffe had unacceptable losses in the Battle of Britain. The equivalent date in the Napoleonic era was 20 July 1804, the day on which the Emperor came to inspect his flotilla at Boulogne. It was blowing a gale and the landing craft were mostly running for shelter at Etaples or St Valery-sur-Somme, others being driven on shore or wrecked near Portet. A scene of disaster, in which 400 men perished, was made worse by the fire of two British sloops, the *Harpy* (18) and *Autumn* (16) and two gun-brigs, the *Bloodhound* and *Archer*. The incident was a small one but the significant fact was that it took

'The Board Room at the Admiralty', drawing by Rowlandson and Pugin, 1808.

Richard, Earl Howe, Commander-in-Chief of the Channel Fleet in 1793. This portrait was painted by John Copley in 1794.

ABOVE LEFT Lord Hood was
Commander-in-Chief of the
Mediterranean Fleet in 1793 but was
replaced by Vice-Admiral Hotham in
1794. Portrait after Sir Joshua Reynolds,
1793.

ABOVE RIGHT Sir Edward Pellew,
Commander-in-Chief of the
Mediterranean Fleet in the final phase of
the Napoleonic Wars. He became
Viscount Exmouth after the Battle of
Algiers in 1816. Portrait by W. Owen,
1819.

LEFT This portrait of Admiral Sir Hyde
Parker was painted by George Romney,
c. 1782. He commanded the Baltic
Fleet which attacked Copenhagen in
1801.

The *Agamemnon*, of 64 guns, commanded by Horatio Nelson from 1793 to 1796. This painting shows the action of 12 March 1795 in which the *Ca Ira* was captured.

Nelson's ship *Captain*, of 74 guns, capturing the *San Nicolas* and the *San Josef* during the Battle of Cape St Vincent, 14 February 1797.

Sir John Jervis, a portrait by Sir William Beechey, c. 1792. He became Commander-in-Chief of the Mediterranean Fleet in 1795 and with little more than half the strength of his opponents he attacked and defeated the Spanish off Cape St Vincent and was created Earl St Vincent.

BELOW Sailors firing a thirty-two pounder cannon of a type widely used in the Napoleonic Wars. From a painting by Frank Dadd.

'The Battle of Camperdown', an oil painting by Philip James de Loutherbourg showing the defeat of the Dutch Fleet by Admiral Duncan in 1797.

BELOW LEFT Captain Richard Bowen gained fame as captain of the frigate *Terpsichore* in which he actually engaged the Spanish flagship *Santissima Trinidad* but had to break off action when more Spanish ships arrived. This portrait c. 1812.

BELOW RIGHT Sir Home Riggs Popham commanded the squadron which recaptured the Cape of Good Hope in 1805. After a disastrous attempt to free Argentina and Uraguay from Spanish rule he was ordered home and tried by court martial. After a painting by M. Brown, 1806.

Admiral Lord Keith by
G. Saunders, c. 1816. He
succeeded Sir John Jervis
as Commander-in-Chief of
the Mediterranean Fleet.

Alexander Hood, Lord
Bridport, was the younger
brother of Admiral Lord
Hood and was
Commander-in-Chief of
the Channel Fleet from
1797 to 1800. Portrait by
Lemuel Abbott, 1795.

A Rowlandson cartoon of 1798, the original title being 'Admiral Nelson recreating with his brave Tars after the glorious battle of the Nile'.

Aerial view of the harbour of Valletta, Malta.

Thomas Rowlandson's drawing of a midshipman c. 1800.

BELOW In an attempt to destroy Linois' squadron, Saumarez raised the blockade of the Spanish at Cadiz and engaged the French at Algeziras. This painting shows the British squadron off Gibraltar, where Saumarez returned after the action and carried out extensive repairs before engaging the French again.

A model, from the Science
Museum, of a British
landing craft used during
the Napoleonic Wars.

The American Robert
Fulton first studied as an
artist before becoming an
engineer. In 1801 he built
a submarine for the
French which was rejected
and eventually he
returned to the United
States.

A view of the harbour at Boulogne in 1803 where many of Napoleon's troops and landing craft were concentrated.

Lord Nelson's squadron blockading Cadiz, a painting by T. Buttersworth.

Lord Nelson's Great Cabin in the *Victory*, restored and refurnished to its state at the time of Trafalgar.

BELOW LEFT Lord Collingwood was second in command of the Mediterranean Fleet at the time of Trafalgar. He succeeded Nelson as Commander-in-Chief, retaining command until his death in 1810.

BELOW RIGHT Admiral Villeneuve, Nelson's opponent at the Battle of Trafalgar.

Horatio Nelson, a portrait by Lemuel Abbott, 1798.

J. M. W. Turner's painting of the *Victory* breaking the enemy line at the Battle of Trafalgar.

Caricature of the British towing the Danish fleet into harbour by Gillray, 1807.

Lord Cochrane led a brilliant fireship attack on the French fleet in the Basque Roads in 1809. Owing to lack of support from Admiral Gambier the operation only partly succeeded. From a painting by W. H. Overend, showing Cochrane signalling for assistance during the attack.

Sir Nesbit Willoughby, 'the immortal', from the painting by Thomas Barber, 1837.

The Battle of Grand Port, the British defeat which preceded the capture of Mauritius in 1810.

Sir Philip Broke, a gunnery expert, proved the value of his training methods when his frigate the *Shannon* captured the American ship *Chesapeake* in 1813. Portrait by Samuel Lane, c. 1814.

Napoleon on board HMS *Bellerophon* from a painting by W. Orchardson.

place in the height of summer. With weather that bad in late July, what might an invasion force expect in spring or autumn? And what losses might be expected if such a gale were to blow up after the whole invasion flotilla had set sail for England? And while the British played only a marginal part in this setback, the fact remained that they were very much present despite the gale and barely beyond the range of the shore batteries. Were the invasion actually taking place, they would be there in greater force and ready to take greater risks. On 16 August the Emperor reviewed his invasion army at Boulogne, there being over 80,000 men on parade. On the 25th he went on to inspect the landing craft, or at least some 146 of them. The parade was also inspected, at a respectful distance, by the British gun-brig *Bruiser*. Admiral Bruix ordered a division of gun vessels to drive the intruder off but this brought on the scene the British frigate *Immortalité* (36). After some confused firing the action ended but with the frigate still within three miles. On the 26th there was another skirmish but this time with the Emperor actually afloat in his barge, attended by Marshals Soult and Mortier. The *Immortalité* was again in action and several French gun-boats were run on shore to avoid sinking. It was now obvious that any scheme for invading Britain, without first removing the British fleet, must be ruled out as impracticable. As Nelson wrote at the time 'This boat business may be a part of a great plan of invasion; it can never be the only one.'

What happened, meanwhile, to Robert Fulton? Having changed sides, he offered the British government a device which he called a catamaran. It was a waterproof box, about 21 feet long, containing forty barrels of gunpowder and, in addition:

'a piece of clockwork, the main spring of which, on the withdrawing of a peg placed on the outside, would, in a given time (from six to ten minutes) draw the trigger of a lock, and explode the vessel.'

This invention was shown to the Prime Minister and a committee comprising Lords Melville, Mulgrave and Castlereagh, Sir Home Popham, Sir Joseph Banks, Mr Cavendish, Sir John Rennie and Major Congreve. After taking all this scientific and technical advice, the Ministers decided to launch a few catamarans against the French flotilla off Boulogne. Admiral Lord Keith directed the operation, which also involved the use of four fireships. October 2 was the chosen day and boats towed the catamarans as near as they dared to the French gunboats. Four or five of them exploded but only one with any effect, the fireships doing as little damage and the whole effort achieving practically nothing. Lord St Vincent, now out of office, recognized the tremendous possibilities inherent in Fulton's discoveries but opposed their use, saying 'Pitt was the greatest fool that ever existed to encourage a mode of warfare which those who commanded the sea did not want, and which, if successful, would deprive them of it.' Fulton was allowed to make another experiment and he used 175 lbs. of powder to blow up the brig *Dorothy* off Walmer in 1805, but St Vincent's view finally prevailed. Fulton returned to the USA and in 1810 was voted £5,000 by Congress to construct the steam vessel *Mute*, the trials of which were incomplete when he died.

William Pitt returned to office on 10 May 1804, with Dundas (now Lord Melville) as his adviser, and began a more offensive policy. With Castlereagh's help, he made alliance with Russia in April 1805. Austria and Sweden were next persuaded to join what became the Third Coalition. Pressure was brought to bear on Spain to cease helping France – a pressure which Spain resisted – and Napoleon came to realize that his enemies were gathering against him. The coalition took time to organize but Napoleon recognized his danger and concluded that his invasion of Britain must take place in 1805 if it was to take place at all. He could not count on naval victory but he began to dream of elaborate plans by which the British fleet might be tricked and lured away from its position in goal. All such plans depended, however, upon the passive co-operation of Spain. Left to themselves, the Spanish would have remained neutral and Nelson, for one, believed that this would be their policy.

I do not think a Spanish war so near. We are more likely to go to war with Spain for her complaisance to the French; but the French can gain nothing, but be great losers, by forcing Spain to go to war with us; therefore, I never expect that the Spaniards will begin, unless Bonaparte is absolutely mad, as many say he is. I never can believe that he or his counsellors are such fools as to force Spain to begin.

(November, 1803)

Spain was in fact forced into war by Britain, Pitt deciding to intercept the annual treasure fleet as an opening move. He also decided to redraw the boundaries of the Mediterranean station, giving Sir John Orde a separate station west of the straits of Gibraltar. Orde's task was to blockade Cadiz and it would now be on his station that the Spanish register ships would be captured. The next order was for Cornwallis to detach two frigates from the Channel Fleet under Captain Graham Moore, who was to collect two frigates from those stationed off Gibraltar and take up a position in the approaches to Cadiz. Nelson was furious and sent an order to Captain Gore, commanding the Mediterranean detachment, forbidding him to molest the lawful commerce of Spain 'with whom we are at perfect peace and amity'. The order came too late and the four register ships were duly intercepted on 3 October 1804. An action followed in which one Spanish ship blew up and the remainder were captured. The cargoes of these ships, including copper, tin, silver and gold, were valued at well over a million pounds and brought instant wealth to the captors. In Nelson's words 'Sir John Orde was sent . . . to take the money . . . and now he is to wallow in wealth whilst I am left a beggar.' Senior to Nelson, Orde should ordinarily have commanded the squadron which Nelson led at the Battle of the Nile; they had not been on speaking terms since then and this latest incident did nothing to promote their friendship. The interception of the Spanish treasure led to Spain's declaring war on Britain on 12 December 1804. There followed, on 4 January 1805, the treaty between France and Spain which put the Spanish forces at Napoleon's disposal. The terms of this treaty are especially interesting in that they contain the allied order of battle, as follows:

FRENCH FORCES

Location	Ships	Troops	Horses
Texel	Transports for:	30,000	
Ostend			
Dunkirk	Flotillas capable		
Calais	of embarking:	120,000	25,000
Boulogne			
Havre			
Brest	21 sail of the line	25,000	
Rochefort	6 sail of the line	4,000	
Toulon	11 sail of the line	9,000	
Ferrol	5 sail of the line		
TOTAL	43 sail of the line	188,000	

SPANISH FORCES

Ferrol	7 or 8 sail of the line	
Cadiz	12 to 15 sail of the line	4,000–5,000
Cartagena	6 sail of the line	
TOTAL	29–25 sail of the line	4,000–5,000
Grand Allied TOTAL	72–68 sail of the line	193,000–192,000

Napoleon had thus, on paper, over seventy sail of the line to deploy against the British strength, on paper, of 105. The actual position was, of course, more complex. If the number of ships refitting at any given time are deducted from the total as listed the British effective strength would be about 80. From these, however, the Admiralty had to provide defensive squadrons in the East and West Indies, at the Cape, at Newfoundland, or Nova Scotia. A precise comparison of strength is difficult but for practical purposes the opposing fleets were of roughly comparable size.

With these facts and figures before him, Napoleon saw that a successful invasion of Britain must hinge on the removal of the Channel Fleet. It must somehow be lured from its post off Brest, leaving Britain momentarily unguarded. What threat elsewhere could bring this about? He decided that a threat to the West Indies would have that effect. Such was the economic importance of the West Indies, he believed, that Britain would react strongly to any French move in that direction. He also possessed, in Martinique, a base from which a fleet could operate. We know that Napoleon considered many operational plans, with Ireland and Egypt studied afresh, but he came back to the West Indies again, convinced that this area was the key to success. Nor was he disillusioned when his first attempt was a failure. Missiessy escaped from Rochefort in January 1805 and Villeneuve, a week later, sailed from Toulon. Losing track of his opponent and influenced by memories of 1798, Nelson looked for him at Alexandria. While Missiessy reached the West Indies and made an attack on Dominica, Villeneuve encountered a gale and put back to Toulon; on news of which Missiessy returned to Europe. Napoleon decided, nevertheless, to try again on a bigger scale. Ganteaume was to sail from Brest with twenty-one sail of the line and raise the blockade of Ferrol, heading for the West Indies with some Spanish ships in company. Villeneuve was to sail from Toulon at the same time, raise the blockade of Cadiz and, adding the squadron there to his own, make for the West Indies in his turn. The two fleets with over fifty ships between them were to rendezvous at Martinique and then re-cross the Atlantic, enter the Channel and, sweeping all opposition aside, escort the invasion flotillas to the English coast. Napoleon had con-vinced himself that the Channel Fleet would hasten to save the West Indies and would not quickly realize that the French, having arrived there, had gone again. Leaving them to fight shadows, the French Admirals would find the coast clear and enable Napoleon to reach London. This was the plan and there was one French Admiral, Alle-mand, who was bold enough and lucky enough to have carried it out. But he was not in high command, nor, in any case, did the British react as Napoleon had assumed they would.

When St Vincent went out of office with Addington he left a time-bomb under the desk of his successor. This was the Commission of Naval Inquiry which continued its work in successive reports. So damaging were many of the facts revealed that Henry Dundas, Viscount Melville, currently First Lord of the Admiralty and a previous Treasurer of the navy was forced to resign. Pitt replaced him by the appointment of Sir Charles Middleton (30 April 1805) who became Lord Barham. Middle-ton's career in the navy had been almost purely administrative, more especially as Comptroller from 1778 to 1790. He, more than anyone else, had been responsible for the good state of the ships when war began. Considered as an administrator he was probably the best available but he was nearly eighty and had last been at sea in 1761. It was a surprising appointment but Pitt's immediate concern was to refit the maximum number of ships and reverse the tendency of St Vincent's economy drive. For such a task Barham was uniquely fitted by long experience. He accepted office with reluctance, induced only by the offer of a peerage. In point of fact, however, Barham was also to prove himself a strategist of the highest ability. In the campaign of 1805 he was to be Napoleon's opponent and we can see the war, at this stage, as a duel between them. But Lord Barham, proceeding methodically, began with an immediate reorganization of the Board itself. He was no lover of com-mittee procedure, his practice being to delegate work to the other members, making each responsible for specific duties. He made this clear in May 1805, allocating work as follows:

First Lord: Superintendence and arrangement of the whole.
First Sea Lord: Correspondence of the day. Ship movements. Promotions and appointments.
Second Sea Lord: Superintendence of the Navy Board, Transport Board, Victualling Board, Sick-and-Hurt Board and Greenwich Hospital.
Third Sea Lord: Commissions and Warrants.
Civil Lords: To sign orders, protections, warrants and promiscuous papers.
The more important work he clearly kept to himself and he paid the penalty in working late hours:

The charge I have taken upon me is, I own, a heavy one and the service so increased in every point of view as to bear no comparison with former times. I seldom have the pen out of my hand from 8 in the morning till 6 at night; and although I see no person but on public business, yet I don't find my own finished at that time; and if I did not make a point of doing so, the current business must overpower us. This labour is very much increased from a want of men, and 'tis mortifying in the highest degree to have no prospect of success, notwithstanding we have removed the grand obstacle in the forwarding ships . . . [1]

Barham's first problem had been with fitting out ships. His second and more difficult problem had concerned the manning of them. He was still at his wits end when the crisis came with news of the French fleet putting to sea. The situation would have been infinitely worse had the admirals and captains been less successful in preserving the health of the men they had.

Napoleon's campaign of 1805 began on 30 March when Villeneuve sailed from Toulon and, shaking off the British frigates, sailed for the Straits of Gibraltar. Reaching Cadiz, the French Admiral raised the blockade of Cadiz, added six Spanish and one French ship to his squadron, crossed the Atlantic and presently reported his arrival at Martinique with eighteen sail of the line. Had all gone according to plan, Ganteaume should have sailed at much the same time from Brest but he sailed no farther than the outer roads, being faced by Admiral Lord Gardner with 21 (and eventually 24) sail of the line. Ganteaume's big effort was made on 15 April, and his 2,000 troops were actually embarked, but he could not leave port without a battle; the very thing he had been ordered to avoid. So the great plan had broken down at the outset. What was still possible, in theory, was for Villeneuve to return and relieve Brest, thus adding Ganteaume's fleet to his own. Where Napoleon's plan had succeeded was in luring Nelson to the West Indies. When certain that Villeneuve had sailed westwards, Nelson followed against contrary winds and did not reach Gibraltar until 6 May. Informed that Villeneuve was bound for the West Indies, he resolved to follow, with 10 sail of the line, leaving Bickerton to command in the Mediterranean. He explained his decision in a letter dated 14 May:

Under the most serious consideration which I can give from all I hear, I rather think that the West Indies must be the destination of the Combined Squadron. A trip to England would have been far more agreeable, and more necessary for my state of health; but I put self out of the question upon these occasions. And although it may be said that I am unlucky, it never shall be said that I am inactive, or sparing of myself; and surely it will not be fancied I am on a party of pleasure, running after eighteen Sail of the Line with ten, and that to the West Indies. However, I know that patience and perseverance will do much; and if they are not there, the Squadron will be again off Cadiz by the end of June – in short, before the Enemy can know where I am gone to; and then I shall proceed immediately to England, leaving such a force as the Service requires; and as the Board will know where the Enemy are, I shall hope to receive their orders off Cape St Vincent . . .

In studying the sequel to this decision, it is interesting to realize that Nelson saw Villeneuve's voyage as a threat to the West Indies and the sugar trade. As he wrote at the time:

'I was in a thousand fears for Jamaica, for that is a blow which Buonaparte would be happy to give us. I flew to the West Indies without any orders, but I think the Ministry cannot be displeased . . . I was bred, as you know, in the good old school, and taught to appreciate the value of our West India possessions . . .'

He had no suspicion that Villeneuve's object was to lure him away from the Mediterranean and prepare the way for a concentration of the allied fleets against England. He and Villeneuve were once within a hundred miles of each other but did not meet in the West Indies. The French knew of his arrival, however, and sailed for Ferrol again without having done any material damage. Villeneuve had, in fact, received orders from Napoleon on 4 June, to relieve Ferrol and collect 15 ships; with 35 ships to relieve Brest, and with 56 ships, to enter the Channel. Nelson guessed that the French had gone and wrote on 16 June: 'My opinion is firm as a rock, that some cause, orders or inability to perform any service in these seas, has made them resolve to proceed direct for Europe.' With his squadron he re-crossed the Atlantic and was back at Gibraltar by 19 July 'without having obtained the smallest intelligence of the Enemy's Fleet'. Landing there, he remarked that it was the first time he had been ashore for two years. Writing to Lord Barham on 23 July, Nelson said 'I have yet not a word of information of the Enemy's Fleet: it has almost broke my heart. . . I shall return to England the moment I know that the Enemy's Fleet is in Port, and out of my reach.' He was back in England, on leave, by 19 August.

On the chessboard of the ocean it was now for Lord Barham to make the next move. He learnt of Villeneuve's approach on 8 July and knew that the Channel Fleet was deployed as follows: Cornwallis with 20–25 ships off Brest, Stirling with 5–6 ships off Rochefort, Calder with 10 ships off Ferrol, and Collingwood with 6 ships off Cadiz. Villeneuve's exact destination was unknown but he was known to be on too northerly a course for the Mediterranean. Barham made a quick decision and conveyed it to Cornwallis by a private letter which preceded the official despatch:

If we are not too late, I think there is a chance of our intercepting the Toulon Fleet. Nelson follows them to Cadiz, and if you can immediately unite the Ferrol and Rochefort Squadron and order them to cruize from 30 to 40 leagues to Nor-Westward and stretch out with your own fleet as far, and continue six or seven days on that Service, and then return to your several Posts, I think we stand some chance of intercepting them. Official Orders will follow as fast as possible.

In other words, Cornwallis was to end the blockade of Brest and go to meet Villeneuve, taking the risk that Ganteaume would sail at once when Cornwallis had gone; and Calder, reinforced by Stirling's squadron, would go to meet Villeneuve on the supposition that he was bound for Ferrol. The calculated risk was based on the fact that the officers of a blockaded squadron when the blockade was lifted were not always aware that they were free to sail. Their opponents were often invisible, represented only by a frigate or two and a known presence beyond the horizon. That the blockading squadron had actually gone would become apparent but not immediately nor with any certainty that it might not return. A week or more might pass before the coast was known to be clear. In that way the relieving force could be destroyed before the blockaded force might give assistance. Obeying orders promptly, Cornwallis sent the Rochefort blockading squadron to join Calder. In this instance the gamble failed because Allemand put to sea almost at once and carried out a feint against Ireland and a damaging raid against British commerce. This did not affect the main campaign, however, and Ganteaume remained in harbour.

Steering for Cadiz, as ordered, Villeneuve was duly intercepted by Sir Robert Calder on 22 July, by which day Cornwallis had returned to his station off Brest. He was a deeply disappointed man 'out of sorts with everyone and everything', cursing his ill-luck at having missed the French. As his fleet of twenty sail included seven three-deckers and two 80-gun ships he was in greater strength than Villeneuve, who was lucky to encounter the weaker force of the two. Calder had only fifteen sail of the line and two frigates but four of his ships were three-deckers and one an 80-gun ship. Villeneuve had four 80-gun ships, seven of 74 guns and seven frigates. Gravina, the Spanish admiral, had two 80-gun ships, two of 78 guns and two of 64. On sighting each other, both fleets formed line of battle, the action beginning rather late in the afternoon and under conditions of bad visibility. After some fighting two Spanish ships surrendered and Calder made the signal to disengage at 8.25 pm as the light failed. Everyone expected to resume battle at daylight but neither fleet attacked and they eventually lost sight of each other. In his subsequent defence Calder explained that:

I could not hope to succeed without receiving great damage; I had no friendly port to go to, and had the Ferrol and Rochefort squadrons come out, I must have fallen an easy prey. They might have gone to Ireland. Had I been defeated it is impossible to say what the consequences might have been.

Calder had done little more than avoid defeat, taking two prizes by way of proof, and the immediate result was that Villeneuve entered Ferrol, making his junction with the squadron he found there and forming a combined fleet of twenty-nine sail. Here was the nucleus of the force which Napoleon wanted to see in the Channel and ministers in Britain expected an invasion that summer. But the Channel Fleet still lay between Villeneuve and Brest, and Cornwallis, joined successively by Calder and Stirling and by Nelson's ships, had a concentration at one time of thirty-five sail. Napoleon learnt on 11 August that Villeneuve had entered Ferrol. He at once sent the admiral his orders to sail for Brest and extricate Ganteaume, fighting if necessary. 'If with thirty ships my admirals fear to attack twenty-four British, we may as well give up all hopes of a navy.' He later wrote to Talleyrand (23 August):

... My squadron sailed 14 August from Ferrol with 34 ships; it had no enemy in sight. If it follows my instructions, joins the Brest squadron and enters the Channel, there is still time: I am master of England. If, on the contrary, my admirals hesitate, manoeuvre badly, and do not fulfil their purpose, I have no other resource than to wait for winter to cross with the flotilla. That operation is risky ... Such being the case, I hasten to meet the most pressing danger: I raise my camp here, and by 23 September I shall have in Germany two hundred thousand men ... I march on Vienna.

On that date the 'Army of England' was still in camp at Boulogne, complete with landing craft, and Napoleon still hoped for better news of Villeneuve. As he said, there was still time. He issued warning orders for the march across Germany but was still awaiting news. Nor did he make his final decision until 25 August.

Ganteaume was still blockaded in Brest and his fleet made no more than a brief sortie, returning to its anchorage after a skirmish in which Cornwallis was very slightly wounded. The question was now whether Villeneuve would come to the rescue. He sailed from Ferrol on 11 August, with twenty-nine sail of the line and headed north-westwards. When Cornwallis heard of this he divided his fleet, retaining seventeen ships with his flag and detaching eighteen under Calder to go in search of Villeneuve. It was a bold decision (showing 'great lack of judgment' according to one great authority) and it produced an unexpected result. One of Villeneuve's advanced frigates spoke to a Danish ship on her way from Lisbon to the Baltic and learnt that the Dane had been boarded earlier that day by a boat from the *Dragon* (74), one of Calder's squadron, and had been told that 25 British sail of the line were in the vicinity. This was not entirely true, but Villeneuve, when he received the report, was inclined to believe it. He soon afterwards altered course and steered southward, being off Cape St Vincent on 18 August and entering Cadiz on the 20th. He was blockaded there by Collingwood and Calder, but that was not important in itself. The significant fact was that he had virtually refused to fight. So far from sailing north to challenge Cornwallis, Villeneuve had turned back at the first whisper of danger and had taken refuge in another Spanish port. Napoleon knew what was happening before his fleet dropped anchor and seems to have made his decision on 25 August. The camp at Boulogne was broken up on the 29th and his army began its march to the Danube. All idea of invading Britain was indefinitely postponed. In making that decision he admitted, in effect, that he had lost the campaign. The truth, not immediately apparent to himself or to anyone else, was that he had lost the war.

EIGHT

Trafalgar

The credit for preventing Napoleon's great design succeeding must
be shared by a number of people including Lord Barham, Admiral
Cornwallis, Lord Gardner and Sir Robert Calder. Nelson had the credit
for preventing Villeneuve from wreaking havoc in the West Indies but
some people were inclined to blame him for allowing the Toulon fleet
to escape in the first place. Calder, who had expected to receive con-
gratulations on his capture of two enemy ships, faced a court
martial, received a severe reprimand and was never employed again.
Confused operations had ended with the combined enemy fleet
anchored off Cadiz. There they were safe for the moment under the
shelter of the Spanish batteries but Cadiz was not a port in which
they could stay indefinitely. There were no means of maintaining so large
a fleet at Cadiz under conditions of blockade. Supplies would ordinarily
have arrived by sea but little could be expected with Collingwood just
outside the harbour mouth. Napoleon must have known this but he
could see no point, anyway, in maintaining a fleet which did nothing.
He was looking now to the Mediterranean and to new conquests in
Italy. Before quitting Paris, therefore, he issued new orders for
Villeneuve dated 14 September. The combined fleet was to enter the
Mediterranean and co-operate with the army against Naples. On the
15th he issued a further order, replacing Villeneuve by another admiral,
Rosilly. The first order reached Villeneuve on 27 September. Some
rumour of the second reached him on 11 October, with news that
Rosilly was already at Madrid. Villeneuve decided to sail before he could
be superseded.

After a period of leave (twenty-five days) Lord Nelson was ordered to resume his command of the Mediterranean Fleet and so rejoined his flagship at Portsmouth:

> *Victory*, at St Helens,
> 14th September, 1805

> *Sir*,
>   You will please to acquaint the Lords Commissioners of the Admiralty that I arrived at Portsmouth this morning at six o'clock, and hoisted my Flag on board the *Victory* at this anchorage about noon. The *Royal Sovereign, Defiance*, and *Agamemnon* are not yet ready for sea, so that I must leave
> *Victory* them to follow the moment they are complete. The ships
> *Euryalas* named in the margin only accompany me.
>   I am, Sir, etc.
> Nelson and Bronte

Sailing from St Helens, Nelson joined the fleet off Cadiz on 28 September, superseding Collingwood, who now became Second-in-Command. 'I have twenty-three Sail of the Line,' he wrote, 'and six occasionally at Gibraltar and to have an eye upon the Ships at Carthagena.' The combined enemy fleet was thought to number thirty-five or thirty-six sail, with eight more at Carthagena, against which the British fleet was 'not so large as might be wished'. With six ships at a time watering at Gibraltar, Nelson had only a minimum strength, weakened when Calder, going home to face his court martial, was allowed to take his flagship, the *Prince of Wales*, with him. Worse still, for immediate purposes, was the shortage of frigates. Nelson had only two and reckoned that his need was for eight. Sloops were also needed and were equally scarce. It was some small consolation when the schooner *Pickle* joined the fleet on 2 October.

Villeneuve came of the provincial nobility and had begun life as a Knight of Malta. He had done his best during his recent cruise but had been plagued by novice crews and damaged ships, as he had pointed out in a letter to Decrès, the Minister of Marine:

I declare to you, my Lord, the ships thus manned, with weak crews, cluttered with troops, with old and badly-made spars and rigging – ships which break their masts and tear their sails when there is a high wind, and when it moderates spend their time in repairing them – handicapped by their weak and inexperienced crews – are not in a state to attempt anything. I had a presentiment of this before I sailed. Now I have had it brought home to me by hard experience.

With ships so worn out and ill-equipped he had been joined at Cadiz by Spanish ships which had, some of them, seen no service at all. His efforts to refit his ships were hampered by lack of funds, lack of supplies and lack of seamen. He had 1,731 seamen in hospital and over 300 had deserted since he left Toulon. Cadiz and the ships there had suffered from yellow fever and the undermanned Spanish ships were brought up to something like strength by detachments of infantry. Villeneuve was himself ill with a bilious colic and was on bad terms with Rear-Admiral Magon, his third-in-command. The Spanish Commander-in-Chief was Don Federico Gravina, a fine seaman, but there was friction between the allies. When Villeneuve summoned a Council of War, a majority of senior officers voted for staying at anchor. But that, as Villeneuve knew, was impossible, for the Emperor's orders were that his fleet should put to sea.

Nelson, on his side, had decided on his tactics before he left England, explaining his plan to Captain Keats and, on another occasion, to Lord Sidmouth. To Keats he said 'I shall form the fleet into three divisions in three lines'. One division was to be a mobile reserve, to windward. 'With the remaining part of the fleet formed in two lines I shall go at them at once, if I can, about one-third of their line from their leading ships.' This was 'The Nelson Touch' and he explained it verbally to all his captains, following this up with his Memorandum issued to them all on 9 October. This plan assumed a total strength of forty ships, eight in the Advanced Squadron and sixteen in either main division, and an enemy fleet of forty-six. Collingwood, as Second-in-Command, was to lead his division so as to cut through the enemy's line 'about their twelfth Ship from the Rear'. Nelson would himself lead his division through 'about their centre'. As for the Advanced Squadron, led presumably by Rear-Admiral the Earl of Northesk, it was to cut through 'two or three or four ships ahead of their Centre, so as to ensure getting at their Commander-in-Chief, on whom every Effort must be made to capture'. In summary:

The whole impression of the fleet must be, to overpower from two to three Ships ahead of their Commander-in-Chief, supposed to be in the centre, to the Rear of their fleet, twenty sail of the Line to be untouched ...

All that is clear enough but Nelson was not to have the number of ships on which his plan was based. On the eve of battle he had, not

40 ships but 23. His original argument, therefore, that it would be impossible to form a single line of battle without waste of time did not altogether apply. What he did on the day of battle was to scrap the Advance Squadron and retain the two Divisions led respectively by himself and Collingwood. One man who had guessed what Nelson's tactics would be was Villeneuve, whose instructions to his fleet were explicit on this point: 'The enemy . . . will endeavour to envelop our rear, and to direct his ships in groups upon such of ours as he shall have cut off. . . .' The forecast was correct but he ordered no suitable riposte. Some scholars have suggested that no counter-move was possible but there were half-a-dozen manoeuvres, surely, which he could have attempted. He might have tried to attack first. He could have fought the battle at night. He could have placed his flagship in the rear, not the centre . . . But his words of encouragement to his men were not alto-gether helpful. 'Nothing in the sight of an English Squadron should daunt us . . . They are skilled in seamanship; in a month's time we shall be as skilful.' Were his men to believe that? But, anyway, the point was that they did not have a month. They would be in battle as soon as they came out from harbour. If we wonder, incidentally, how Villeneuve came to foretell what Nelson would do, we should perhaps remember that his attack was all but a copy of Duncan's tactics at the Battle of Camperdown. Nelson claimed for his plan that, 'It was new – it was singular – it was simple!' Simple it may have been but new it was not. And that is why Villeneuve knew beforehand what Nelson was likely to do. What he may not have foreseen is that Nelson's flagship would lead the attack, for that was very singular indeed.

All British schoolboys used to be exposed, at some time, to diagrams of the Battle of Trafalgar, whether accurate or fanciful. They are so much part of the legend that we have grown up with the idea of an Admiral leading his column into battle. We incline to assume that this was the naval practice. It was, in fact, nothing of the sort. All tradition placed the Commander-in-Chief in the centre of his line. This had been Howe's position at the Battle of the First of June. That was where Jervis had been at the Battle of St Vincent. At the Battle of the Nile Nelson's flagship had been sixth in line. At the Battle of Copenhagen his flagship had been again in the middle. If there was an exception to the rule it was again provided by Duncan, who formed no line at Camper-down but certainly led the division under his direct command, just as Onslow seems to have led the other. There was this difference, however, that Duncan's ships were not in a strict line ahead, so that the Dutch fire was not concentrated, of necessity, on the leading ship. Nelson's Memorandum before the Battle of Trafalgar is not explicit on this point but he and Collingwood led their respective divisions into action, more or less (one must assume) as planned. As a practice, it certainly allowed the Commander-in-Chief to set an example of gallantry: as against which it deprived him of all further control over his fleet. His officers vainly expostulated with him about this but he insisted on being first into battle and was aided in his obstinacy by the *Victory*'s superior speed. This was not an example to follow and it is arguable that Nelson's victory would have been more complete had he lived to direct the final phases of the action. Nelson did nothing to advertise his joining the fleet off Cadiz but his presence was known and so was the fact that the *Victory* was his flagship. We have seen that he planned the capture of the French Commander-in-Chief. Can we doubt that there were similar plans on the French side? Earlier in the year Nelson himself wrote that, had he been in Calder's place, the enemy 'meant to take a dead set at the *Victory*'.

Villeneuve finally sailed on 20 October, his force comprising thirty-three sail of the line, five frigates and two corvettes. In worsening weather and with great difficulty, he formed his Order of Sailing in three columns. His course at first was WNW but the wind came westerly and he steered south. This move was reported to Nelson, who followed suit, but realized that he was ahead of the enemy and so turned northward again. At daylight on the 21st he signalled the fleet, twenty-seven sail of the line by this time, to form the order of sailing in two columns, and presently followed that with the signal to prepare for battle. Ships individually cleared for action and beat to quarters. The guns were loaded and run out. Seeing that the British fleet was heading to cut off his rear ships, Villeneuve ordered his fleet go to about and head northwards again for Cadiz, adding to that the signal to form the order of battle. These different evolutions, performed by a fleet never before exercised together, were indifferently and slowly performed. The allied fleet was in some sort of a line by 10 am, but in a crescent formation with the centre ships to leeward. The two nationalities were somewhat mixed, Villeneuve's flagship being supported, ahead, by the *Santissima Trinidad* of 130 guns (the biggest man-of-war afloat) and, astern, by the *Redoutable*, probably the best-trained ship in the French fleet. Gravina, the Spanish Admiral, in the *Principe de Asturias* was in the rear of the column but the *Neptune* was in the lead. Of the patriotism of the French and of the courage of the Spanish there can be no doubt at all but they were ranged in battle against professionals.

The wind had died away to a fitful breeze, making the British approach all too slow. The enemy opened fire on the *Victory* at fifteen minutes after noon but she was still out of effective range, over a mile distant. First broadsides were fired at about 12.20 pm and the *Victory* was under fire for perhaps twenty-five minutes before she replied. She was to suffer 159 casualties in the course of the battle and many of these fell, no doubt, during this opening phase. By way of comparison the *Britannia* (100) sixth in line (which was the position of Nelson's flagship at the Battle of the Nile) had ten men killed and forty wounded. The *Victory* broke the allied line just astern of Villeneuve's flagship, the *Bucentaure*, and just ahead of the *Redoutable* (74) being closely supported by the *Temeraire* (98) and *Neptune* (98). It was with the *Redoutable* that the *Victory* closed, coming at once under heavy musketry fire. In the meanwhile, Nelson had made a last and probably fatal decision. Eight marines drawn up on the poop had been killed by one cannon ball and Nelson ordered the other marines to disperse and take cover. The result was that the enemy marksmen, who should have been under small-arm fire, could make target practice at their leisure. At about 1.25 pm, Nelson was hit by a musket ball and carried below with an obviously fatal wound. He was to die about three hours later. The Commander-in-Chief had been lost but the battle went on. Out of the battle, at this stage, were the six or eight leading ships on the allied side, which had no opponents. Led by Dumanoir, they eventually entered the battle two hours late. Nelson had done what Villeneuve expected, enveloping the rear of the opposing fleet. There followed a series of conflicts during which the allied ships of the centre and rear were pulverized by gunfire. The *Victory* with her immediate consorts, *Temeraire, Neptune, Leviathan, Conqueror, Ajax* and *Britannia*, overwhelmed the allied centre of six ships. The *Royal Sovereign*, followed by the *Belleisle, Mars* and *Tonnant*, broke through the enemy line and crushed the *Fougeux, Santa Ana* and *Monica*. The *Bellerophon*, with the *Colossus, Swiftsure* and *Orion* dealt with another group round the *Bahama*, and the *Colossus* with the *Achilles* and *Revenge* took the *Argonauta* and *San Idelfonso*.

So far, Nelson's tactics had thrown his twenty-seven ships against twenty-three opponents, actually outnumbering them on occasion. Then Dumanoir came belatedly into action with ten ships, seven of his

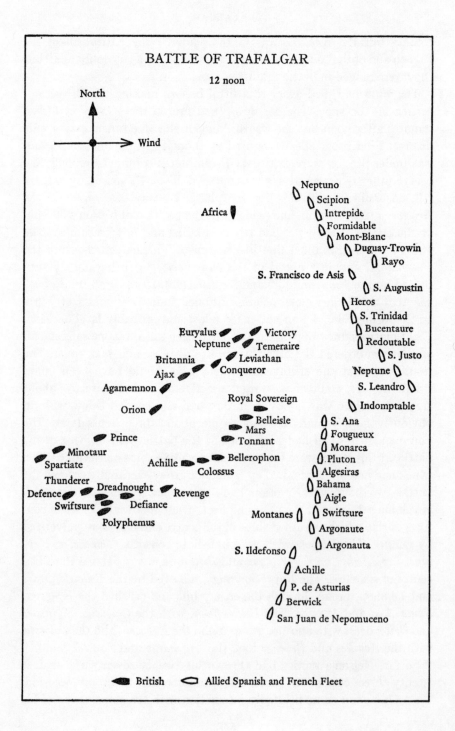

BATTLE OF TRAFALGAR

12 noon

North

Wind

Africa

Neptuno
Scipion
Intrepide
Formidable
Mont-Blanc
Duguay-Trowin
Rayo

S. Francisco de Asis

S. Augustin

Heros
S. Trinidad
Bucentaure
Redoutable
S. Justo
Neptune
S. Leandro
Indomptable

Euryalus   Victory
Neptune   Temeraire
Britannia   Leviathan
Ajax   Conqueror
Agamemnon
Orion

Royal Sovereign

Belleisle   S. Ana
Mars   Fougueux
Tonnant   Monarca
Pluton
Prince   Algesiras
Minotaur   Bellerophon   Bahama
Spartiate   Achille   Colossus   Aigle
Thunderer   Swiftsure
Defence   Dreadnought   Revenge   Montanes   Argonaute
Swiftsure   Defiance   Argonauta
Polyphemus

S. Ildefonso
Achille
P. de Asturias
Berwick
San Juan de Nepomuceno

◗▬ British   ◖ Allied Spanish and French Fleet

own division and three stragglers. He might have made a considerable impact – he even dreamed of victory – but only four ships followed his lead. These were beaten off by the *Spartiate* and *Minotaur* and, of the remainder, only two, the *Intrepide* and *San Augustin*, tried to plunge into the battle around the *Bucentaure*. The *Intrepide* fought a very gallant battle and suffered very heavy casualties before she finally surrendered. The other three ships made no real effort and were chased off the battlefield. Firing ceased at 5.30 pm at about the time the French *Achille* blew up and Gravina and Dumanoir withdrew with such ships as remained to them, reaching Cadiz in a somewhat damaged state. A gale that evening, which continued for two days, added confusion to the scene, some of the prizes being wrecked and others deliberately destroyed. In the words of William James,[2]

To sum up the results of the battle of Trafalgar, the French, out of 18 sail of the line, preserved only nine, and the Spaniards, out of 15 sail of the line, lost all except six. Of the 19 French and Spanish ships, including the *Rayo*, which the British captured, one, the *Achille*, was accidentally burnt, and 14 were recaptured, wrecked, foundered, or destroyed; leaving but four ships, one French and 3 Spanish 74s, as trophies in the hands of the conquerors.

Of the ten allied ships which reached Cadiz only three, it is said, were fit for service. Taken prisoner, Villeneuve was exchanged and came back to France, where he apparently committed suicide.

Nelson's death, killed as he was in the hour of victory, was enough to confirm his legend as a hero. Nor can it be denied that stories of heroism have their permanent value, perfected in this instance by the fact that there was no old age to dim the brightness of his greatest achievement. Nelson was to give inspiration to all flag-officers who came after him but what, specifically, were the lessons he had to teach them? We may be tempted, at this point, to dwell on his tactical skill which was indeed impressive. We know, however, that an Admiral's most important work is done before the enemy is sighted. His fleet has to be formed, organized, equipped, disciplined, trained, tested, rehearsed and (finally) inspired. The victory was not won by manoeuvre in the enemy's presence. It was mostly won by efforts previously made, some of them by men who took no part in the battle itself or indeed in any other battle. But Nelson was lucky in many ways. By the time he became a flag officer, the problem of discipline had been solved. He could be humane, considerate and popular, knowing that some of his predecessors had been very tough indeed. He was faced, as he knew, by opponents who were many of them badly officered, demoralized, ill-trained and inexperienced. His plan at Trafalgar, open to criticism in any case, would have been highly inadvisable against a better antagonist, and depended for its success on the enemy being demoralized. But, having those advantages and making the most of them, he had his own contribution to make. What was it? First and foremost, he sought to destroy the enemy. Urged to pursue the French after the Battle of the Saints, Rodney had said 'Come, we have done very handsomely' and had allowed his opponents to escape. But Nelson had moved away from the eighteenth-century tradition. He wanted not merely victory but annihilation. Told on his deathbed by Hardy that fourteen or fifteen of the enemy had been taken he replied at once 'That is well, but I had bargained for twenty.' In other words, he wanted a more complete victory than could be paralleled in modern times. He wanted to do at sea what Napoleon was doing at Austerlitz and Ulm.

In the last resort, Nelson was ruthless, but this was only a small part of the example he was to leave. For he had, above all, the qualities of leadership. He had imagination, first of all. He knew what he wanted. He knew what his men were thinking and he knew what the enemy would do. He had a deep knowledge of his profession, especially on the tactical side. He had the ability to organize and direct his forces. He had determination, a belief that the task would be accomplished, coupled with a gift for conveying his own confidence to the rest of his team. Such was his influence over his officers that they would all do what he wanted whether they saw the signal or not. He had determination to spare, enough to share out, so that his men never doubted that they were going to win. He had, finally, the gift of attraction; not attractiveness in the ordinary usage of the word so much as attraction in the magnetic sense. He was a centre to which people were drawn not from which they were repelled. He was seen and recognized and was hard to ignore. He was talked about in his absence, a subject for anecdote, the central figure in stories which were repeated. His influence permeated his fleet and could be seen in the special insignia, the white ensign, the chequered paintwork, the yellow mast-hoops, all of which gave his men their sense of membership in a specially chosen team. Nelson was genuinely interested in other people and their problems, their limitations and their potential. He knew his men and paid them the compliment of believing that they were worth knowing. His arrival brought about an instant raising of morale. As St Vincent said at the time 'There is only one Nelson.'

Having said that, we must avoid the mistake of thinking that the war at sea ended with Nelson's death. It did nothing of the kind. It continued for another ten years with plenty of incident. All that was lacking was an enemy fleet ready to give battle. Fleets there would be and often in considerable strength, but Trafalgar had been a terrible blow to French and Spanish morale. Villeneuve had tried to hearten his men with the words 'Nothing in the sight of an English Squadron should daunt us.' But why had he to say that if his men were not already daunted? And if their morale was low before the battle had begun, to what depth had it fallen before the battle had ended? It would take years for Britain's opponents to regain any confidence in battle, more years than the war was to last. The French revival had begun, indeed, before peace was made, the work of officers who were too young to have known the old regime, but it was no more than a beginning and it began too late. The British, by contrast, could draw on a great reserve of talent, no one man exactly replacing Nelson but some of them better than he was in various ways; Collingwood better as an administrator, Keats better as a seaman, Popham more original in some ways and Saumarez destined to gain a high reputation as a diplomatist. Nelson died with his reputation at its peak and it is not too easy to see him in the roles he would have had to fill in the years to come. He had made himself a heroic legend and that is what he has remained.

The story of Trafalgar is incomplete without describing what happened to the remains of the combined fleet. Coming to take command at Cadiz, Rosilly found himself with one undamaged ship, the *Héros*, in which he hoisted his flag, and four ships more or less disabled. His Spanish allies had eleven or twelve sail of the line, all in reasonable order or at least capable of repair. There might have been four more French ships but Rear-Admiral Dumanoir, with the *Formidable* (80), *Duguay-Tronin* (74) *Mont-Blanc* (74) and *Scipion* (74), escaped southwards from the battlefield. He would have made for Toulon but he knew that Rear-Admiral Louis was near the Straits with the British ships that had missed the battle. He therefore headed north again and was sighted by the *Phoenix* frigate (36) in the latitude of Finisterre. The French ships chased the *Phoenix*, which led them towards the British squadron blockading Ferrol. Under the command of Captain Sir Richard Strachan this detachment comprised the *Caesar* (80), the *Hero* (74), the *Namur*

(74), the *Courageux* (74) and *Bellona* (74), together with two frigates, the *Santa-Margarita* (36) and *Aeolus* (32). It was dark when the *Phoenix* reported to Strachan but there was moonlight enough to distinguish the French ships. The chase began and the *Caesar*, leading the hunt, was within six miles of the *Scipion*, the sternmost French ship, at daylight on 5 November. Sailing faster than the ships of the line, the frigates *Santa-Margarita* and *Phoenix* came up with the French rear and did their best to cripple the *Scipion*. Dumanoir realized that he would have to give battle and formed line-ahead, being presently attacked by the *Caesar, Hero* and *Courageux* – the *Bellona* having lost track and the *Namur* being far astern. A spirited action followed, Strachan at one stage firing two guns at the *Namur* by way of underlining the signal for close action. Sir Richard 'whose impatience' we read 'is not always of the most discriminative kind' seems to have apologized afterwards.

The action, meanwhile, continued, and the French ships finally hauled down their colours. What is remarkable about this action is the scale of casualties on the French side:

Formidable	200 incl. Rear-Admiral, wounded
Scipion	200 incl. Captain, wounded
Mont-Blanc	180
Duguay–Tronin	150 incl. Captain, killed
TOTAL	730

The British, by comparison, had 135 casualties: an indication of superior gunfire on the one side and considerable courage on the other.

At the end of 1805 two French squadrons escaped from Brest, the one comprising five sail of the line, two frigates and a corvette, commanded by Vice-Admiral Leissegues; the other comprising six sail of the line, two frigates and two corvettes, commanded by Rear-Admiral Willaumez. Having given up his more grandiose plans, Napoleon had authorized the sending of these two squadrons on a mission of commerce destruction to the West Indies. When news of Leissegues' operation reached Vice-Admiral Sir John Duckworth, who, with six of the line and two frigates, was blockading Cadiz, he sailed with six sail of the line for Madeira. He finally caught up with the French squadron off Santo-Domingo in the West Indies. Here the five French ships were all captured or driven on shore, only the smaller vessels escaping. There were heavy losses again, over 1,500 men in all, over 500 of them aboard the three-decked flagship *Imperial* (130). By contrast, Willaumez's squadron was never brought to action. One ship, the *Impetueux* was taken and destroyed but the other ships made their way separately back to France.

If we add these later losses to those incurred at the Battle of Trafalgar, we should be tempted to conclude (and some historians have in fact concluded) that the allied fleet had ceased to exist as a fighting force. As far as morale went, this may in a sense have been true. In mere numbers, however, the picture is different, the French having 32 ships afloat in 1806 and at least 21 under construction, making 53 in all. Nor was this all for there were other ships within Napoleon's grasp, ships belonging to Spain, Portugal, Holland, Denmark or Venice; or potentially in alliance like those of Sweden and Russia. As for the need to maintain the blockade of Brest, so far was it from lessening that the aged Earl St Vincent was brought back from retirement, following Pitt's death, and given the command of the Channel Fleet. He re-hoisted his flag in the *Hibernia* on 22 February 1806, a month after his seventy-first birthday. His immediate impression, after four years ashore and out of office, was that the service had gone to the dogs.

How the unaccountably lost spirit of discipline and animation of it is to be recovered, I cannot tell, but I really think that starvation (entre nous) is the only mode. Sure I am that an over-increase of full and half-pay will dish it completely. . . .

This vast overflow of young nobility into the service makes rapid strides to the decay of seamanship, as well as subordination, and I wish with all my heart we had no captains with seats in Parliament. . . . I can perceive no principle of laudable ambition or patriotic spirit anywhere.

We are familiar with the idea that the service lost its impetus with the death of Nelson. But the change described by Lord St Vincent comes rather too suddenly. In October 1805, we have Nelson's band of brothers, patriotic, selfless and brave. By February 1806, all discipline has gone and all laudable ambition has disappeared. But it is the same men we have to consider and they are only about three months older. We cannot really suppose that there could have been so much change in so short a time. Nelson inspired the fleet he led but the men of Trafalgar were relatively few and only a minority of seamen served in any fleet at any given time. Frigates rose in number during the war from about 90 to about 150, sloops and other small men of war from about 50 to about

340, all forming part of the Royal Navy but none likely to play any significant part in a general engagement. For most seamen the actual work that had to be done and the fighting in which they were likely to be engaged was little changed by the Battle of Trafalgar and changed still less by the death of Nelson. Nor would it have occurred to people at the time that there was any faltering in the direction of the naval effort. Some flag officers had retired, notably Cornwallis and Keith, but St Vincent and Collingwood held high command and Strachan might be said to have completed Nelson's victory. The coming man was Sir Charles Cotton whose abilities would seem to have been mainly administrative, but it was not unreasonable to expect great things of Admiral James Gambier, who had been prominent in the Battle of the First of June and who was related to Lord Barham and incidentally, to William Pitt. No one could suppose that there was any shortage of talent.

That the Royal Navy was declining in efficiency would be difficult to prove. What it lacked, however, was the sort of immediate threat which caused the crisis of 1804. Napoleon might be conquering Europe but he was no longer to be seen at Boulogne. Britain was safe from invasion and there was no immediate threat to India. Officers who had accepted St Vincent's rules about shore leave were no longer so willing to be perpetually at their posts. As against that we should bear in mind that the Admiralty had never been obsessed with the invasion threat. The main threat, as seen at Whitehall, was still what it had always been; the danger to British commerce. That individual merchantmen should be captured by the enemy was plainly inevitable. What ministers feared was the capture of a whole East India or West India convoy, for which purpose the French had enough ships, even after Trafalgar. Squadrons like that of Dumanoir and Willaumez could have done appalling damage and Linois in the East Indies had done quite enough. It was Britain's good fortune that Napoleon never fully understood the importance of commerce or its relation to sea-power. It was natural for a soldier to think of marching his army into London. The truth was that the military invasion, without sea-power, was more or less impossible. Given sea-power, on the other hand, it was not even necessary.

NINE

Deadlock

When William Pitt died in January 1806 his death was said to have been hastened by the news of Austerlitz, marking the collapse of the Third Coalition. Seeing a map of Europe, he said bitterly 'Roll up that map! It will not be wanted these ten years.' Lord Grenville was the new Prime Minister, who formed the Ministry of All-the-Talents with Fox as Foreign Secretary and Lord Howick as First Lord of the Admiralty. When Fox died in September 1806, Howick went to the Foreign Office and the Prime Minister's brother, Thomas Grenville, went to the Admiralty. He in turn was succeeded by Lord Mulgrave in April 1807. St Vincent described Grenville as 'the truest patriot, the most upright man, the most faithful, straightforward servant of the public that I ever met with in any situation'. Mulgrave was a General and had been one of Pitt's military advisers. Behind Howick and Grenville stood Admiral John Markham, First Sea Lord of whom St Vincent wrote to Grenville 'You will find in Markham firmness and integrity to the backbone, happily combined with ability, diligence and zeal.' The Admiralty, thus effectively manned, inherited the situation which was created by the victory at Trafalgar. Their lordships also inherited, however, the situation created by Napoleon's victories on land. He had done more than merely crush the Third Coalition. He was now able to force other countries into war on his side; notably Turkey in 1806 and Russia in 1807. He could not invade England; nor with the British in Malta and Sicily, could he dream of returning to Egypt. He could build up his navy again, however, and he did so. He also knew that with Sweden, Denmark, Portugal and Austria on his side, he would have a hundred ships with which to challenge Britain again.

Such was Napoleon's military position that he still held the initiative in 1805–1806. The British efforts were all purely defensive and began with retaking the Cape of Good Hope, an operation planned so as to prevent Napoleon making another attempt to reach India but by a different route. The operation, mounted in the autumn of 1805, involved a small squadron – three ships of the line, one 50-gun ship, two frigates, a sloop and a gun-brig – with transports (East Indiamen included) in which were embarked 5,000 troops under Major-General Sir David Baird. The naval commander was Commodore Sir Home Popham, the signals expert who had perfected the current system. Popham was not a typical officer but a good linguist, born in Tetuan and educated at Cambridge, having commanded an Austrian East Indiaman and been given naval promotion for service on land under the Duke of York. He had been knighted by the Tsar of Russia and made a Fellow of the Royal Society. The landing was successful and led to a rapid conquest of the colony. There followed, however, an extraordinary sequel. Having heard that the inhabitants of Montevideo and Buenos Aires were restive under Spanish rule, Popham now planned to attack the River Plate. Borrowing some troops from Baird, under Major-General Beresford, and a further detachment from the garrison of St Helena (about 1,200 all told), he set off to conquer South America. Buenos Aires duly surrendered and over a million dollars were sent to England in specie. When the Spanish realized, however, that the invaders were so few, they rallied in force and compelled Beresford to capitulate. Popham blockaded the River Plate and waited for the reaction from London. Puzzled and confused by these unexpected events, the government sent military reinforcements under Major-General Whitelocke. These forces were also defeated and Whitelocke was cashiered. As for Popham, he was superseded by Rear-Admiral Stirling and sent home to face a court martial. Stirling was then superseded by Rear-Admiral George Murray. He had been assured beforehand that the Spanish in South America were 'generally disaffected and ready to throw themselves into the arms of any nation powerful enough to protect them . . .' After some experience of the River Plate he changed his mind and wrote that 'The inveteracy of the Spaniard is not to be conceived . . . not a single deserter has come in since we have been in the country . . .' As against that, the British soldiers and sailors were very much inclined to desert, seeing around them 'A fine country and climate, plenty of every necessary of life, and nothing to do.' It was time to withdraw and this was finally accomplished, not without casualties, humiliations and expense.

The main point of naval interest in this improbable affair is that Popham, when court-martialled, was told that 'withdrawing, without orders so to do, the whole of any naval force from the place where it is directed to be employed . . . may be attended with the most serious inconvenience to the public service.' He was severely reprimanded but had influence enough to obtain further employment. That an officer should remain on the station to which he was appointed might seem fairly obvious but the rule had been twice broken in recent years, establishing what might seem an awkward precedent. First of all, Nelson had gone to the West Indies while serving as Commander-in-Chief, Mediterranean. His excuse was that the Toulon fleet had gone to the West Indies and that his duty was to follow where his opponents had gone. It is still a question whether he was right to do this. He escaped any public censure at the time and criticism within the service ended of course with his triumph and death. So the precedent existed and gave Sir John Duckworth a good excuse to do the same thing. Under the orders of Vice-Admiral Lord Collingwood, he had been given the task of blockading Cadiz, which harbour contained the French and Spanish survivors of Trafalgar. When he received information that a French squadron was at sea, he raised the blockade and sailed for Madeira and the West Indies, where he eventually fought a successful action against an inferior force (see page 126). Lord Collingwood blamed Duckworth for having disobeyed his orders and deserted his post. The result was that Rear-Admiral Louis, Duckworth's second-in-command, was given a baronetcy, the honour which Duckworth himself did not obtain until 1813. His claims were pointedly ignored after the action off Santo Domingo and with good reason. For Nelson, in quitting the Mediterranean, had gone in pursuit of the squadron he had been blockading but Duckworth had gone after another squadron, releasing for possible mischief the ships he had been ordered to blockade. This gave Sir Home Popham his excuse to leave his station at the Cape and stage his attempted conquest of South America. The time had clearly come to draw the line and Popham was lucky, perhaps, to escape with a severe reprimand. From the Admirals' point of view, one of the strongest objections to initiative on this scale was the confusion it introduced into questions of prize-money. Who had the flag officer's share when ships under the orders of Admiral A had invaded the carefully defined territory of Admiral B?

The Cape recovered and garrisoned, the government's next concern was with the Baltic. Last of the continental powers to be defeated by Napoleon was Russia, the war ending with the Treaty of Tilsit in 1807. This, it was suspected, would give Napoleon the use of the Russian fleet. With his armies on the borders of Holstein and Swedish Pomerania, it seemed likely that he might also secure the Danish and Swedish fleets. Adding these to the French and Dutch ships at Antwerp and Flushing, he might have anything between thirty and sixty sail of the line; enough, it was rumoured, for a possible invasion of Ireland. Incidentally, and of more immediate importance, the Baltic would be closed to British commerce. To this threat the British government, on Canning's advice, responded with vigour, demanding from Denmark the temporary custody of her fleet. The expected refusal led to an expedition sailing from Yarmouth on 26 July, commanded by Admiral Gambier and Lieutenant-General the Lord Cathcart. The campaign which followed was to involve no heavy fighting, neither on sea nor land, but is of great interest from another point of view. When Lord Keith and General Sir Ralph Abercromby invaded Egypt in 1801 (see page 71) with over sixty men-of-war and 16,000 soldiers, there had been no previous combined operation on a comparable scale over a comparable distance. This second expedition against Copenhagen was far more ambitious. The fleet which left Yarmouth comprised 17 sail of the line with 21 frigates, sloops, bomb-vessels and gun-brigs. It was gradually reinforced, bringing the ships of the line to a total of 25 with 40 smaller vessels and no less than 377 transports carrying 27,000 troops, half of them German. Nor was there any shortage of naval and military talent. Sir Home Popham was Captain of the Fleet, one of the Rear-Admirals was Richard Goodwin Keats (Keats of the *Superb*), reputedly the best seaman in the Navy, another Rear-Admiral being Sir Samuel Hood, and the captains included such men as Robert Stopford, Samuel Hood Linzce, Charles Ekins, Thomas Graves and Charles Dashwood. With Lord Cathcart served Major-General Sir Arthur Wellesley, the future Duke of Wellington. For its given task the expedition was one of overwhelming force, the result being that fewer lives were lost and less damage done.

First move in this campaign was to station Keats, with a squadron, in a position to cut off Zealand from Holstein, thus isolating Copenhagen from the rest of Denmark. On 15 August a landing took place at Wedbeck, between Elsinore and Copenhagen. A further landing followed in

Keoge Bay and a regular bombardment of Copenhagen began on 2 September. By the evening of the 5th much of the city was on fire and on 6th–7th the defending general capitulated, agreeing to surrender the Danish fleet. This was found to comprise eighteen ships of the line, ten frigates and some smaller craft and gunboats. Of the fifteen line-of-battle ships brought back to England only four were added to the Royal Navy, the remainder being rejected. More valuable were the masts, yards, timber, sails and cordage removed from the Danish arsenal. In the war which followed the Danish colonies were occupied and another minor acquisition was the previously Danish-held island of Heligoland at the mouth of the Elbe. What was more important was the demonstration of British sea-power, a fact not wasted on Sweden and Russia. An eventual sequel was a war with Russia which began in 1808, and a British alliance with Sweden. Some operations took place between Vice-Admiral Sir James Saumarez and his Russian opponents but with no dramatic result and no obvious relevance to the war as a whole. What emerged, first and foremost, was the technical gap which had come to exist between the combatant navies and the fleets maintained by countries which had been more or less neutral. It transpired, to begin with, that the Swedish ships were not coppered and were no good at working to windward. To make matters worse they were unused to being at sea for long periods and lacked any knowledge of scurvy, its prevention and cure. A third of their seamen were sick at any given time, many of them dying, and those actually on deck were anything but smart in sail drill. They were saved from disaster by the fact that their Russian opponents were no more competent. On the subject of health, Valentine Dyke (surgeon, R.N.) reported as follows to Saumarez on 12 September 1808:

> . . . I am decidedly of opinion that scurvy of the most obstinate and dangerous nature, threatens the safety of the whole [Swedish] fleet . . .
>
> The rapid progress which this disease is making cannot fail to excite the greatest alarm, as already twelve hundred men have been sent to the hospital (every hour is adding to the number of sick); and it is painful to remark that not less than four hundred have died on one ship since yesterday . . .[1]

These ships had been at sea for eight or nine months without any regular supply of fresh provisions. Lime juice had been issued but 'insufficient to effect a radical cure'. In fact, as we know, lime juice is not a cure at all. If the British ships remained healthy, it was because they obtained fresh supplies of vegetables and, possibly, lemon juice instead of lime. Pre-scorbutic symptoms were observable, incidentally, in the Swedish seamen supposed to be in good health.

As for the Russians, the Baltic campaign affords only one example of their prowess as between one ship and another. In 1808 the *Implacable* (74) fought an action with the *Sewolod* (74), which hauled down her flag in less than thirty minutes, having 48 killed and 30 wounded as against 6 killed and 26 wounded in the *Implacable*. The *Sewolod* was afterwards recovered by the Russians and taken for a second time by the *Centaur*, this time with 180 killed, wounded or missing as against 3 killed and 27 wounded in the *Centaur*. Captain T. Byam Martin of the *Implacable* wrote afterwards that Rear-Admiral Sir Samuel Hood, in the *Centaur*, had performed 'the most determined, well-arranged, glorious act that I think our naval history can boast of', done in defiance of 23 sail of Russians. He went on to add:

The spirit, the love, the enthusiastic kind of attachment formed between our officers and ships' companies is one of the most interesting things I ever witnessed. It is a matter of doubt to me which is greatest, the wonder and admiration of the Swedes, or the terror of the Russians; the effect on each will be highly conducive to the interest of our dear country. The captain of the Swedish fleet actually shed tears on board the *Centaur* this morning in admiration of what had passed.[2]

The action was of no great importance but the comparative casualties explain why the Russian admiral was reluctant to risk a general engagement. The same reluctance would have been shared by most other admirals with a mainly neutral background. All sorts of progress had been made in the belligerent navies, especially in the British, and the paper strength of other fleets which might be added to the French were to that extent somewhat theoretical.

Outside the Baltic the year 1807 began with a somewhat irrelevant setback and ended with a modest but useful success. The Turks having been persuaded into alliance with France, Lord Collingwood was instructed by the Admiralty to send a squadron to the Dardanelles under the command of Sir John Duckworth. The main interest of the events which followed was that the mistakes made were exactly those which would be made again in World War I. Duckworth duly entered the Dardanelles and might have destroyed the Turkish fleet, but argument was allowed to take the place of action. What could have been achieved at the outset became impossible as time passed and as the

Turks strengthened their defences. Duckworth withdrew under fire, more or less defeated. This operation was followed by the British capture of Alexandria but here again the Turks reacted with vigour and Egypt had to be evacuated again. Later that year Napoleon tried to coerce Portugal into joining the alliance against Britain. Wavering at first, the Prince Regent of Portugal finally agreed to accept British protection and transfer both his fleet and his capital to Brazil. Rear-Admiral Sir Sidney Smith appeared off the Tagus with a squadron and was joined there by eight Portuguese sail of the line, four frigates, three corvettes and twenty merchantmen. The French general Junot entered Lisbon on the following day, beginning an occupation which differed from others in that there existed in this instance a government in exile which was pledged to return. Apart from these events the year 1807 was one in which Napoleon, at the height of his power in Europe, tried to exclude British trade from the continent while Britain, still defiant but without strength for a war on land, could retaliate only by a blockade of the European coastline. Nor was the situation greatly changed until the autumn of 1808. That year, however, did see two earlier events of some significance: the cruise of Admiral Ganteaume and the surrender of Admiral Rosilly.

Among the blockaded French ports was that of Rochefort, watched by Sir Richard Strachan with 7 sail of the line. Strachan withdrew for some distance to meet with some expected victuallers and Rear-Admiral Allemand, seizing his opportunity, put to sea with six ships of the line, one frigate and one corvette. One ship was crippled in a gale and returned to Rochefort but Allemand brought the remainder safely to Toulon. Strengthened by this reinforcement, Admiral Ganteaume sailed from Toulon with ten sail of the line, three frigates and two corvettes, his object being to occupy the island of Corfu. He carried out this mission and returned safely to Toulon, sighted, pursued but never intercepted by Collingwood's ships. This was a disquieting event in itself but the whole situation began to change when the Spanish rose against French domination in June 1808. The movement began in Seville but led to a startling development in Andalusia, where the French General Dupont, with 18,000 men, found himself confronted by a Spanish army under a Swiss General. Defeated at Baylen, Dupont finally surrendered, revealing to the world that Napoleon's armies were not necessarily invincible. The sequel to this Spanish rising was the surrender of Admiral Rosilly, who had been blockaded in Cadiz since his predecessor's defeat at Trafalgar. The Spanish applied pressure by opening fire on the French ships from shore batteries and from gun and mortar boats. Escape was impossible, there being a British squadron off the harbour mouth under the command of Rear-Admiral Purvis, and Rosilly had finally to surrender. He had five ships of the line, a frigate and a corvette, all now lost to France. It would be quite wrong to imagine that the French navy was by this time negligible, because new ships were being built, but the present situation left the British with fewer ports to blockade and with new friends upon whom they could rely. With the Portuguese following the Spanish example, Britain was no longer without allies and the Napoleonic system had begun to break down. In 1808 it became possible for Britain to resume offensive operations on land with good prospects of success.

British historians of the Napoleonic Wars have often tended to go from the death of Nelson to the burial of Sir John Moore; a narrative of naval prowess turning gradually into the epic story of the Duke of Wellington. Few of them have paid much attention to the history of combined operations and fewer still have seen the Peninsular War as an extension of sea-power. Napier is content to explain that Sir Arthur Wellesley's expedition sailed from Cork on 20 July 1808, without mentioning the transports in which the soldiers embarked or commenting upon the presence of a naval escort. Fortescue is as laconic about the convoy but could not avoid the fact that Mondego Bay, where Wellesley agreed to disembark his troops, had already been occupied by 400 Royal Marines. This earns Admiral Sir Charles Cotton a passing mention but little further notice until page 236. One man of this period whose views were in sharp contrast was Sir Arthur Wellesley or (as he soon became) Lord Wellington. On this subject Rear-Admiral T. Byam Martin wrote as follows:

In the course of our conversation, Lord Wellington, alluding to naval assistance, made a very remarkable observation. His words were: 'If anyone wishes to know the history of this war, I will tell them that it is our maritime superiority gives me the power of maintaining my army while the enemy are unable to do so.'

So Wellington on this subject had no illusions, his complaint being merely that the Navy were not, on occasion, giving him enough support. The fact was that Spain was a poor country, quite unable to support an army in the field, let alone two armies in action against each other. The central problem was one of supply but it was made easier for the British because their supplies came by sea and could be diverted from one port to another as the campaign went on. It was also fortunate that Spain and Portugal shared a peninsula, the internal communications of which were poor so that much of their internal trade went by sea. With British men-of-war blockading the ports which were in French hands this coastal traffic dwindled to nothing and added to the French logistic problems. But the Royal Navy did more than that. When the first campaign ended in disaster at Corunna the Navy brought the troops away, much as at Dunkirk in World War II.

A south-westerly gale drove the transports home in four or five days; and it is said that some officers, worn out with the exertions of the previous three weeks, fell asleep when the ships weighed anchor and never woke till they reached Portsmouth. All ranks landed as they had embarked, in the clothes which they had never changed for three weeks, unwashed, unshorn, unspeakably filthy. The people at the various ports were horrified . . .

But the Navy, which removed Moore's troops and would soon land others in Portugal, did useful work in distracting the French by other operations along the Spanish coast. The roads between France and Spain are close to the sea on either side of the peninsula and were vulnerable to British attack. The supreme exponent of the coastal raid was Lord Cochrane of the frigate *Imperieuse*. Operations such as his – the destruction of telegraph stations, the blowing up of batteries, the interception of coastal shipping – used up French troops in coastal defence. A typical description of a raid is taken from Cochrane's Autobiography:

The whole coast was now swarming with troops and hastily prepared fortifications. That morning a small fishing town was sighted, which appeared to have added to its peaceable occupation the business of veritable armouries, barracks and stables. . . . The small boats of both ships were manned with the ships' boys dressed in the scarlet jackets of the marines and sent towards the right of the town. The French sent off a body of cavalry to oppose them. Meanwhile the ships approached the town, under continual fire, and began a succession of broadsides which lasted for an hour, during which distraction the real marines, thirty from the *Imperieuse* and twenty from the *Spartan*, landed on the left. As they did so the enemy fled from the battery in their front, the guns of which were spiked, the ships moved in still further, and opened a heavy fire of grape-shot upon the cavalry, which was now returning, disillusioned, to the rescue of the guns; and the marines leisurely returned to their boats.

Of more importance locally was Cochrane's help in defending Fort Trinidad at Rosas. The main attack was successfully beaten off but the place became untenable. Three British men-of-war moved in to cover the landing place and the whole garrison was embarked after the fort had been blown up. The Spanish were then landed at Scalla and continued the war from there. This was one instance of what could be done by close co-operation between the Spanish insurgents and their British allies.

The peninsula of Spain had become the grand arena where France and England were to decide their quarrels. The British army, under Lord Wellington, occupied the lines of Torres Vedas; the fleet lay in the Tagus, and afforded supplies of every description. Massena commanded the French armies, but was not so well provided with the means of conducting his campaign as his fortunate opponent; who, with Lisbon in his rear, and the Tagus at his side, had every thing he could desire. Sir William Beresford was on the south side of the river. A strong squadron of ships of war and transports, under the command of Rear-Admiral Sir Joseph Yorke, lay in the Tagus: they had arrived in February, with a reinforcement of 6,500 men – Lieutenant Claxton, of the *Barfleur*, the flag-ship, commanded the gun-boats attached to the army. This officer perceived, on the 5th of March, that the French had broken up from Santarem, and had fled in disorder. He immediately crossed the river, and gave the intelligence to Lord Wellington . . .

So writes Captain Brenton, describing the situation in 1810. He goes on to deal with a combined operation of great interest:

We now return to the siege of Cadiz, which, during the winter, had been defended by the combined forces of England, Spain and Portugal, and closely invested by the French under Marshal Soult. The British land forces were commanded by Sir Thomas Graham, the squadron by Sir Richard Keats.

Early in 1811 a powerful expedition was formed, composed of British and Spanish troops, commanded by Sir Thomas Graham and General Lapena, with a view to land on the coast to the westward, and to make an attack on the rear of the enemy, while the rear-admiral at the same time, with a body of seamen, royal marines, and the Spanish regiment of Toledo, was to make a diversion to the eastward, by way of drawing the enemy's attention . . .[4]

That was a relatively large scale operation in which the French were to lose 3,000 men in killed, wounded and prisoners. Other raids were mere pin-pricks. Captain Kittoe RN, thus destroyed the coastal defences between Rota and Catalina. Captain Spranges, RN, landed between Catalina and St Mary's, his marines ashore being supported by gunboats.

... These operations compelled the enemy to detach a column of about 2,000 troops for the protection of Catalina, and that part of his line [of communication] thereby fully answering the purpose of diversion for which it was intended.[5]

It was eventually thought necessary to co-ordinate these operations and Commodore C. V. Penrose did this from a headquarters at Gibraltar. To describe all these activities would mean writing a book but we do well to have a general idea of the work done by officers like Codrington and Collier. In the Peninsular War the Royal Navy played a significant part.

Of more vital importance than these raids, alarms and excursions was the less spectacular task of transporting and maintaining the army. At this period Britain was sufficiently defended by the militia, numbering up to about 100,000. The regular army, available for service overseas, comprised:

Cavalry	30,000
Foot Guards	6,000
Infantry	170,000
Artillery	14,000
TOTAL	220,000

Of this number up to 60,000 were stationed in India and the colonies, leaving 160,000 (and 30,000 marines) for more active service. The force which embarked for Portugal and Spain in 1808 numbered over 48,000. It was opposed by a French army of over 100,000 men, the strength of which was finally raised to over 240,000. To maintain such an army in the field against the French, present in such strength, continual reinforcements were needed, together with a transport system to remove prisoners and wounded. Of the shipping involved we gain a glimpse in the memoirs of William Richardson who was then serving in the *Caesar*:

All the transports, more than three hundred sail, have dropped down to Belem to be ready to embark the army in case of emergency....
(18th October, 1810)
This day all the boats of the transports assembled on the south side of the Tagus, and brought over to Lisbon 15,000 Spanish troops, under the command of General Romana; they marched away immediately to join Lord Wellington.

25th-Arrived the *Dreadnought* (Captain Linzee), which makes our number as follows:

Barfleur   Admiral Berkeley, Commander-in-chief
              Capt. Sir Thomas Hardy   98 guns
Dreadnought (Capt. Linzee)   98 guns
Hannibal   (Rear-Admiral Sir T. Williams)   75 guns
Caesar (Capt. Granger)   84 guns

He then lists 7 other ships of the line, a frigate and 3 troopships.

. . . and between three and four hundred transports. The carpenters of the line-of-battle ships are fitting some of them up to carry 6,000 prisoners to England. . . .

There has been a great desertion of the German troops from the French army to ours, and 8,000 were shipped off to-day for England. Report says that there has been a mutiny among them, and Massena has ordered every fourth man in two German regiments to be shot.

(12th April) – Having got all ready for sea at ten this morning, we got under way and bade a final adieu to Lisbon, having the *Cyene* (20-gun ship) and eighty-two transports and merchantmen with us . . .

It will be noticed that Richardson makes a clear distinction between a troopship and a transport. The ordinary transport was a merchantman chartered by the government on a temporary basis. The troopship was often an obsolete man-of-war and was commanded, in any case, by a naval officer and manned by a crew under naval discipline. We know of one troopship from Sir William Dillon. In March, 1811, Dillon was posted, much to his annoyance, to the command of the *Leopard*, which he knew was to become a troopship. The *Leopard* built at Sheerness in 1790 was a 50-gun ship built on the same lines as the *Portland* of 1770, one of a practically obsolete class. Her great claim to distinction lay in the fact that she had fought and captured the United States frigate *Chesapeake* in 1807 at a time when Britain and the United States were at peace. The incident was followed by explanations and apologies and Britain renounced, at this point, the right to search foreign men-of-war for deserters. Since then the British 50-gun ship had been modified and partly disarmed. Although thus adapted for trooping the *Leopard* was still a man-of-war and still a suitable command for a Captain, RN.

When the ship was nearly ready for sea, I received from the Admiralty some instructions relating to the treatment of the troops that would be embarked, as well as a set of regulations signed by the Duke of York directing the Commanding Officer of any detachment sent on board to conform to the discipline of the ship. In plain terms, they were to consider themselves during the passage under the naval Articles of War. These documents were satisfactory as, by them, my authority as captain was not interfered with, and in the event of meeting with any troublesome characters, I had the power of controlling them. I was employed upon a service altogether new to the Navy. Consequently it was necessary to be armed with sufficient authority for the occasion . . .[6]

The *Leopard* as a troopship, was not fitted with the rigging allowed to a 50-gun ship, but that of a frigate of 28 guns, and a crew suitable to that class.

. . . On the 30th we embarked a battalion of the Guards, and sailed next day for Cadiz.[6]

The *Leopard* had clearly lost many of her guns in providing more space for the troops. For purposes of war, she was of no more use than a small frigate with a reduced spread of canvas. On her return voyage to England the *Leopard* carried invalids from the army and French prisoners of war. At Plymouth she embarked 457 French prisoners bound for Leith. Later we find the *Leopard* in a squadron with five other troopships, the *Diadem, Latona, San Fiorenzo, Mermaid* and *Brune*, all on their way back to Lisbon. When Dillon sailed again he embarked 70 invalid soldiers and had charge of a convoy. After refit, the *Leopard* sailed for Lisbon once more in May 1812, embarking 450 men of the 5th Regiment at Cork. On the return voyage Dillon embarked 258 British and 150 Portuguese artillerymen – and so the work went on until the war ended. It would be natural to suppose that Dillon's active career would end with this rather humdrum command. He was, however, to have a frigate as his next command and lived to attain the rank of Vice-Admiral. Commenting on his troopship experience he wrote:

On this subject I cannot omit my observations. The troopship had been introduced solely for the accommodation of the Army, because so many accidents had happened to the transports. All the naval captains out of employ dreaded the idea of being appointed to one of them. However, whatever the feelings of the whole Service towards those officers who accepted the commands of them, the Admiralty had selected for the Captains of the frigates [i.e. the frigates re-rated as troopships] men of title and of the first families in the kingdom. They were in rank Commanders, and in accepting their appointments were sure in the end of obtaining promotion. Among the

Post Captains chosen for that duty I noticed some of our most distinguished officers . . . Therefore, though not overpleased when I received my appointment to the *Leopard*, I found officers, my seniors, in a similar position; which circumstance in some degree enabled me to bear with patience the chances of my profession. Now I had gone through the ordeal, and in consequence thereof had received a distinguished appointment . . .[7]

It would seem that the Admiralty handled the troopships with some care. Some, probably the larger ones, like the *Leopard*, were given the post captains who would eventually have more active commands. Others, probably of smaller size, were given to commanders, or perhaps to lieutenants who thus achieved commander's rank, and these included men with a definite future in the service – men with parliamentary or other interest who could expect early promotion. Where some were unfortunate, however, was in holding such an appointment when the war ended, leaving them with no further chance of distinction. Even for them, however, there was one opportunity left, and that was the war with the United States. To quote from Dillon again:

I had now to commence a new career, but the thought that plagued me most was that the war had nearly reached its termination in Europe. But there was still America open for a chance.

TEN

Successes and Setbacks

The French had lost or were to lose most of their colonial possessions during the Napoleonic Wars. An exception was Martinique in the West Indies and it was generally assumed that this too would be conquered by Britain. Any plan Napoleon might have had for the re-establishment of French power in the West Indies would have to hinge on Martinique, the base he possessed and from which further efforts might some day be made. If Martinique were to be held the island would have to be reinforced, it was thought, in 1809. The man to do this was Rear-Admiral Willaumez, assisted by Rear-Admiral Gourdon, whose squadron at Brest comprised the *Ocean* (120) and seven other ships of the line with two frigates, a corvette and a schooner. Blockading Brest was Admiral Lord Gambier, assisted by Rear-Admiral Stopford, whose squadron included the *Caledonia* (120) and ten other sail of the line. On 21 February 1809, Gambier being blown off station by a westerly gale, Willaumez put to sea. His orders were to chase Commodore Beresford's blockading squadron from Lorient, thus releasing Commodore Troude with his three sail of the line and five frigates, chase Rear-Admiral Stopford's squadron away from the Basque Roads and finally sail for Martinique with a considerable force, troops included. The plan miscarried at the outset; Willaumez being seen and his movements reported to Gambier. Three frigates from Lorient were trapped at Les Sables d'Olonne by Stopford's squadron, driven ashore and wrecked. Willaumez succeeded in releasing Troude but ended in the Basque Roads, blockaded again by Lord Gambier.

The Basque Roads are part of a complex coastline north of the Gironde Estuary, largely sheltered behind the Ile de Ré and the Ile d'Oleron. The anchorage can be approached from the north by the Pertuis Breton, from the south by the Pertuis Maumusson, but the more direct and obvious approach is by the Pertuis d'Antioche. The River Charente enters the Rade des Basques behind the Ile d'Aix and Rochefort lies up the river. Rochefort, founded by Colbert in 1666, was more of a shipbuilding centre than a naval base, the river being too shallow for the entry of men-of-war when fully armed and laden. At this time the Ile d'Aix was known to be fortified, with a citadel at its south end. The French squadron took up a position between that citadel and the Ile Madame but lost one ship in the process, the *Jean-Bart*, wrecked on the Palles shoal – a reminder in itself that the Charente estuary is complex and dangerous. Unable to sail for Martinique and unable to take refuge at Rochefort, Willaumez took up a defensive position. Following cautiously, Lord Gambier dropped anchor about eight miles away. Writing to the Admiralty on 11 March he said:

The enemy ships lay very much exposed to the operation of fire-ships; it is a horrible mode of warfare, and the attempt very hazardous, if not desperate; but we should have plenty of volunteers for the service.

This was no new idea to their Lordships because another French squadron had found refuge at the same anchorage in 1807 and Captain Keats had then suggested an attack by bomb-vessels, fireships and rockets, to be protected by a squadron in close support. Anticipating Lord Gambier's needs, the orders had already gone forth for the preparation of fireships, the fitting-out of bomb-vessels and the embarkation of Mr Congreve with a supply of the rockets he had invented. On the French side Willaumez was replaced in command by the abler Vice-Admiral Allemand.

At this time Admiral Lord Gambier was aged 53, his reputation resting firmly on the second bombardment of Copenhagen, the action which had earned him his peerage. He was well-connected, the nephew of an earlier Admiral Gambier, and had served at one time (1795–1801) on the Board of Admiralty under Lord Spencer. He was chiefly known for his rather obtrusive and evangelical piety, his men being constantly pestered with hymn-books and tracts. Rumour had it that the best way to promotion under his command was through Methodism. His Captain of the Fleet was Sir Harry Neale, whose career had been more administrative than distinguished. Gambier and Neale were not the men to hazard all and gamble with death and destruction. This appears to have been realized at the Admiralty, where an attempt was made to find the ideal leader for a hazardous enterprise; an officer who would serve under Gambier but who would himself, in fact, lead the attack. Their lordships' choice fell on Lord Cochrane, captain of the frigate *Imperieuse* (38), who was known to be familiar with the French coast. Cochrane was reluctant to accept the task but was told by Mulgrave 'My lord, you must go. The Board cannot listen to further refusal or delay.' Cochrane obeyed but with misgivings about the reaction of the officers who were already on the scene; misgivings which were more than justified in the event. He also distrusted the government of the day, thinking that they would snatch credit from his success but would be at least equally pleased to see him fail. He was not, he realized, the most popular man in the service.

Cochrane was the elder son of the eccentric, ingenious and impoverished Earl of Dundonald. He was Scottish, red-haired, clever, brave, insubordinate and obstinate. A Member of Parliament, he was, by politics, a radical, a man of the extreme left. The nephew of an Admiral, Sir Alexander Cochrane, he gained rapid promotion. When commanding the sloop *Speedy* he became a legend in the Mediterranean, crowning his reputation when he actually captured a Spanish frigate. His next ship was the *Arab* (20), from which he was promoted to the *Pallas* frigate in which he made some prize money and came to know the approaches to Rochefort. Later, in the *Imperieuse* he had young Frederick Marryat as a pupil, who wrote:

I never knew any one so careful of the lives of his ship's company as Lord Cochrane, or any one who calculated so closely the risks attending any expedition. Many of the most brilliant achievements were performed without the loss of a single life, so well did he calculate the chances . . .

The same point is made by Captain E. P. Brenton, RN who wrote of Cochrane:

No officer ever attempted or succeeded in more arduous enterprises with so little loss. Before he fired a shot he reconnoitred in person, took soundings and bearings, passed whole nights in the boats, his lead line and spy glass incessantly at work . . .

That was his best side. St Vincent took a different view, writing that 'The Cochranes are not to be trusted out of sight. They are all mad, romantic, money-getting and not truth-telling.' Keith reached much the same conclusion, describing Cochrane as 'wrong-headed, violent and proud'. He was certainly better liked by his subordinates than by his superiors. The First Lord of the Admiralty must have been an optimist indeed to foresee a happy partnership between Gambier and Cochrane. The younger officer had enterprise and brains, the older officer was the man responsible.

On 26 March 1809, Lord Gambier replied to the Admiralty letter in which he was directed to attack and try to destroy the French squadron:

The enemy's ships are anchored in two lines, very near to each other, in a direction due S from the fort on the Isle d'Aix . . . The most distant ships of their two lines are within point-blank shot of the works upon the Isle d'Aix: such ships, therefore, as might attack the enemy would be exposed to be raked by the hot shot etc. from the Island; and should the ships be disabled in their masts, they must remain within the range of the enemy's fire until destroyed, there not being sufficient depth of water to allow them to move to the south-ward out of distance . . . I beg leave to add, that, if their Lordships are of opinion that an attack on the enemy's ships by those of the fleet under my command is practicable, I am ready to obey any orders they may be pleased to honour me with, however great the risk may be of the loss of men and ships.

It is clear that Gambier disliked the whole project and had decided to keep his fleet out of it. There would be a fireship attack because their Lordships had so decided 'however great the risk'. Cochrane should direct it, again as ordered, even if a better choice could have been made. But his ships of the line were not going near the Ile d'Aix. That, he ruled, was out of the question.

Lord Cochrane arrived with the *Imperieuse* on 3 April. Twelve fire-ships were to follow from the Downs and 6 from Plymouth with a shipload of explosives from Woolwich. Other fireships were prepared before these arrived and Cochrane supervised the equipment of three explosion vessels. Meanwhile, however, there was an even more explosive scene on the flagship itself. Rear-Admiral Sir Eliab Harvey, who had commanded the *Temeraire* at Trafalgar, came on board the *Caledonia* with a list of officers and men who had volunteered for special service. Told that Cochrane was to direct the attack (he himself being passed over) he announced that he would haul down his flag and quit the service. Given the chance and given any rotten ship available, he would have gone in and taken the *Ocean* (120) by boarding. He told Sir Harry Neale that he never saw a man so unfit for the command of a fleet as Lord Gambier. He had nothing against Lord Cochrane personally but Gambier's conduct was insufferable, the old psalm-singing 'so-and-so' etc. All this was to end in a court martial and his being dismissed from the service. (He was later reinstated, however, given the KCB and promoted, although never employed again.) Other captains senior to Cochrane were as disgruntled if less outspoken.

On the 3rd, 4th and 5th Cochrane did what Gambier should long since have done. He took the *Imperieuse* in to reconnoitre the enemy and reported that the batteries on the Ile d'Aix were far from formidable, being in process of reconstruction. He also reported on the French squadron which had sent down their topmasts and unbent their sails. About 100 yards in front of their line was a boom made of cables $31\frac{1}{2}$ in. in diameter, supported by buoys and moored in position by $5\frac{1}{4}$ ton anchors. The French were in no doubt as to what they might expect and had their boats out rowing guard. The longer the attack was delayed the more complete their defences would become. The French admiral had moored three frigates in advance of his line proper, the *Pallas, Hortense* and *Indience*. His front line comprised the *Calcutta, Cassard, Regulus, Ocean* (flagship) *Varsovie* and *Foudroyant*. Covering the gaps between his front ships were those in the second line, the *Elbe, Tourville, Aquilon, Jemappes, Patriote* and *Tonnere*. Allemand's right flank was protected by the batteries on the Ile d'Aix, mounting perhaps 30 guns. Besides his eleven ships of the line, Gambier had seven frigates, five sloops, two bomb-vessels, six gun-brigs and some smaller craft fitted for firing rockets. He had, in addition, the explosion vessels and fireships. It was for Cochrane to make the detailed plan. It was to be a night-attack and would begin with the *Imperieuse* and three other frigates anchoring in a position near the Boyart Shoal together with three rocket vessels. The *Aetna* bomb-vessel (the only one which had arrived) would take up a position north-west of the Ile d'Aix, covered by the *Indefatigable* and *Foxhound*. The *Emerald*, with three sloops or gun-brigs, was to make a feint attack on the island itself, and two other gun-brigs, the *Redpole* and *Lyra* were to mark, with lights hoisted, the target area. Between those lights the explosion vessels would be launched and would destroy the boom, followed by the fireships, which would drive among the enemy men-of-war and destroy them; the French formation making them, incidentally, an ideal target for such an attack. Finally, the boats of the fleet, under Rear-Admiral Stopford, were to follow up the fireships and complete the enemy's destruction.

The evening of 11 April was chosen for the operation, the fireships having arrived the day before. The night was uncommonly dark with a high wind from the right quarter and a heavy sea. One part of the plan had to be cancelled almost at the outset because Stopford's boat attack was foiled by rough weather. This meant that there was no follow-up for the fireship attack unless Gambier brought his ships of the line into action; and his doing so was no part of the scheme as agreed. The defending French boats were as completely frustrated and from the same cause. In other respects the operation went according to plan with all hell let loose as the night went on. Lord Cochrane took command of one explosion vessel, waiting to light the fuses himself until within fifteen minutes (as he estimated) of the enemy. The explosion was premature but impressive, involving 1,500 barrels of gunpowder, several hundred shells and nearly 3,000 hand-grenades. The other two explosion vessels achieved nothing but this one was enough to destroy the boom. The fireship attack now developed, only four out of twenty-one reaching the target and no single French ship being destroyed, although three, including the flagship, had a narrow escape. But here again the small success was enough. Alarmed by the approach of the blazing fireships, the French ships of the line all cut their cables and five of them ran aground on the Palles shoal. Others grounded elsewhere in the estuary, being left immovable as the tide ebbed.

At daylight Lord Cochrane saw that the French were making every effort to re-float their ships. He therefore made a series of telegraphic signals to Gambier:

5.48 am:	Half the fleet can destroy the enemy
	Seven on shore
6.40 am:	Eleven on shore
7.40 am:	Only two afloat
9.30 am:	Enemy preparing to heave off

These signals were acknowledged but no action was taken until the flagship at 9.35 am made the signal for the fleet to weigh anchor. The execution of that signal was annulled by another calling all captains on board the *Caledonia*. The fleet finally sailed at 10.45 am but presently dropped anchor again about three miles from the Ile d'Aix, six miles from the stranded enemy ships. Gambier then signalled the *Aetna* bomb-vessel to move towards the Aix roads under the protection of the gun-brigs *Insolent, Conflict* and *Growler*. Captain Bligh was ordered in with three sail of the line to support this rather feeble attack but he dropped anchor again when still a mile distant from the grounded enemy ships. Seeing the ineffectiveness of this movement, Cochrane with the *Imperieuse* went in to attack the *Calcutta, Varsovie* and *Aquilon*. On a signal from Gambier, the *Indefatigable* frigate (44) came to join in the battle, assisted eventually by the *Valiant* (74), Captain Bligh's ship, the *Revenge* and the *Pallas*. The *Varsovie* and *Aquilon* surrendered and were burnt, the *Tonnerre* and *Calcutta* were set on fire and blew up. Five more French ships of the line were still on shore and vulnerable and one of these, the *Ocean* three-decker, was resolutely attacked by the *Beagle* sloop but was finally floated again. The action continued for some days but little more was achieved. When Rear-Admiral Stopford staged a further attack on the remaining enemy ships the *Caesar* ran aground and the attack was called off. The operation finally came to an end on the 29th, the day on which Gambier sailed for England.

Among the records of this affair, perhaps the most revealing document is the letter addressed by Gambier to Cochrane on the 13th, following up a signal of recall and sent in reply to Cochrane's signal 'The enemy can be destroyed'. The letter had no great influence on events but it gives a clue to character:

My dear Lord – You have done your part so admirably that I will not suffer you to tarnish it by attempting impossibilities, which I think, as well as those captains who have come from you, any further effort to destroy those ships would be. You must, therefore, join us soon as you can, with the bombs etc. as I wish for some information, which you allude to, before I close my despatches.

Yours etc.
Gambier

P.S. – I have ordered three brigs and two rocket-vessels to join you, with which, and the bomb, you may make an attempt on the ship that is aground on the Palles, or towards Ile Madame, but I do not think you will succeed; and I am anxious that you should come to me, as I wish to send you to England as soon as possible. You must, therefore, come as soon as the tide turns.[3]

Argument is possible on either side about what Gambier could or should have done – and Captain Brenton, for one, thinks that Gambier was right to avoid risking his fleet – but this letter is proof in itself of a twittering ineptitude. Gambier begins by recalling Cochrane. Why? Because he can help the Admiral complete his despatch; the document mattering more, seemingly, than the success of the operation. Then he changes his mind and promises to send help with a view to Cochrane

149

destroying a ship which is very vaguely described. But the attempt, he thinks, will not succeed. If success is unlikely, however, we are left to wonder why the attempt should be authorized? Then the order is repeated for Cochrane to report to the Admiral. Why is that a matter for such urgency? Cochrane might conclude, on receiving this letter, that he was to be the bearer of the despatch. But that honour was to be reserved for Sir Harry Neale who, like Gambier himself, had never been within range of the enemy's guns. Gambier was not unfair to Cochrane, who on his recommendation was to be made a Knight of the Bath, but he was perfectly satisfied with his little victory and could not see the point of view of an officer like Nelson or Cochrane who wanted, not victory, but annihilation. In the opinion of men like these it was a disgrace to quit the Basque Roads until the enemy fleet had been completely destroyed.

Back in England the news of Lord Gambier's victory was received with enthusiasm and not entirely without reason. Whatever opportunities had been lost, the fact remained that the Brest fleet had been utterly humiliated and had virtually ceased to exist. Of its eleven ships of the line four had been destroyed, several had been damaged by grounding and gunfire, others had saved themselves by cutting away their masts and throwing their guns overboard. As for morale, what could be done with seamen who had been chased up the Charente, whose flagship had been engaged by an 18-gun sloop, and one of whose captains had been afterwards shot for cowardice? We do wrong, therefore, to conclude that nothing had been achieved. To many it must have seemed right and proper that Lord Gambier should receive the thanks of Parliament. On hearing of this proposal, however, Cochrane warned Lord Mulgrave that he would oppose the motion in the House of Commons. Faced by this threat, Lord Gambier had no alternative. He applied for a court martial and prepared to defend himself before it. The court duly assembled on 26 July 1809, on board His Majesty's Ship *Gladiator* at Portsmouth. Admiral Sir Roger Curtis sat as President, supported by Admiral Young, Vice-Admirals Campbell, Sir John Duckworth and Douglas; Rear-Admiral Sutton and Captains Irwin, Dickson, Hall and Dunn. In his letter of 10 May, laid before the court, Gambier stated what was to be the gist of his defence:

... I was obliged to have a second object in view, for besides the destruction of the enemy's ships, the greatest care was required that his Majesty's fleet should not be sacrificed ... nothing can better exemplify the limited space and danger of the navigation, than the circumstance of one of the enemy's line-of battle ships having, on their fleet entering the Roads in February last, run on shore on the shoal of the Pallas, and being there totally wrecked.

After all the evidence had been heard, Gambier summed up the defence by emphasizing that seven of the enemy's ships of the line were 'never in a situation to be assailed'.

I concluded by observing that the service actually performed has been of great importance, as well in its immediate effect as in its ultimate consequences; for the Brest Fleet is so reduced as to be no longer effective. It was upon this fleet the enemy relied for the succour and protection of their West India Colonies; and the destruction of their ships was effected in their own harbour, in sight of thousands of the French . . .

All this was true enough. The question remained as to whether more might have been done. What decided the matter was the evidence given by the other officers who had been present in the action. There was, first and foremost, the testimony of Rear-Admiral Stopford:

Question: When the *Imperieuse* made the signal that the enemy's ships were on shore, and the fleet might destroy them, would you, with the experience you have as a flag officer, have thought it prudent or proper to send or lead the fleet to destroy them?
Answer: In my opinion the dislodgement from the anchorage of the enemy's ships by fireships removed but a small part of the obstacles. With the wind as it then was, and the broadside of the enemy's ships still commanding the passage, we should have been so crippled in going in and in working out a passage a little more than a mile. I think I should not have risked the ships had they been under my command.

Much the same opinion was expressed by others:
Captain Bligh, of the *Valiant*, examined by Lord Gambier – he expressed his opinion, that had any of the line-of-battle ships been sent in, they could never have returned, but must inevitably have been destroyed. Captain Bligh thought that nothing further could have been practicable. There had been no neglect or delay on the part of Lord Gambier.
Captain Beresford – no blame attached to the conduct of Lord Gambier.
Captain Kerr, of the *Revenge* – deposed to the same effect as the last witness.
Captain Douglas of the *Bellona*, and Captain Godfrey of the *Aetna* – deposed to the same effect.

Captain Hardiman, of the *Unicorn*, sworn and examined – he spoke in favourable terms of the exertion of the *Beagle*. There had been no neglect or delay on the part of the Commander-in-Chief.

Captain Seymour, of the *Pallas* – thought that everything practicable had been done.

Captain Newcombe, of the *Beagle*, sworn and examined. He entered into a detail of the particular part his ship took in the action, which bore no reference to the charges exhibited against Lord Gambier, but reflected considerable credit on his own activity and exertion:

Question: Under the circumstances of the case, would you, had you been commander-in-chief have sent the ships earlier in to attack those of the enemy on shore?

Answer: The risk, I think, as the wind and tide were, was rather too great.
. . .

Captain Malcolm. . . . Every practicable effort was made to destroy the ships of the enemy that had got into the entrance of the Charente. . . .

Captain Burlton, Captain Ball and Captain Newman were not aware of any blame attaching to Lord Gambier.

Only one captain, Broughton of the *Illustrious*, gave evidence helpful to Cochrane and he backed down under Lord Gambier's questions. The result of the trial was, therefore, inevitable. Gambier was acquitted with the comment that his conduct had been 'marked by zeal, judgment and ability'. Was that, in fact, the truth? In reaching a conclusion on a question of some complexity and doubt, there are two facts to be borne in mind. First, Cochrane's behaviour after the action was regarded as deplorable. He had shown too little loyalty to the service. Gambier might be an old woman but he did not merit public disgrace. He had done his best. He had been unfailingly polite. Psalm-singing apart, he was fairly competent. He was better liked than Cochrane, a demagogue and a damned radical. The other fact to remember is that the government of the day had formed its own opinion of Gambier. When Lord Collingwood died at sea in 1810 he was succeeded in the Mediterranean by Admiral Sir Charles Cotton. Replaced by Vice-Admiral Sir Edward Pellew, Cotton was chosen to succeed Gambier as Commander-in-Chief of the Channel Fleet. Gambier saw no further service at sea and held no other active command. Perceval proposed at one time to make Gambier First Lord of the Admiralty, but was saved from what would have been a fatal mistake by the common sense of George III. The tragedy is that

Gambier's court martial also ended Cochrane's career so far as the Napoleonic Wars were concerned. Britain's most brilliant naval officer was lost to the service for thirty-nine years; and virtually, indeed, for good.

The year which saw the action in the Basque Roads also saw the expedition to the Scheldt. Napoleon had his northern shipbuilding yard at Antwerp; his actual naval base at Flushing. There were 10 ships of the line there under Rear-Admiral Missiessy and as many again under construction. Napoleon was known to have spent some £2,640,000 on the fortifications, basin, dockyard and arsenal. To destroy Flushing and Missiessy's fleet was a reasonably sensible idea and one under discussion early in 1809. The government of the day, however, saw this planned operation as part of a campaign intended to bring about Napoleon's downfall. To quote the words used by Captain E. P. Brenton, RN:

It was reasonably conjectured by the Ministers of George III that the moment was at length arrived when, by a great and simultaneous movement of England, Austria and Spain, the idol of the French revolution might be broken in pieces. Bonaparte had begun his campaign on the Rhine and Danube; Spain was up in arms; the best generals and the choicest troops of France were employed in that country; and the British ministers began to prepare such an armament for the invasion of Holland as it was conceived would put down all opposition, and give to the friends of the house of Orange, in that country, an opportunity of declaring themselves.

The Admiral chosen to command was Sir Richard Strachan and his orders were simply to destroy the enemy's ships, dockyards and arsenals at Antwerp and Flushing. The unstated objects were a great deal more ambitious and it was thought proper to appoint, as military Commander-in-Chief, an officer with great political experience. William Pitt's elder brother, the second Earl of Chatham, had served in the army until, at the age of thirty-two, he had become First Lord of the Admiralty. He held merely political office for most of the years between 1788 to 1801 but had commanded a brigade without discredit in 1799. On the basis of this limited experience he expected to be given the military command in Spain. This was denied him but he was consoled as Lieutenant-General, with the Command-in-Chief of the Scheldt expedition. Had he returned from it victorious he would almost certainly have become Prime Minister after the expected resignation of the invalid Lord Portland. The force now put at his disposal amounted to over 39,000 men, including 3,000 cavalry, and was excessive for the task immediately in hand. Chatham was not without abilities and had been a useful member of the Cabinet but he was so hesitant and unpunctual that he was commonly called the late Lord Chatham. Strachan had been in action (see page 125) and was described by Captain Graham Moore, RN (Sir John Moore's brother) as 'an excellent seaman, and, tho' an irregular, impetuous fellow, possessing very quick parts and an uncommon share of sagacity and strong sense'. All these gifts he would certainly need when placed in command of 27 sail of the line, five ships of 50 or 40 guns, 23 frigates, 32 sloops, 5 bomb-vessels, 23 gun-brigs and 120 smaller craft and gunboats, making 245 men-of-war, forming the escort for about 400 transports measuring between them over 100,000 tons. As his chief assistants in an operation of daunting magnitude, Strachan had Rear-Admiral Lord Gardner, Rear-Admiral Sir Richard Keats and, among other captains, Sir Home Popham. Of Strachan, or 'Mad Dick', his men said that when he swore he meant no harm, and when he prayed he meant no good. He was a poor choice for this particular command but he had very good support from Keats and Popham. Chatham's divisional commanders were Lieutenant-Generals the Marquis of Huntley, the Earl of Rosslyn and Thomas Grosvenor. The expedition sailed from the Downs on 28 July 1809 and the first landing took place on the 30th. Missiessy, meanwhile, withdrew his ships up the Scheldt towards Antwerp. Flushing was taken on 13 August and Antwerp was the next objective. By this time that fortress was defended by 35,000 men.

The Earl of Chatham learnt also, for the first time, that Antwerp was strongly fortified; that the approach to it could be completely inundated, that the citadel commanded the arsenal and dock-yard; that the ships of war, with their guns and stores in, could retire to a spot within one mile of Kuplemonde, which is five miles above Antwerp; and that, by taking out their guns and stores, they could go to Dendermonde, a fortified town situated 15 miles higher. These and other causes led to a council of war on the 26th; and a council of war, as it more commonly does, determined that to abandon the enterprise was better than to run the risk of failing to accomplish it.

Most of the army was now re-embarked. A force was left to occupy Walcheren Island until the end of the year. The fortification, basin and arsenal at Flushing were then destroyed and the evacuation completed. What turned this fiasco into disaster was the polder fever which at one time put 14,000 men on the sick list; an illness of which a quarter of them died and from which none completely recovered. The concept of this expedition was not entirely wrong but it was based on scanty information and confused aims and was led by the wrong general. What little was accomplished might have been achieved by a fraction of the force in a fraction of the time. Three operations of this period, that in the Dardanelles, that in the Basque Roads and this of Walcheren or the Scheldt, all illustrate the need to be careful and deliberate in planning but swift as lightning in execution. In each of these instances the planning was hurried and slipshod, the action appallingly slow. The intolerable Lord Cochrane knew how to do it but one of the minor blemishes on the Scheldt expedition was that the frigate *Imperieuse* was there but commanded by someone else.

Chatham had to take the blame for the failure but the ministers were now in complete disarray, with great friction especially between Castlereagh and Canning. The situation was described by Lord Folkestone in a letter to Thomas Creevey:

Brook's Sept 21, 1809

Dear Creevey,

I cannot help writing to tell you what a curious scene is going on here. Old Portland is going both out of the Ministry and out of the world – both very soon, and it is doubtful which first; but the doubt arises from the difficulty of finding a new Premier, though both Perceval and Canning have offered themselves. Mulgrave is going too, they say – Castlereagh is quite gone, and Canning too, and the latter well nigh this morning quitted this sublunary globe, as well as the Foreign Office, for his friend Castlereagh on Wimbledon Common about 7 o'clock this morning as neatly as possible sent a pistol ball through the fleshy part of his thigh. These heroes have quarrelled and fought about the Walcheren affair – Castlereagh damning the execution [i.e. the performance] of Lord Chatham and Canning the plan of the planner, and being Lord Chatham's champion, Lord Chatham's friends, too, say that he is not at all to blame, that he has a complete case against Castlereagh. . . . On the other hand, Castlereagh's friends are furious too – say that never man was so ill-used, and that he never will have any more connection with his present colleagues.

In the event, Chatham had to resign office as Master-General of the Ordnance. Forming his ministry, Perceval removed Mulgrave – for his mismanagement of the Basque Roads expedition – and gave him the Ordnance Department. Hawkesbury (later to become Earl of

Liverpool) became Secretary of State for War. Lord Wellesley took the Foreign Office and Charles Yorke was made First Lord of the Admiralty. With Robert Jenkinson, second Earl of Liverpool, there came into the government the man who was destined to finish the war, serving as Prime Minister from 1812 to 1827. Yorke was at the Admiralty only a short time, being succeeded by Robert Dundas, the second Viscount Melville, who held this office for the remainder of the war.

Among the Admirals, reputations were crumbling and no great future could be foreseen for Gambier, Duckworth or Strachan. Absent from the European scene was the man whose reputation now stood highest. Sir Edward Pellew had sailed for the East Indies in 1804, that lucrative command being his reward for the political support he gave to Addington. As Addington (now Lord Sidmouth) said to Pellew's third son in after years 'There were three persons Pitt never forgave for their adherence to me – Lord Cornwallis, Sir Will'm Grant, and your father.' In Pellew's case vengeance took the form of dividing the East Indies Command and giving half of it to Lord St Vincent's closest follower Sir Thomas Troubridge. The result was an acrimonious quarrel between these two officers, one which endangered British interests in the whole Indian Ocean. When things were at their worst in 1806 Pellew wrote to Sir Evan Nepean: 'I wish to God that I was out of it. I would rather command a Frigate with her Bowsprit over the rocks of Ushant all my Life . . . for Heavens sake call one of us home. . . .' This the Admiralty finally did, transferring Troubridge to the Cape. His flagship, the *Blenheim*, was lost on the way there and one more aspiring flag-officer was removed from the list. Pellew did well in India and ended his tour of duty with a successful raid on Java. Having made a fortune and promoted both his sons to the rank of post-captain, he sailed for home, hauling down his flag on 14 July 1809. He was ashore for nearly a year and was then appointed Commander-in-Chief in the North Sea, entrusted with the blockade of the Scheldt. Among the first to congratulate him was Lord Chatham who wrote:

I have many acknowledgements to offer you for your very kind Note, as well as to congratulate you, which I do most sincerely, on your appointment to a command now of very considerable importance. Had you fortunately possessed it last summer, it would, I am confident, have ceased, comparatively to be of any, and my individual happiness would not have been less secured by it, then the honor and interests of the Country.

Would Pellew's presence in the Scheldt have made all that difference? It is difficult to say but he was himself probably glad to have been elsewhere. He remained at his post until April 1811, when orders came for him to haul down his flag and come ashore. He had been appointed Commander-in-Chief in the Mediterranean.

ELEVEN

The American War

When Lord St Vincent hauled down his flag for the last time in 1807, he had a private audience with George III. Some record exists of the conversation, as thus:

The King: Well, Lord St Vincent, you have now quitted active service, as you say, for ever. Tell me, do you think the naval service is better or worse than when you first entered it?

St Vincent: Very much worse, may it please your Majesty.

The King: How so? How so?

St Vincent: Sire, I have always thought that a sprinkling of nobility was very desirable in the Navy, as it gives some sort of consequence to the service; but at present the Navy is so overrun by the younger branches of nobility and the sons of members of Parliament, and they so swallow up all the patronage and so choke the channel to promotion that the son of an old officer, however meritorious both their services may have been, has little or no chance of getting on.[1]

St Vincent's own service included the period of the Seven Years War; a time, he was apt to suggest, when men were men. By the time of his retirement he was convinced that the service was going to the dogs. It is fair to ask at this point whether he was right. There is, to begin with, little evidence of deterioration due to the cause he was apt to stress. As against that, we have reason to believe that success had made people complacent. The French navy had been more or less ruined by the revolution, the Spanish navy by Bourbon neglect, the Dutch navy by alien conquest and resulting disunity. With British supremacy thus established, all the British opponents began to suffer from the effects of blockade. This led in turn to heavier casualties and more serious manning problems. The British were themselves short of men and especially so with the expansion of Wellington's army after 1808, but they retained their confidence. Given anything like equal force on either side, a British victory could be assumed. There were, however, a growing number of men-of-war which had never been in battle. On stations where the enemy was unlikely to give serious trouble, officers laid more stress on sail drill than gunnery. Even when exercising the guns there was more emphasis on rapidity of fire than upon accuracy of aim. In some ways the standard of training declined. Instead of striving for perfection some officers were content to ensure that their men were better than their probable opponents. After about seventeen years of warfare some older officers were fairly worn out and some younger officers commissioned who would not have been accepted in peace time. At the same time there were signs of revived morale in the French Navy. A setback for the Royal Navy was not impossible and it actually happened in 1810.

In that year, the operations had begun which would lead to the conquest of the French island of Mauritius, for years the base of marauding cruisers and privateers. As one of the preliminary moves a frigate squadron under Captain Pym descended upon Grand Port, Mauritius, and captured the Ile de la Passe, situated in the harbour mouth. He then went with the *Sirius* (36) to join the *Iphigenia* (36) off Port Louis, leaving Captain Willoughby at Grand Port with the *Nereide* (36) and the brig *Staunch*. Then a French squadron entered the harbour comprising the *Bellone, Victor, Minerve* and a prize, *Ceylon*. The French were in the harbour, sustaining little damage, and Willoughby was still at the entrance. He sent a boat to Pym, who arrived with three frigates, the *Sirius, Iphigenia* and *Magicienne*, and decided to attack before the expected arrival of another French squadron. A battle followed, Pym with four frigates to deploy against two heavier French frigates, a corvette and a captured Indiaman. Owing to navigational errors it was initially a fight between two frigates on either side. The final result was to reduce the *Nereide* to a wreck with 230 casualties (92 dead) out of her original complement of 281 officers and men. The *Magicienne* had to be set on fire and was destroyed. The same fate accounted for the *Sirius*, and Pym, with the remainder of his force, had to capitulate when the expected French squadron appeared under the command of Commodore Hamelin. The wrecks of the *Sirius* and *Magicienne* are still there at the bottom of the harbour and some of their guns have recently been salvaged.

In the campaign for the conquest of Mauritius the Battle of Grand Port was of only momentary importance. The situation was brilliantly saved by Commodore Josias Rowley and bigger forces soon over-whelmed all French forces in the area. In the meanwhile, however, the British frigates had been badly defeated by the French. To make matters worse, the frigate *Africaine* (38) engaged two French frigates off Port Louis, suffered 163 casualties out of a crew of 295 and finally struck her flag. She was actually retaken that evening but the fact remains that she had been defeated in an absurdly unequal conflict. Some British captains were arrogantly over-confident and some British crews were not nearly as good as they thought they were. Their fighting spirit was not in question, as we know from the numbers of killed and wounded, but their gunnery was not good enough and they seriously underrated their opponents. The French navy was recovering its morale – too late in the day so far as this war was concerned – and it should have been clear by now that some British ships needed re-training. No such conclusion was drawn at the time and the appropriate lessons had to be learnt more dearly at the hands of a still more formidable foe. This last phase of the Napoleonic War was notable, in fact, for the appearance of the American Navy. It was no threat, of course to British sea-power but it was to provide a salutary lesson in terms of naval gunnery. In a war between frigates and sloops on either side it was to appear that the American officers and men were as good as the British and that their ships were better. Some lessons were to be learnt the hard way.

Until this late stage in the world conflict the United States had been neutral. A traditional dislike of Britain, dating back to the War of Independence had been balanced by a close relationship in terms of commerce. A traditional sympathy for France had been weakened by tales of bloodshed and atheism. There was already an isolationist senti-ment, a desire to watch European quarrels from a geographical distance and a moral height. Few Americans asked themselves what sort of a Europe (and America) it would be if Napoleon won. More were inclined to remember that George III, Britain's present king, was the same man who had resisted all their just demands and so forced them to seek their independence. He was, in their opinion, as bad as Napoleon or worse. Whatever their attitude to George III, however, the Americans depended heavily upon Britain as a market and a source of supply. To Britain they exported their tobacco, timber, turpentine and tar, their rice and indigo, potash and flour. From Britain they obtained their beer and coal, their hardware and salt, their playing cards and cheese. They traded also with the Mediterranean, with the West and East Indies, but most of the goods to be found at Boston, Salem and New York, had been carried, before the war, in British ships. Since the war began American ships had multiplied, shipowners profiting largely from their neutral position. In going further afield, however, they came more into contact with the navies of Britain and France and began to be accused of harbouring deserters. Until about 1806 relations between Britain and the United States were tolerably good, and relations between America and France were often very strained indeed. Then the blockade system began to create causes of disputes. Argument centred upon definitions of contraband, methods of blockade and unjust decisions of prize-courts. On the British side irritation was caused by the big profits made by American shipowners, by the extent to which American trade was supplanting British and by the desertion of British seamen to American ships. The blockade of May 1806, absolute between the Seine and Ostend conditional from the Elbe to Brest, raised a new and acrimonious issue. There followed the Berlin Decree of November, followed in turn by the British Orders in Council of 1807 and 1809. Numbers of American ships were seized and resulting complaints began to multiply. The American government retaliated by refusing entry to a number of British imports.

At this juncture came the unfortunate encounter between the *Leopard* (50) and the USS *Chesapeake* (36), ending in apologies. This was followed by the American Embargo Act, designed to prevent American ships from entering European waters. The theory was that American seamen would now be safe from impressment and that Great Britain, missing American goods and markets, would make terms. Trade died away, ships sailing to Britain from New York numbering 211 in 1807, 13 after the Act took effect. The embargo did not produce the expected result. After an outbreak of illicit voyages in 1809 the Act was allowed to lapse. But Congress, in freeing trade again, declared that if either combatant revoked its policy and the other (after three months) did not follow suit, non-intercourse would be enforced against the delinquent. Seizing his opportunity in 1810, Napoleon announced that he would revoke the Berlin and Milan decrees as from 1 November. The British replied, accurately, that Napoleon had not done what he said he would. It was 20 May 1812, before the British could be presented with any proof that French policy had actually changed. It was not until 23 June that the Orders in Council were revoked, and the United States Congress had declared war five days earlier. When news came that the Orders in Council no longer applied, Congress agreed to continue the war on the grounds of impressment alone. Napoleon could claim a considerable success for his diplomacy.

On the American side the British press-gang bulked large in argument and larger in propaganda. What was the extent of the grievance? First of all, the British Admiralty reported that they had 2,548 seamen who refused duty on the grounds of being United States citizens. Not all refused duty who could claim American nationality. Castlereagh admitted in Parliament (1811) that American seamen in the Navy numbered over 3,300. The State Department in Washington received 6,257 protests about individual men impressed. Some American historians have claimed that Americans in the Royal Navy numbered over 20,000. Others have admitted that many of the claims were bogus and that other Americans had been impressed into the French Navy. What was the truth? There is no means of knowing. But a fact we need to bear in mind is that the 18th century seaman was often a polyglot character, belonging more to the sea than to any particular country. Documents proving American citizenship were bought and sold on the quayside and claims of nationality were framed according to the needs of the moment. An odd fact is that, although the war was fought to protect American seamen, the people of Massachusetts and New England generally – where the seafaring population lived – were utterly opposed to the war and to Jefferson. A Massachusetts ballad of 1808 reads thus:

> Our ships all in motion once whitened the Ocean,
> They sailed and returned with a cargo;
> Now doomed to decay, they have fallen prey
> To Jefferson – worms – and embargo

The New Englanders who lived by trade, made little of the impressment grievance and turned rather reluctantly to privateering. Privateers put to sea in approximately these numbers: 58 from Baltimore, 55 from New York, 41 from Salem and 31 (a very low number) from Boston.

The War of 1812 was essentially one of Napoleon's contrivance and the Madison government, keen as it was to conquer Canada, had made no preparation for a naval war. The US Navy comprised, at the outset, seventeen vessels (two of them soon condemned) with the following squadron immediately available in New York harbour:

Frigate   *President* (44)
Frigate   *United States* (44)
Frigate   *Congress* (38)
Sloop   *Hornet* (18)
Sloop   *Argus* (16)
To these were added:
Frigate   *Chesapeake* (36)
Frigate   *Essex* (36)
Frigate   *Adams* (26)

It will be seen that the US Navy included no single ship of the line. As against that, the frigates were in a class by themselves. An Act of Congress had been precise in authorizing the construction of frigates but had been vague on the subject of cost. This had allowed Joshua Humphreys to build frigates more powerful than any then in existence. Their dimensions approached those of a 64-gun ship, making them the equivalent of what the 20th century German would call a 'pocket battleship'. First ships of this class were the *United States* and *Constellation* of 1797, followed by the *President* and *Philadelphia* of 1798. The *President*, the most beautiful and the fastest of them was pierced for 54 broadside guns and could actually mount 62. The guns normally comprised thirty 24-pounders on the main deck, eighteen 42-pounder carronades on the quarterdeck and six more on the forecastle, with two more long 24-pounders as bow chasers, making 56 guns in all. Ships of this class were manned by 475 men and boys. The *Chesapeake, Congress* and *New York* were of a smaller class, each mounting up to 54 guns with a crew of about 440. All these ships were of an exceptional size and fired a broadside of considerable weight.

To put this conflict into its proper perspective, we do well to summarize the results or, rather, the British losses:

1812   *Guerriere*   (38)   taken by   *Constitution* (44)
        Java   (38)   taken by   *Constitution* (44)
        Macedonian   (38)   taken by   *United States* (44)
        Alert   (16)   taken by   *Essex* (32)
        Frolic   (18)   taken by   *Wasp* (18)

1813	Peacock	(18)	taken by	Hornet (18)
	Boxer	(12)	taken by	Enterprise (16)
	Dominica	(14)	taken by	Decztar, privateer (7)
1814	Avon	(18)	sunk by	Wasp (18)
	Eperirer	(18)	taken by	Peacock (22)
	Reindeer	(18)	taken by	Wasp (18)
	Picton	(16)	taken by	Constitution (44)
1815	Cyane	(20)	taken by	Constitution (44)
	Levant	(22)	taken by	Constitution (44)
	Levant	(22)	taken by	Constitution (44) (Retaken)
	Penguin	(18)	taken by	Hornet (18)
	St Laurence	(12)	taken by	Chasseur, privateer

Taken in the context of the Napoleonic Wars these losses were, of course, trifling. Three frigates were taken in 1812, thirteen sloops were lost in 1812–15, four of them taken by American frigates. What is significant is not the list of captures but the repeated failures in British gunnery. Following on the Battle of Grand Port, they all point to errors in training which had now to be remedial and were largely remedied before the war came to an end. The British had to learn the hard way that rapidity of fire is not enough and that accuracy of aim is actually more important. From a technical point of view a number of these actions justify careful consideration and study.

In the action between the *Macedonian* and *United States* the British frigate was crippled at fairly long range, her mizzen topmast gone and her carronades mostly dismounted. When at closer range the *Macedonian* lost her mizzenmast and mainyard. She had soon received over a hundred shot in her hull. Of her crew of 254 men the British frigate had 36 men killed and 68 wounded. The *United States* was, by contrast, very little damaged, her casualties numbering no more than 5 killed and 7 wounded (2, mortally). It is apparent that both sides fought well but that the *United States* was a more formidable ship in every way; bigger and more strongly built, better armed and better manned. Nor was the story very different when the action was between two sloops. In June 1814, the British sloop *Reindeer* engaged the US sloop *Wasp*. In the action which followed the *Reindeer* lost her captain, officers and more than half her men, the ship being surrendered by the captain's clerk. In the *Wasp* only eleven men were killed and fifteen wounded. After refitting she was at sea again in August and this time fell in with the

British sloop *Avon*. At the end of the action the *Avon* was sinking, her crew being lucky to be rescued by another sloop, the *Castilian*. The *Wasp* received only four shot in her hull, her casualties amounting to two killed and one wounded. Finally, and after the war had ended, the US Sloop *Hornet* (18) fell in with the British sloop *Penguin* (18). The action was as brief, the British gunnery as ineffective and the result the same. The *Penguin* had been hurriedly built, poorly armed, badly manned and insufficiently exercised. The point has been made that many trained British seamen were serving in American ships. So indeed they were, but that is no explanation for the defeats here listed. The British failed in all these instances from over-confidence. They believed that any ship would do, however badly built and armed, however badly manned and trained. There are few examples of failure through coward-ice but many of failure to damage the enemy.

The situation changed as the French war came to an end. Napoleon came back, defeated, from Russia. In Spain the Duke of Wellington was driving Marshal Soult back into France. Then Napoleon was defeated at the Battle of Leipzig and his empire began to collapse, his own Marshals deserting him. Early in April 1814 Napoleon was persuaded to abdicate and left France, on 28 April, reaching the island of Elba on 4 May in the British frigate *Undaunted*. With peace in Europe Britain could now use almost limitless forces against the United States, a sparsely populated country which still possessed no single ship of the line. Losses continued in 1813, vessels captured including the *Peacock* (18), *Boxer* (12), *Dominica* (14), and *Highflyer* (8). The tide turned on 1 June 1813, with the action between the *Shannon* and *Chesapeake*; a victory which had nothing to do with reinforcements coming from Britain but much to do with the careful training of one ship that was already there. This single ship duel is of great technical interest and it so happens that we have an unusually detailed account of what happened. The result had a great psychological effect at the time but its importance lies not in the history of the war – the result of which was not in doubt – but in marking the progress of British naval gunnery. To the *Shannon* can be traced a new school of thought and a new standard of gun-laying competence.

Captain Philip Broke took command of the frigate *Shannon* (38) on 31 August 1806 and joined the American station in 1811. He was from the outset a gunnery specialist and he instituted a rigorous system of training:

The guns were manned from the larboard and starboard watches *alternately* – the odd-numbered guns from the larboard watch, the even-numbered guns from the starboard watch; the idea was that the watch below should not be disturbed, and that those men who *fought* together ought to be exercised together.

In exercising with shot at a mark each gun was allowed three shots. The mark was a beef-cask, with a square piece of canvas of about four feet. It was always cut to pieces, the distance about three to four hundred yards.

There was also an occasional exercise: this was to lay the ship to, throw a beef-cask over board, and at the *same time*, pass the word 'Numbers two and four main-deck guns, up to your quarters.' Then the captain gave the word to 'Clear for action and fire at the cask.' It was, in most instances, sunk; but the shot always went close enough to be called *effective. All* the guns and carronades had dispart sights on them, and a wooden quadrant for degrees of elevation. Besides these, to every post a compass was inscribed on the deck, by cutting grooves in the planks and filling them up with white putty.[2]

The first exercise described was evidently carried out with the ship under sail, the slower gun-crew being thus penalized by having to fire at a longer range. The second exercise was rather like a pistol competition in which the marksman starts with his pistol in the holster and his back to the target. It had to be done quickly and yet accurately. The dispart is the difference between the semi-diameter of the gun at the base-ring and the muzzle. The dispart sight corrects the inaccuracy which results from this difference so that the line of sight is parallel to the axis of the bore. The quadrant and plumb bob, together with the lines of bearing cut in the deck, allowed an early and primitive form of predictor shoot.

To suppose a case: you are coming up with your enemy on a dark night; the Captain judges what her distance *will* be and how many degrees of the wooden quadrant (tangent scale) will give that distance. Then he orders the guns to be so elevated and trained to so many points before the beam. All being ready the Captain watches the bearing of the enemy by the [fixed] compass . . . and when that bearing corresponds with the point to which the guns are trained, he gives the order to fire.

By this system Broke ensured that his shot would skim the surface horizontally to full point-blank range. Nor did it matter if the gunners were blinded by smoke or darkness provided that the controlling officer could see the enemy's topmast. As Broke said afterwards 'one constant main object was to give a man *confidence* in his gun and shew him what service he alone might effect against an enemy by cool courage and practical skill'. Broke's scientific improvements had a psychological as well as a technical value. One should perhaps note that he was an officer with private means who almost certainly paid for the dispart sights out of his own pocket and probably paid, in addition, for most of the gunpowder used in practice shooting. The Admiralty allowance for this was minimal.

All this care and training was put to the test when the *Shannon* met the *Chesapeake* on 1 June 1813. The *Shannon* was smaller than her opponent by seventy tons and her crew numbered ninety less, the ships being otherwise fairly matched. The effect of the *Shannon*'s first broadside almost decided the battle.

A hurricane of shot, splinters, torn hammocks, cut rigging and wreck of every kind, was hurled like a cloud across the deck. Of 150 men quartered thereon, more than 100 were instantly laid low.

The action lasted no more than thirteen minutes and was ended when Broke boarded the *Chesapeake* at the head of his men. 'In this brief space 252 men were either killed or wounded in the two ships' – as compared with 296 in the Battle of St Vincent. The *Chesapeake* had about 170 casualties, her captain being mortally wounded and calling out as he died 'Don't give up the ship!' She was examined carefully after being taken and it seemed that the *Chesapeake* received 25 thirty-two pound shot, 29 eighteen-pound shot and 306 grape shot. A final calculation showed:

18 pdr shot fired at the *Chesapeake*		82
32 pdr		30
	TOTAL	112
18 pdr shot accounted for		29
ditto, by carpenter's statement		35
32 pdr shot accounted for		25
TOTAL number of shot accounted for		89
TOTAL shot unaccounted for 112 — 89 =		23

Comparing the two sides, the *Shannon* was hit by 158 projectiles (including grape shot) and the *Chesapeake* by 362, 28 shot every minute. If the grape shot are ignored, the *Shannon* received four hits a minute and the *Chesapeake*, nine. To quote from Broke's biography:

One question is 'How many such shot must enter a frigate's hull before she is crippled or silenced?' Is it thirty? Fifty is certainly a large allowance if the fight is a sea fight; but say forty shots must silence and capture a frigate, then it is *clear* that *whatever* frigate opposed herself to the *Shannon* must either take her in half an hour or be herself taken, for as it is allowed that forty shot in the hull will cripple and silence her, the *Shannon* would have placed there 270 in the half hour, or 230 shots more than is supposed to be required . . .

What reliance can be placed on this calculation it is difficult to say but it suggests that the accuracy of aim during the Napoleonic Wars must have been appallingly bad on all sides, the British superiority being mainly in rapidity of fire. It was the Americans who were responsible for this eleventh-hour improvement in gunnery.

The *Shannon* was an exceptional ship but her opponent, we should note, was not a 'pocket battleship' of the 'United States' Class. The honour of capturing the *President* in January, 1815, fell to the frigate *Endymion* (40) which eventually had the co-operation of the *Pomone* (38). While the arrival of the second frigate put an end to the *President's* resistance, she had already been defeated by the *Endymion*, a smaller ship with fewer guns and a smaller crew. The fact that the *President's* hull was riddled and that her casualties numbered 35 dead and 70 wounded is enough to show that the *Endymion's* gunnery was not to be despised. A general improvement had evidently begun and this was shown again in the capture of the *Essex* (32) by the *Phoebe* (36) slightly assisted by the sloop *Cherub*. The advantage here was on the British side partly because the *Phoebe* was a bigger ship and partly because the *Essex* mounted only carronades on her main-deck and was compelled to fight at long range; an interesting reversal of British tradition. Of this action C. S. Forester writes:

The *Phoebe's* long guns, well served, caused frightful havoc in the *Essex* during half an hour's bombardment. . . . The losses on board the *Essex* were appalling, there were something near a hundred and twenty casualties, more than half the ship's company; the British ships were firing into her hull with a steadiness and accuracy comparable with the best of American gunnery.

Standards of marksmanship were rising but the guns themselves were not very accurate, there being too much windage, the cannon ball fitting too loosely into the bore. If the shot were allowed to rust, the round was too large. When the rust was chipped off it became too small. But much was achieved when the gun captains realized that gunnery is a science. A leading specialist was Captain Sir John Pechell, whose interest dated from the day on which he saw the damage sustained by the *Chesapeake*. When HMS *Excellent* was established in 1830 as the naval gunnery school at Portsmouth, Pechell wrote to tell Broke that his dream had at last come true: 'I could not deny myself the pleasure of being the first to apprise you of it, feeling as I do that visiting the *Chesapeake* was the origin of my taking up the subject.' Scientific gunnery began with Sir Charles Douglas in Rodney's time but it was the American War, a life-time later, which finally turned theory into practice.

When the American War began the British squadron on the American station comprised one ship of the line as flagship, the *Africa* (64), three 38-gun frigates, two smaller frigates and six sloops. These had initially to confront three heavy frigates (*Constitution, President, United States*) and about sixteen smaller frigates and sloops. Admiralty policy, explained to Sir John Borlase Warren in January 1813, was to provide him with 'upwards of ten of the line, exclusive of the six sail of the line appropriated to the protection of the West India convoys' and exclusive, we may note, of other ships patrolling the Atlantic especially between the Cape Verde Islands and the Azores. The Secretary to their Lordships concluded:

It has not been without interfering for the moment with other very important that my Lords have been able to send you this re-inforcement, and they most anxiously hope that the vigorous and successful use you will make of it will enable you shortly to return some of the line of battle ships to England, which, if the heavy American frigates should be taken or destroyed, you will immediately do, retaining four line of battleships.

The interesting point is the way those three American heavy frigates, having no exact British counterpart, tied up so many British ships of the line. Only one of them was taken, the *President* as we have seen, and her last action actually took place after peace had been made. In the meanwhile and until the war ended the mere existence of these three ships imposed on Britain a disproportionate waste of effort. It is a question, however, whether Sir John Borlase Warren made the best use of his squadron. He had been distinguished as a frigate captain but he may have been worn out by the time he hoisted his flag. He was not without sympathy for the Americans, moreover, and was reluctant to do them any 'serious injury'. Greater energy and ruthlessness were shown by his second-in-command, Rear-Admiral Sir George Cockburn. In the end Warren was superseded by Vice-Admiral Sir Alexander Cochrane (Lord Cochrane's uncle) who took command on 1 April 1814. 'I have it much at heart' he wrote 'to give them a complete drubbing before peace is made.' He did not succeed because, for one thing, there was not enough time. Peace between Great Britain and the United States was signed at Ghent on 24 December 1814. The plenipotentiaries included Admiral Lord Gambier, making his last appearance in history. It was a war of which nobody, in retrospect, is particularly proud. It was a conflict which began over nothing, proved nothing and settled nothing. It is an episode of history which most people – gunnery specialists apart – would prefer to forget.

TWELVE

The Battle of Algiers

On 20 April 1814, Louis XVIII made his public entry into London, following a long period of retirement, and went on the following day to Dover, where the *Royal Sovereign* yacht awaited him, together with an escorting squadron, under the command of Vice-Admiral Foley. The Prince Regent, on board the yacht, took leave of His Majesty, the Duchess of Angouleme and the princes of the blood royal.

As soon as the Prince Regent had quitted the yacht, the royal standard of England, and the flag of the Admiralty, which had been flying, were struck. The royal standard of France, surmounted by a British pendant, was hoisted at the main, and saluted with 21 guns, by the castle, the batteries, and every ship of the squadron. The *Royal Sovereign* proceeded to sea, followed by the other yachts, in which the royal family and suite were embarked. As the *Royal Sovereign* passed the outward pier head, his Royal Highness the Prince Regent, who stood at the extremity, gave the signal for three cheers, which was obeyed with enthusiasm by his subjects, who thronged every part of the shore. This last mark of affection was received by the royal family of France with unutterable feelings of gratitude and attachment to the prince and the nation.

In two hours and fifteen minutes the royal yacht entered the harbour of Calais and France received from the British navy the descendant of the Capets, Louis le Desiré. Such was the termination of the great struggle between France and England, which had continued, with the exception of the truce of Amiens, for 21 years.

So wrote Captain Brenton but without complete accuracy. Napoleon left Elba on 26 February 1815, and began his last campaign which was to end at Waterloo. During the 'hundred days' the Commander-in-Chief of the Channel Fleet was Lord Keith, who had seemingly retired from active service when he married in 1808; his bride being the daughter of Mrs Thrale (Dr Johnson's friend). He hoisted his flag again in February 1812, but regarded his command as a shore appointment, he himself being more often to be found in Harley Street or at his country house, Purbrook Park in Hampshire. When peace was made following Napoleon's abdication he retired once more but was re-appointed to the Channel Fleet when the news came of Napoleon's landing in France. It was an anxious time, for many ships had been paid off and dismantled. The process had now to be reversed, ships being hurriedly refitted and again commissioned. There were no naval operations and two months of suspense ended with the news of Napoleon's defeat and abdication. He had left Paris and was at Malmaison, having demanded from the provisional French government two frigates to take him and his immediate followers to the United States. His request was refused but it seemed possible that Napoleon would find some other means of leaving France. As a first move in that direction he reached Rochefort on 3 July 1815. He still had his supporters, frigate captains included, and some were willing to aid him in the attempt. His intentions were known, however, and Lord Melville sent full information to Lord Keith whose cruisers were ordered to detain him. Commanding on the French coast around Rochefort was Rear-Admiral Sir Henry Hotham. One of the ships under his orders was the *Bellerophon* (74) commanded by Captain Frederick L. Maitland, stationed with two frigates off the Charente. Napoleon reached the Ile d'Aix on 3 July and soon realized that he had no hope of escaping to sea while the blockading ships were there. He finally came on board the *Bellerophon* and gave himself up as a prisoner of war. While on board this ship he was impressed by the cleanliness, order and routine silence. In conversation with Captain Maitland he said:

'I can see no sufficient reason why your ships should beat the French with so much ease. The finest men-of-war in your service are French; a French ship is heavier in every respect than yours; she carries more guns; those guns are of larger calibre; and has a great many more men.'[1]

On a later occasion, while the ship was at sea, he discussed with Maitland the defence of Acre, in which that officer had taken part. Napoleon ended by saying:

'If it had not been for you English, I should have been Emperor of the East; but wherever there is water to float a ship, we are to find you in our way!'

Although the *Bellerophon* went to Plymouth, Napoleon never set foot ashore. He was transferred to the *Northumberland* and sent to his place of exile. With his landing in St Helena the Napoleonic Wars came finally to an end. Once more the orders came to pay off the ships of the Channel Fleet, the *Bellerophon* included, and the Navy returned gradually to a peacetime footing, much to the disappointment of many of the officers, much to the joy of most of the men.

During the last years of the war Sir Edward Pellew had been Commander-in-Chief in the Mediterranean. As second-in-command he had Sir Richard Keats and later, Sir Sidney Smith. To blockade Toulon he had twelve or thirteen sail of the line, his French opponents having about twenty ships but all undermanned as a result of demands made by Napoleon's armies. The French, under Emeriau, came out to exercise but put back to port when Pellew approached, sometimes after the exchange of a few distant shots. There was no real prospect of battle and Pellew, as he said, had more annoyance from his own fleet than from the enemy. Writing to Keats, now Commander-in-Chief on the Newfoundland station, he complained (12 Sept 1813):

I don't know if the thought ever occur'd to you, but it does frequently to me, that Captains of the Navy are very like spoilt Children, every thing out of common course goes ag't the grain and the subjects of discontent are infinite.

Scarcely any do their Duty from Principle, Zeal is out of the Question. He is the ablest Man who can get offnest into Port and do less than his neighbour – such bouncing and flouncing, such black looks – such reluctance to pay even the Common forms of Civility are quite disgusting.[2]

The truth was, as Pellew said, that 'we all grow tired'. When the war ended he was directed, on 29 April 1814, to return home and bring his three-decked ships with him. He hauled down his flag on 19 August and received his peerage at about the same time, becoming Lord Exmouth as the reward for his services. His retirement was brief, however, for he was recalled to active service when news came of Napoleon's escape from Elba. He hoisted his flag once more and sailed for the Mediterranean, superseding Rear-Admiral Penrose, who now became his second-in-command. Exmouth was at Naples when Murat, who had been king there, fled to France. From there he sailed to Genoa where he embarked

Sir Hudson Lowe and part of the garrison. These he landed at Marseille which had risen for the Bourbons against Napoleon. No battle resulted and the war came to its final end with Exmouth on horseback leading an army against Marshal Brune. At this point Exmouth must have expected his recall but he was ordered instead to conclude certain treaties with the Barbary States; a task which he would have to postpone until the following year.

The Barbary States were the Muslim powers of North Africa; Tripoli, Tunis and Algiers. They lived by piracy, maintaining perpetual war against the smaller European countries but not against France or Britain. It was their practice to enslave their christian prisoners, accepting ransoms in respect of some but keeping as slaves the poor seamen or fishermen of Sicily, Naples and Sardinia. Some smaller countries like Sweden and Denmark purchased immunity by annual tribute. During the 18th century it was British policy to be on friendly terms with the Barbary States. Being frequently at war with France and Spain, the fleet had to have a source of supply and so had the garrison of Gibraltar. There had to be a constant traffic in bullocks from Bona and Tetuan. With the end of the Napoleonic Wars British forces were largely withdrawn from the Mediterranean, ending the need for supplies on a large scale, and apart from that Britain had now a number of allies, Spain included. The Barbary States were no longer essential nor even particularly useful. At the Congress of Vienna, moreover, Castlereagh was urging on the other Powers the morality and expedience of suppressing the negro slave trade – only to be asked, in return, why the British were solely concerned with *black* slaves. What had the leading naval power done to abolish white slavery in North Africa? It was an awkward question and it resulted in Exmouth being ordered to visit the ports of Barbary and secure the release of the slaves. No force was to be used in the first instance for force might easily lead to the slaves being massacred. The slaves were, in fact, to be ransomed, with Exmouth as intermediary between the Barbary States and the governments immediately concerned. Exmouth recognized, however, that his proposals might be rejected. So his first move was to send Captain Warde to reconnoitre Algiers and Captain Pechell to make a careful report on Tunis. Either or both of these places might have to be bombarded; Tripoli being thought less of a problem, unlikely to give trouble. On 24 March Lord Exmouth appeared off Algiers with five sail of the line and seven frigates or sloops. The Dey of Algiers yielded readily to reason and the Sicilians and Neapolitans were ransomed at 1,000 Spanish dollars a head, the Sardinians and Genoese costing only half as much. Peace was made with these various countries but nothing was said about piracy in general. Exmouth then sailed on to Tunis where 524 slaves were ransomed rather cheaply and 257 freed unconditionally. The Bey of Tunis agreed that future captives should be treated as prisoners of war. Exmouth went on to Tripoli where he had no difficulty at all. Influenced by the example of Tunis the ruler of Tripoli accepted 50,000 Spanish dollars for 468 slaves, and agreed to abolish slavery in future. So Exmouth decided to revisit Algiers and extract a similar promise from the Dey. He had a long discussion with that potentate on 15 June but this time met with resistance. Algiers, as its ruler suddenly remembered, owed allegiance to the Sultan of Turkey. He expected to have the Sultan's decision in six months' time. But would he accept the decision when it came? The discussion having ended on a note of disagreement, the Dey assumed that war had begun and sent messengers to warn his provincial governors. After a day or two negotiations were resumed with a measure of agreement and then the British squadron sailed for England, arriving at Spithead on 24 June. Exmouth struck his flag on the 26th and reported progress at the Admiralty. Almost at the same time came the news that 200 local fishermen (Corsicans, Sicilians etc.) had been massacred at Bona apparently on the Dey's orders. He was not, in fact, entirely at fault but the news came at an opportune time when the government was under attack for treating the Algerines too leniently. Exmouth had hardly reached Charing Cross before he was on his way back to Portsmouth, armed now with orders to teach the Dey a lesson.

The Admiral's first problem was to man the squadron he would need, for his ships had been paid off. With his flag in the *Queen Charlotte*, he offered, as he had been authorized, a bounty of two months' pay to seamen who would volunteer for this particular service. An effort was made to collect and man five sail of the line, a 50-gun ship, four frigates and smaller craft; enough for his purpose when joined by the ships which Penrose already had in the Mediterranean. The force, gradually assembled and officered, was not the old Mediterranean Fleet but a squadron formed for the occasion and manned at least partly by volunteers. It comprised two three-decked ships, the *Queen Charlotte* (100), Exmouth's flagship, the *Impregnable* (98) (Rear-Admiral Milne); three other sail of the line, the *Superb* (74), *Minden* (74) and *Albion* (74); two 40-gun frigates, *Severn* and *Glasgow*; two 36-gun frigates, *Granicus* and *Hebrus*; five sloops and four bomb-vessels. Lord Exmouth sailed with part of this force on 24 July and was joined by the remainder at Plymouth. Penrose was to have joined the fleet at Gibraltar but never received the despatch addressed to him. Instead, Exmouth found at Gibraltar the Dutch Admiral, Van de Capellan, who offered his co-operation with five frigates and a corvette; an offer which Exmouth was glad to accept. Five gunboats fitted out at Gibraltar brought the total number of vessels to thirty-five, less one sloop sent home with despatches. It was at Gibraltar that all the final arrangements were made and the detailed orders issued.

In making his plan, Lord Exmouth had this great advantage, that he knew the place he had to attack. A careful study had been made by Captain Warde, who had checked the soundings and counted the embrasures, and Exmouth had himself been ashore there quite recently. Algiers, as he knew, had a fortified sea front about a mile long behind which the town (of about 50,000 inhabitants) rose to a citadel on the landward side. In front of this was a heavily fortified island, joined to the waterfront by a breakwater which formed the harbour, open only to the south. Where the breakwater joined the island was the lighthouse battery with three tiers of cannon, those in the lowest tier mounted in casemates and all protected by solid five-foot-thick stonework. There was another three-tiered battery immediately south of the lighthouse, beyond which a two-tiered battery extended to the harbour mouth. (see diagram of the Battle 'as planned'.) Covering this on the landward side was the fish-market battery, and there were other batteries to the north and south. In the harbour would be the Algerine men-of-war which might play some part in the defence. Ships apart, the Dey had perhaps a thousand cannon facing seawards, backed by a garrison of 8,000 men, with some 30,000 Moorish auxiliaries who would be brought in from the surrounding countryside. It was to be assumed that the Dey's artillery-men had been trained and that they would fight with fanaticism. It was also to be assumed that he had ample replacements for all casualties and plenty of ammunition for all guns. Nor was there any hope of making a surprise attack. The Dey knew what was coming and when. So Algiers, 'the warlike city' was clearly very formidable indeed. Exmouth's task was to destroy the Algerian navy, silence the batteries and induce the Dey to make peace on British terms. Whether anything he could do would alter the Algerine way of life may be doubted but the main object was to strengthen Castlereagh's position at the Congress of Vienna; and this, at least, was possible. Exmouth had been briefed verbally and knew well enough what was required of him.

Studying the fortifications, Exmouth realized that he had to avoid the fire of the lighthouse and the other three-tiered batteries. He could do this by anchoring three ships in a central triangle of water at x (see diagram of the Battle 'as planned') on which the heavy batteries would not bear. The water was too shallow for any use to be made of the area at z. At x there was depth of water enough and the height of the mole would protect the attacking ships from all but the nearest batteries. To help destroy these it was essential to place a three-decked ship in an enfilading position at y. That would be the place for the flagship. To destroy the ships in the harbour it would be necessary to place a heavy frigate in position at y but it would also be necessary to protect that frigate by sending in other frigates to engage the waterfront batteries. All depended, however, on the bigger ships keeping to the left of the line A – B (see diagram of the Battle 'as planned'). If all were done correctly the enemy three-tiered battery would be left without a target. The apparent flaw in the plan, obvious to everyone, was that ships would have to pass through the danger zone on the way in and again on the way out. It was a question whether the ships would ever reach their allotted positions. Exmouth decided to take that risk. The Dey, Omar Pashaw, had said that he would not fire the first shot and the Admiral believed him. Nor did he intend to fire the first shot himself, assuming that someone on the enemy side would eventually fire without orders. As for his withdrawal, that would be at night and the enemy cannon should by then have been largely silenced.

As a tactician, Lord Exmouth was as masterly as Nelson had been at Copenhagen, although his problem was on a smaller scale. But he was faced with something different in kind; permanent fortifications built in stone. Whereas Nelson's gunners had to aim at an opposing ship or floating battery, Exmouth's men had to fire at the enemy embrasures, knowing that a hit on the stonework would be useless. For each of them the target was an enemy cannon framed in solid masonry. Accuracy was essential and this is where the lessons of the American War were made to apply. Exmouth was himself a gunnery specialist but, apart from that, several of his ships (the *Severn, Superb* and *Leander*) had been on the American station, two of his captains (Brisbane and Ekins) had been at Copenhagen, one of them (William Paterson) at the capture of Mauritius, and five had seen service in America. These were the Hon. Anthony

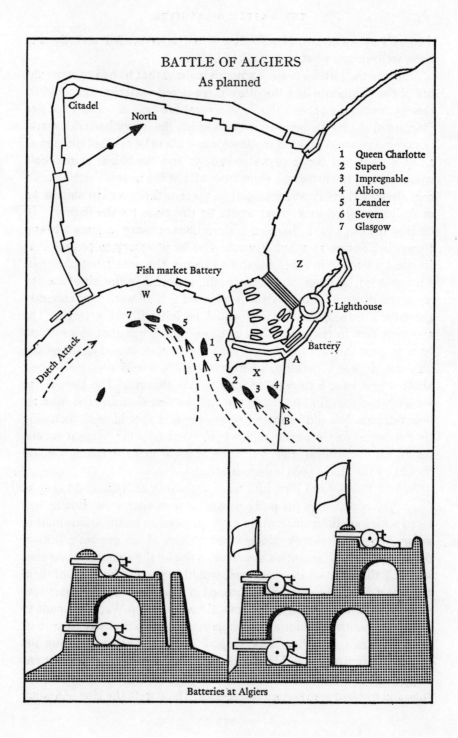

BATTLE OF ALGIERS
As planned

1 **Queen Charlotte**
2 Superb
3 Impregnable
4 Albion
5 Leander
6 Severn
7 Glasgow

Citadel

North

Fish market Battery

Lighthouse

Battery

Dutch Attack

Batteries at Algiers

Maitland, once captain of the *Pique* which came near to fighting the US *Constitution*, Edmund Palmer, George Bentham and the Hon. George Percival. Most important of all was Captain Samuel Pechell (see page 169) who had commanded the *Guerriere* shortly before she was captured and who had since become a gunnery expert. All this expertise was important but so was the knowledge that a battle was certain. On this subject a naval author wrote:

Had Lord Exmouth gone to Algiers direct from Toulon, with five ships, the chances are that he would have been beat. I believe the squadron he took to Algiers, though fitted out in a hurry, knew more about their guns than ships that had been in commission all the war: they knew they were going to fight, and took pains to qualify themselves: the fleet in the war never expected it, and never were prepared, and the officers generally were too old to exert themselves without a stimulus. The Government also were not without their share of blame, for allowing so small a proportion of powder and shot for exercise . . .

It would seem that Exmouth obtained an extra supply but, apart from that, his ships could use their annual allowance in four weeks. They certainly must have done so for the training programme was intensive, all guns being fitted with dispart sights (see page 166), and after leaving Plymouth each ship fired six broadsides every Tuesday and Friday. In addition the first and second gun captains were given daily target practice, firing from the quarterdeck at a target hung forward from a studding-sail boom. Further preparations were made at Gibraltar involving launches armed with carronades, flat-bottom boats equipped for launching Congreve rockets and a sloop fitted as an explosion vessel with 143 barrels of gunpowder on board. The marines were organized for a possible landing and all captains were issued with a plan of the Algerine fortifications.

The fleet was near Algiers on 27 August and a boat was sent in to convey an ultimatum. No reply being received, the signal for battle was made and the attack began at 2 pm, the *Queen Charlotte* leading the column of ships in line ahead. Gaze, Master of the Fleet, brought the flagship in so close that there were only two feet of water under the keel when anchor was dropped and only fifty yards between the ship and the shore but the Admiral had chain lashed to the hempen cable (this was a new idea) and veered out a few fathoms so that the final range was about eighty yards. The *Leander* passed ahead of the flagship as ordered. Just

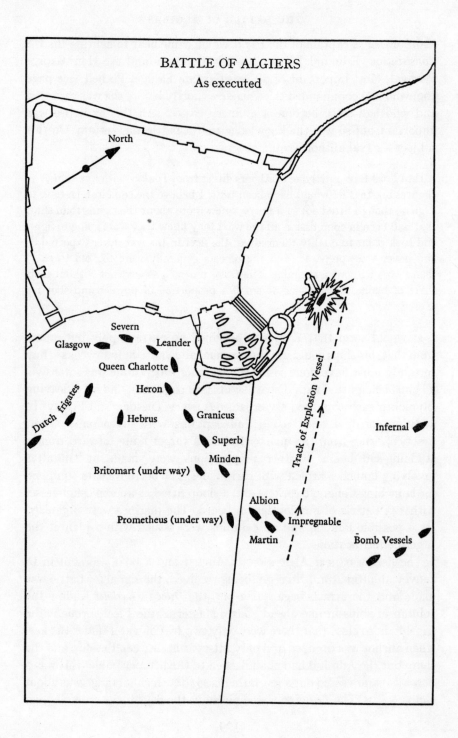

BATTLE OF ALGIERS
As executed

North

Severn
Glasgow   Leander
      Queen Charlotte
          Heron

Dutch frigates
          Hebrus   Granicus
                        Superb
                      Minden
Britomart (under way)

Track of Explosion Vessel

Infernal

Albion
Prometheus (under way)   Impregnable
          Martin   Bomb Vessels

before 3 pm, a shot was fired from the fish-market battery, followed by a second, and Lord Exmouth gave the order to open fire. The *Queen Charlotte* and *Leander* fired their broadsides simultaneously and so the battle began. Pandemonium was to continue for five hours and could be heard from sixty miles away. While the firing intensified the *Severn* and *Glasgow* took up their positions as ordered and the Dutch frigates did the same further to the south. The *Superb* was two hundred yards out of her position when she dropped anchor and twice the distance she should have been from the batteries. The *Impregnable*, Milne's flagship, lagged behind disgracefully and dropped anchor when the flagship did, four hundred yards out of position and well within the arc of the lighthouse battery. The *Minden* promptly passed the *Impregnable* and anchored astern of the *Superb*. The *Albion* anchored ahead of the wretched *Impregnable* but made sail again and ended up just astern of the *Minden*. There was an unfortunate gap astern of the *Queen Charlotte* but this was nobly filled by the frigate *Granicus* and (still more nobly) by the sloop *Heron*. The other sloops kept under way so as to present a moving target, their function being to tow out any bigger ship that might be dismasted. By way of contrast, the *Queen Charlotte* silenced the batteries near her in about twenty minutes while the *Impregnable* fought her lonely battle for hours, engaging the heaviest batteries at the most unfavourable range. At 4 pm, the vessel moored across the harbour mouth was burnt and at 4.24 the flotilla assembled alongside the flagship and then took up position to bombard the harbour and town, the Algerine fleet being totally destroyed by 8.30 pm. Before then, at 8.0, Exmouth ordered the explosion vessel to be used against the lighthouse battery in an attempt to divert attention from Milne. It went off near the wrong battery at 9.10, doing little damage, and then the firing died away and the signal was made to withdraw. It was a slow process and Exmouth ordered the *Minden* to cover the retirement, that ship ceasing fire at 11.30 pm, when her magazine was empty. There was desultory firing from the forts until long after midnight and the *Queen Charlotte* finally dropped anchor again at 1.30 am. In the words of Exmouth's interpreter, Salamé:

After we had anchored, his Lordship, having ordered his steward in the morning, to keep several dishes ready, gave a grand supper to the officers of the ship, and drank to the health of every brave man in the fleet.

We also drank to his Lordship's health, and then everybody went to sleep, almost like dead men.[3]

At noon on the following day Exmouth sent the Dey a carefully phrased message, offering him peace on the terms proposed the day before. Failing acceptance of these terms 'I shall renew my operations at my own convenience'. Three guns were fired in token of acceptance. When the negotiations were concluded over a thousand slaves were set free, the money paid for those previously freed was repaid and a treaty signed by which the Dey promised never to enslave christians again. The object of the operation had been achieved.

Lord Exmouth had played his cards well but his threat to renew the bombardment was mere bluff. He could have done little more because he had practically no ammunition left. The gunpowder expended amounted to 118 tons, the weight of shot to about 500 tons. Returns of round shot fired were as follows:

Queen Charlotte	4,462
Impregnable	6,730
Superb	4,500
Minden	4,710
Albion	4,110
Leander	3,680
Severn	2,920
Glasgow	3,000
Granicus	2,800
Hebrus	2,755

It would be interesting to know exactly what ammunition was left. The *Minden* had none (or was it her gunpowder that had been expended?) which would lead one to suspect that she sailed with 6,000 rounds and had expended the rest in practice. The *Queen Charlotte* had used fewer rounds in battle than the *Impregnable*, the magazines of which were probably about empty, but she previously used more, one might suspect, in exercising her gun captains. In time of a general war, ships would never have dared used up their ammunition in this way, assuming (as they would have to do) that they might be in action again before reaching their home port. The Battle of Algiers was different in this way from any other action of the period. The allied squadron fired over 50,000 round shot, mostly in five hours. The bomb-vessels, in firing off 960 bombs, had probably expended nearly all they had, and the same might be true of the rocket boats. There was probably no other action of the period in which the expenditure of ammunition was comparable.

As for the casualties, they were exceptionally heavy, the returns reading as follows:

	KILLED	WOUNDED	
Queen Charlotte	8	131	
Impregnable	50	160	
Superb	8	84	
Minden	7	37	
Albion	3	15	
Leander	17	118	
Severn	3	34	
Glasgow	10	37	
Granicus	16	42	
Hebrus	4	15	
Infernal	2	17	
TOTAL BRITISH LOSS	128	690	(818 casualties)
DUTCH LOSS	13	52	
TOTAL ALLIED LOSS	141	742	

The British casualties amounted to 16 per cent of those present. Even at the Battle of Copenhagen, the proportion was only 12·5 per cent, while the losses at the Nile were 11 per cent and at Trafalgar still less, at 9 per cent. This was the hardest fought action of the whole period and was gallantly fought by better-trained men than Nelson ever commanded. It was the finish to crown the whole.

John Wilson Croker called Edward Pellew, who now became Viscount Exmouth, 'the greatest Sea Officer of his time'. In the literal sense this is probably true. It was his capture of the *Cleopatre* which fairly began the war in 1793, his battle at Algiers which closed what we may call the classic age. He had been on active service for twenty years and was still not worn out when his final opportunity came. He and many others fought on for ten years after Nelson died. He must have the credit for a tactical brilliance not inferior to that of Nelson, for the seamanship in which he was second only to Sir Richard Keats, for the application of gunnery skills acquired in the American War and for the courage, resolution and speed of thought he applied to every situation he was in.

For nearly every purpose in war Exmouth was incomparable. Like Nelson, however, he had his faults and nepotism was the chief of these. In seeking his own advancement, in which he was fairly persistent, he equally pressed the claims of his brother, Israel, and his two sons, Pownall and Fleetwood. Israel was never more than average as an officer and both boys – the younger especially – were ruined by absurdly early promotion. At the Battle of Algiers this nepotism worked in reverse. Besieged by applicants who saw in this voyage a last chance of distinction for perhaps a lifetime, he rejected all his relations and most of his followers. He thought that the operation would be extremely dangerous, doubted whether he would himself survive, and chose rather to be surrounded by strangers. His only known followers to be present were John Gaze, Master of the Fleet, and William Kempthorne, Captain of the bomb-vessel *Belzebub*. He might surely have demanded a Rear-Admiral from among his friends or one known to him by reputation, like Sir Josias Rowley. But he seems to have been chiefly anxious to exclude those whose lives he thought valuable. The result was that the Admiralty sent Rear-Admiral David Milne to the *Impregnable*, with Edward Brace as flag-captain; two of the stupidest men in the service. Exmouth admittedly expected Penrose to join him at Gibraltar but he should in any case have been more careful in his choice of senior officers. For all practical purposes Lord Exmouth was left without a Second-in-Command. He was justified in placing the *Queen Charlotte* near the harbour mouth, for that was to be the middle of the line, but he temporarily lost control of the battle after firing began, the subsequent mistake being hidden from him by smoke. This would not have mattered if the next flag-officer had obeyed orders and signalled the other ships into their right positions. As things were, Milne made the worst possible mistake and made no effort to rectify it. The result was that the *Impregnable* had two hundred and thirty-three shot holes in her hull and the appalling casualty list we have seen. Her men fought magnificently, it should be added, and had at one time almost silenced the lighthouse battery. The trouble was, of course, that the enemy casualties could be and were replaced as the battle went on. We should also remember that the defenders of Algiers could fire at a ship while the attacking gunners had to fire at an embrasure. The *Impregnable* was lucky, in fact, to survive the battle at all. There is nothing in the story of Algiers to justify the theory that the service had declined in efficiency after Trafalgar. If there was a real decline it would have been in 1810–12, marked by the

Battle of Grand Port and the early frigate actions of the American War. By 1816 the lessons had been learnt and the Battle of Algiers is proof of it.

Why should the classic age end at this particular point? It ends there because the age of steam had dawned. The *Comet* of 1811 had already appeared and there were five steamships on the Clyde by 1814 and two on the Mersey by 1816. Some ten steamships were built by 1815 and the steam vessel *Argyle* was doing seven knots in service between Limehouse and Margate. The first regular sea-going steamship was the *Rob Roy*, built by William Denny of Dumbarton and engined by David Napier of Glasgow, operating successfully between Greenock and Belfast. By 1821 the *James Watt* of 420 tons was in service between London and Leith. At about the time the Battle of Algiers was fought the *Greenock* Steam Packet reached the Mersey from the Clyde, the *Duke of Wellington* was in service between Liverpool and Runcorn, and the *Princess Charlotte* steamship was launched at Liverpool. This last vessel made history when she towed the *Harlequin* sailing ship to sea in October of the same year. The first steamship to cross the Atlantic was the *Savannah* of 350 tons, built in New York. Her only voyage (which was hopelessly uneconomic) took place in 1817. The first successful steam vessels were ferry boats, to be followed by tugs and dredgers. They developed in the triangular area of water between Glasgow, Belfast and the Mersey and spread from there to the seas beyond. But the steamships which excited other people made no immediate impact on the Lords Commissioners of the Admiralty. To them the paddle-wheel steam vessel seemed vulnerable, costly and rather vulgar. Years were to pass before there would be a steam-driven warship under the white ensign. In this respect, however, the East India Company took the lead and the armed steamship *Diana* played a significant part in the Burmese War of 1824. Prominent on this occasion – with Captain Marryat the novelist – was Sir James Brisbane, C.B., Exmouth's flag-captain in the *Queen Charlotte*, who thus lived to see the advent of the steamship at war.

Still more significant was the French expedition to Algiers in 1830. The Algerines, not mending their ways after Exmouth's visit, were invaded by a French army. It was brought to the scene by Victor-Guy, Baron Duperré, known with Bouvet and Hamelin as one of the three heroes of the Battle of Grand Port in 1810. His was an impressive fleet and it included no fewer than seven steamships, one of them the *Sphinx* of 780 tons and 160 horse-power, built at Rochefort in 1829. The army was landed not at Algiers but at Sidi-Ferruch, the city being finally attacked on the landward side. The bombardment from the sea was merely a diversion but one planned in the knowledge that the men-of-war could, in the last resort, be towed out of action. The *Sphinx* did not, apparently, appear in the navy list of the time but it helped to illustrate the fact that the steamship era had dawned. Still more dramatic was the part played by Lord Cochrane in the Greek War of Independence. Appointed to command the Greek Navy in 1825, he made plans to build 'Six steam vessels having each two guns in the bow and perhaps two in the stern, not less than 68-pounder long guns.' Only one of these vessels reached the Aegean, the *Perseverance* (later re-named the *Karteria*) which actually made an attack on Turkish shipping in the Gulf of Corinth, destroying them with red-hot shot. It would take many years to introduce the steamship into the navies of the world but the process had begun in 1824–25 and the end of the sailing ship era was already at least in sight.

The Navy of the classic age, disciplined by St Vincent, inspired by Nelson, and held together by such men as Collingwood, Pellew and Saumarez, ceased to exist when the ships were paid off after their return from Algiers. Men who could remember the great days were old now and many of them were coming ashore. British sea-power was firmly established and there was no rival fleet in sight, no serious fighting to be foreseen for years to come. It was now to be a mainly peacetime navy, inheriting a great tradition but lacking the sort of men who had created it in the first place. Technical progress would take the place of individual exploit. And while there has always been an expressed veneration for the past, no great historian has ever told us the story of the classic age. There has been no official history compiled by an S. E. Morison or a Stephen Roskill, no naval equivalent of a Napier or a Fortescue. We know all too little about the period which we regard as our greatest. Is it not time that something were done? Is it not time that the epic were fully told?

List of References

CHAPTER 2

1 Codrington, *Memoirs*, p 15
2 Navy Records Society, *Spencer Papers Vol 1*, pp 321–2
3 *Spencer Papers Vol 1*, p 326
4 J. S. Tucker, *Memoirs of Admiral the Rt. Hon. Earl of St. Vincent, Vol 1*, p 149
5 Admiral Sir William James, *Old Oak*, 1950, pp 66–8
6 Edward Pelham Brenton, *Life and Correspondence of John, Earl of St Vincent, Vol 1*, 1838, pp 338–44
7 Admiral James, *Old Oak*, p 71
8 Edward Pelham Brenton, *Earl of St. Vincent, Vol 1*, pp 349–50
9 Edward Pelham Brenton, *Earl of St. Vincent, Vol 1*, pp 144–5
10 Edward Pelham Brenton, *Earl of St. Vincent, Vol 1*, p 145
11 Adm James, *Old Oak*, p 109
12 Adm James, *Old Oak*, p 84.
13 Nelson, *Despatches and Letters, Vol 2*, 1845, pp 290–1
14 Nelson, *Despatches and Letters Vol 2*, p 26

CHAPTER 3

1 *The Naval Atlantis*, 1788, pp 98–9
2 E. H. Stuart Jones, *An Invasion that Failed*, Oxford 1950, pp 190–1
3 Captain Brenton, *Naval History, Vol 1*, 1837, p 340
4 Christopher Lloyd, *St. Vincent and Camperdown*, London 1963, p 47

CHAPTER 4

1 *Annual Register*, 1797, p 208
2 James Dugan, *The Great Mutiny*, New York 1965, p 283
3 William James, *Naval History, Vol 2*, p 348

CHAPTER 5

1 Navy Records Society Vol 48, *The Spencer Papers Vol 2*, 1914, p 439
2 J. S. Tucker, *Memoirs of Earl St. Vincent Vol 1*, pp 355–6
3 H. Raikes, *Memoirs of the Life and Services of Vice-Admiral Sir Jahleel Brenton*, London 1846, pp 112–13
4 E. P. Brenton, *Naval History of Great Britain Vol 3*, London 1837, p 39

CHAPTER 6

1 Leslie Gardiner, *The British Admiralty*, London 1968, p 188
2 Navy Records Society Vol 58, *The Spencer Papers Vol 3*, 1924
3 Navy Records Society Vol 58, *The Spencer Papers Vol 3*, 1924, p 314
4 W. V. Anson, *The Life of John Jervis, Admiral Lord St. Vincent*, London 1913, p 276
5 *Naval Chronicle*
6 E. P. Brenton, *Life and Correspondence of John Earl of St. Vincent, Vol 2*, London 1838, p 157
7 W. V. Anson, *Life of John Jervis*, p 200
8 E. P. Brenton, *Life of Earl St. Vincent*, p 155
9 E. P. Brenton, *Life of Earl St. Vincent*, pp 159–61

CHAPTER 7

1 Navy Records Society edited by Sir John Knox Laughton, *Letters and Papers of Charles, Lord Barhan, Vol 3*, 1911, p 95
2 Admiral James, *Naval History, Vol 3*, p 458

CHAPTER 9

1 Navy Records Society Vol 110, edited by A. N. Ryan, *The Saumarez Papers*, 1968, p 46
2 Navy Records Society Vol 1898, edited by Sir R. Vesey Hamilton, *Letters etc. of Sir Thomas Byam Martin*, II 47–8
3 Navy Records Society Vol 1898, edited by Sir R. Vesey Hamilton, *Letters etc. of Sir Thomas Byam Martin*, p 409
4 E. P. Brenton, p 395
5 E. P. Brenton, p 398
6 *A Mariner of England 1780–1817*, edited by S. Childers, 1968
7 Navy Records Society Vol 97, *Narrative of Sir William Dillon, Vol 2*, 1956, p 173
8 Navy Records Society Vol 97, *Narrative of Sir William Dillon, Vol 2*, 1956, p 281

LIST OF REFERENCES

CHAPTER 10

1   F. G. Twitchett, *Life of a Seaman, Thomas Cochrane, 10th Earl of Dundonald*, 1931, p 128
2   Christopher Lloyd, *Lord Cochrane*, 1947, p 61
3   F. G. Twitchett, p 139

CHAPTER 11

1   William James, *Old Oak*, p 209
2   J. G. Brighton, *Admiral Sir P. B. V. Broke, A Memoir*, 1866, p 149

CHAPTER 12

1   Sir F. L. Maitland, *Surrender of Napoleon*, 1904, p 75
2   C. Northcote Parkinson, *Edward Pellew, Viscount Exmouth*, 1934, p 404
3   Parkinson, p 464

Index